Palgrave Studies in Animals and Literature

Series Editors
Susan McHugh
Department of English
University of New England
Biddeford, ME, USA

Robert McKay
School of English
University of Sheffield
Sheffield, UK

John Miller
School of English
University of Sheffield
Sheffield, UK

Various academic disciplines can now be found in the process of executing an 'animal turn', questioning the ethical and philosophical grounds of human exceptionalism by taking seriously the nonhuman animal presences that haunt the margins of history, anthropology, philosophy, sociology and literary studies. Such work is characterised by a series of broad, cross-disciplinary questions. How might we rethink and problematise the separation of the human from other animals? What are the ethical and political stakes of our relationships with other species? How might we locate and understand the agency of animals in human cultures?

This series publishes work that looks, specifically, at the implications of the 'animal turn' for the field of English Studies. Language is often thought of as the key marker of humanity's difference from other species; animals may have codes, calls or songs, but humans have a mode of communication of a wholly other order. The primary motivation is to muddy this assumption and to animalise the canons of English Literature by rethinking representations of animals and interspecies encounter. Whereas animals are conventionally read as objects of fable, allegory or metaphor (and as signs of specifically human concerns), this series significantly extends the new insights of interdisciplinary animal studies by tracing the engagement of such figuration with the material lives of animals. It examines textual cultures as variously embodying a debt to or an intimacy with animals and advances understanding of how the aesthetic engagements of literary arts have always done more than simply illustrate natural history. We publish studies of the representation of animals in literary texts from the Middle Ages to the present and with reference to the discipline's key thematic concerns, genres and critical methods. The series focuses on literary prose and poetry, while also accommodating related discussion of the full range of materials and texts and contexts (from theatre and film to fine art, journalism, the law, popular writing and other cultural ephemera) with which English studies now engages.

Series Board:
Karl Steel (Brooklyn College)
Erica Fudge (Strathclyde)
Kevin Hutchings (UNBC)
Philip Armstrong (Canterbury)
Carrie Rohman (Lafayette)
Wendy Woodward (Western Cape)

More information about this series at
http://www.palgrave.com/gp/series/14649

André Krebber • Mieke Roscher
Editors

Animal Biography

Re-framing Animal Lives

palgrave
macmillan

Editors
André Krebber
University of Kassel
Kassel, Germany

Mieke Roscher
University of Kassel
Kassel, Germany

Palgrave Studies in Animals and Literature
ISBN 978-3-319-98287-8   ISBN 978-3-319-98288-5   (eBook)
https://doi.org/10.1007/978-3-319-98288-5

Library of Congress Control Number: 2018957697

Cover credit: Details/parts of painting "Ocean Being", by Zhong Hao Chen (2008), oil on canvas and panel, copyright and owned by the artist

This Palgrave Macmillan imprint is published by the registered company Springer Nature Switzerland AG
The registered company address is: Gewerbestrasse 11, 6330 Cham, Switzerland

To Gorilla Biscuits

Acknowledgments

The contributions in this volume were selected and adapted from a conference on animal biographies at the University of Kassel in 2016 that was generously funded by the German Research Foundation (DFG). We would like to thank the students from the history department at Kassel University who supported us throughout the conference: Johanna Wurz, Marc Liebke, Nora Fährmann, Basti Skutta, Tanita Schmidt, and Julian Herlitze. In addition, we would like to thank Basti Skutta for his careful support in preparing the manuscript for publication.

CONTENTS

NOTES ON CONTRIBUTORS

Matthew Chrulew is a senior research fellow in the Centre for Culture and Technology at Curtin University. He is the editor, with Dinesh Wadiwel, of *Foucault and Animals* (Brill, 2016), with Deborah Bird Rose and Thom van Dooren, of *Extinction Studies* (Columbia, 2017), and, with Brett Buchanan and Jeffrey Bussolini, of three special issues of *Angelaki* on philosophical ethology.

Margo DeMello, Ph.D. is an adjunct faculty member in the Anthrozoology Master's Program at Canisius College, the program director for Human-Animal Studies at the Animals & Society Institute, and has written widely in the area of human-animal studies.

Hilda Kean is a visiting professor at the University of Greenwich and a senior honorary research fellow at University College London. As a cultural and public historian she also works on animal-human history. Her many books include *Animal Rights. Political and Social Change in Britain since 1800* (2000) and *The Great Cat and Dog Massacre*, University of Chicago Press (2017–2018). She is jointly editing *The Routledge Handbook for Animal–Human History* with Philip Howell, forthcoming in 2018.

André Krebber is Lecturer in History and Theory of Human-Animal Relations at Kassel University. He researches and teaches in the areas of human-animal studies, intellectual history, and critical theory. His current project explores natural beauty as a noninstrumental category of cognition in nineteenth-century philosophy and science.

Markus Krzoska is Lecturer in History at Justus-Liebig-University Giessen and University Siegen, Germany. He obtained his doctorate at Berlin Free University in 2001 and did his habilitation at Giessen in 2012. He studied history and political science at Mainz University.

Susan McHugh is Professor of English at the University of New England, USA, and the author of *Animal Stories: Narrating across Species Lines* (2011) and *Dog* (2004). She co-edited *The Routledge Handbook of Human-Animal Studies* (2014) and *Literary Animals Look* (2013), as well as a special issue of *Antennae: The Journal of Nature in Visual Culture*.

Frederike Middelhoff is a literary scholar at the University of Würzburg, Germany, with a special interest in the history and poetics of knowledge. She is finishing her PhD thesis *Literary Autozoographies—Narrating Animal Life from a First-Person Perspective in German Literature (1787–1922)*.

Dominic O'Key is a doctoral researcher and teaching assistant at the University of Leeds. His research explores the concept of the creaturely in novels by W. G. Sebald, J. M. Coetzee, and Mahasweta Devi.

Mieke Roscher is Assistant Professor for the History of Human-Animal Relations at the University of Kassel. Her academic interests center on colonial and gender history as well as animal historiography. Her current project is on writing the history of animals in the Third Reich.

Mira Shah is a comparatist and cultural studies scholar by training and is working on a PhD thesis on "Ape and Affect. The Rhetoric of Primatology" at the University of Bern, Switzerland.

Aaron Skabelund is an associate professor in the Department of History at Brigham Young University, USA, and the author of *Dogs of Empire: Canines, Japan, and the Making of the Modern Imperial World* (Cornell UP, 2011) and "Dogs at War: Military Dogs in Film" in *Cinematic Canines: Dogs and their Work in the Fiction Film* (Rutgers UP, 2014).

Kim Stallwood is a vegan animal rights advocate who is an independent author, consultant, and scholar. He co-founded the Animals and Society Institute in 2005 and was the volunteer Executive Director of Minding Animals International (2011–2017). He is the author of *Growl: Life Lessons, Hard Truths, and Bold Strategies from an Animal Advocate* (2014).

Radhika Subramaniam is a curator, editor, and writer interested in urban crises and surprises, particularly crowds, cultures of catastrophe, and human-animal relationships. She is an associate professor of visual culture at Parsons School of Design/The New School where she was the first Director/Chief Curator of the Sheila C. Johnson Design Center from 2009 to 2017.

Daniel Wolf is working on his dissertation about the relevance of pictures for animal-human relations at the University of Kassel. He studied philosophy and sociology, and holds a master's degree in history and theory of art.

LIST OF FIGURES

CHAPTER 1

Introduction: Biographies, Animals and Individuality

André Krebber and Mieke Roscher

To observe dogs, say, in a park, interact with their kin, including their human kin, is a curious thing. We are not talking about the distant, dissecting, deterministic kind of observation here, but the kind that suspends rational correction and attempts to lose itself in its object. In these moments, it seems almost inescapable to recognize within their play individual personalities, tastes, characters and forms of waywardness. Yet, taking animals seriously as individuals, and even more, attempting to substantiate and portray such individuality in scholarly terms, proves a daunting exercise. As one approach, scholars have turned to reconstructing and shining light on animal biographies.[1] The biography seems an obvious choice for the challenge. While history is dominated by attempts that try to standardize, de-individualize and automatize the behavior of animals, it also proves to be littered with records of the exceptional lives of unusual animals. Far from being just

---

[1] For example, Baratay, *Biographies animales*; DeMello, *Speaking*; McHugh, *Animal Stories*; Kean, "Balto"; Pycior, "First Dog"; Witz, "Making"; Fudge, "Animal Lives."

A. Krebber (✉) • M. Roscher
University of Kassel, Kassel, Germany

© The Author(s) 2018
A. Krebber, M. Roscher (eds.), *Animal Biography*,
Palgrave Studies in Animals and Literature,
https://doi.org/10.1007/978-3-319-98288-5_1

1

a (post)modern sentimental interest, individual animal lives, both real and fantastic, seem to have captivated the human imagination for a long time. Examples reach from Bucephalus, antiquity's enduringly famous horse of Alexander the Great,[2] to Greyfriars Bobby[3] and William Bingley's four-volume *Animal Biography, or, Popular Zoology; Illustrated by Authentic Anecdotes of the Economy, Habits of Life, Instincts, and Sagacity of the Animal Creation*[4] in more recent times. A biography, it is hoped, projects, almost by definition, the possession of emotions, personhood—a self. Moreover, the personal element of the biography proves popular and promises to tie a knot between the biography's subject and its reader.

Hence, biographical writing surfaces both as an approach to capture the individuality of animals as well as make animals visible as individuals. Animal biographies are not meant to say—as one can hear the critics of such scholarship chuckle—that animals themselves would experience or even construct their lives in (auto)biographical terms. On the contrary, animal biography entails exactly the attempt to account for their individuality without having to read their minds, reconstruct their feelings or infer their intentions. As such, animal biographies remain external to the cognitive experience of the animals' worlds and their relations to it. Rather, the animal biography responds to and tries to capture *our* experience of other animals as individuals, with their own personalities, idiosyncrasies and each and every one with a self of its own, as well as our desire to lend voice and recognition to these individual creatures. We understand this enterprise as an attempt to make animal subjects visible as each possessing individual traits of their own. It is an attempt to study and show cultural and local characteristics of both groups of animals and certain individuals within those groups, with the hope of breaking the mold of identity that lumps together all animals as principally the same. Finally, the writing of animal biography also points to the intimate interlacing of the lives of animals and humans. With this volume, we want to explore the practicalities of reframing animal lives through the biography, but also to evaluate the biography as theoretical frame for animal lives.

[2] Winkes, "Boukephalas."

[3] Kean, "Exploration."

[4] Bingley, *Animal Biography* (first published in 1802 in 3 volumes, noteworthy as: *Animal Biography; or, Authentic Anecdotes of the Lives, Manners and Economy of the Animal Creation, Arranged According to the System of Linnaeus*).

(ANIMAL) BIOGRAPHY: A HISTORICAL SYNOPSIS

Coming from the Greek words of *bios* for life and *graphein* for writing, biography has a long tradition. For historians, the method of biography has been a longstanding tool in recounting the past. By way of exemplifying a life history, one hoped also to reconstruct the historical possibilities of one person's life in the past. Studying a human life in its entirety by considering the historical context and the interdependencies between the individual and society can therefore rightly be termed one of the master narratives in historiography. Looking as far back as antiquity, one cannot fail to notice that recounting the life of so-called great men is the most dominant and maybe one of the oldest forms of literary as well as historical narration. Over the centuries it has remained a widely used practice for recounting and interpreting historical processes. As such, it was not always clear what the genre of biography entails, as it was flexible enough to contain encyclopedic accounts, lyrical verses and memoirs. It was usually defined by its chronological narration, its sequencing and the presentation of important occurrences in the life presented. However, the literary tradition of biography from its beginning strayed from these rather rigid specifications, which led to a distinction between an esthetic and a scholarly biographical genre.[5] That these differences have become significantly blurred following Hayden White's critique of the distinction between facts and fiction has also impacted on the genre of biography.[6]

Biographical research may be much younger than biography itself, but here also there has been a considerable amount of disagreement on what the term implies. The research, depending on which discipline is consulted, was challenged and rejuvenated especially by advances in oral history and narration, as well as in women's and gender studies.[7] The sole focus on the so-called great man as the presumed only agent influencing the course of history has been called into question by these new perspectives. The "noteworthiness" of the biographical subject has been significantly altered, if not abolished, especially with the advent of the biographical method in sociology. Even if not explicitly addressed however, this "noteworthiness" is the central factor for why early attempts at animal biographies have been dismissed as banal or profane. Some say that the general denunciation of

---

[5] Zymner, "Biographie."
[6] White, *Tropics.*
[7] Ferres, "Gender."

biography as a suitable tool was based on the assumption that all lives are inherently constructed. Likewise, the construction of certain lives as privileged over others has led to some historians questioning the suitability of biography as a tool for recreating the past in general.[8] More to the point, however, is the fact that the influence of the social sciences, especially in the 1970s, and the linguistic turn have together had an immense effect on biographical research, also with regard to the innate interdisciplinary character of the biographical genre.[9] Thus, what formerly had been characterized and described as a constant shift between the focus on the individual or on society was now being reread as a way of drawing attention to the abilities of the individual and the individual's agency.[10] The acting subject, his or her practices and dynamic interaction with the surroundings were to become central for the idea of the individual's "making" of his or her biography. The question of animal agency can therefore be regarded as being closely linked to the question of animal biography without however being identical. In addition, biographical research has reacted to transformations in society. Historians have therefore taken to micro-historical approaches and the history of everyday life in their attempts to retell individual biographies, whereas the method of collective biography has been applied in ways that include social, political and structural historical dimensions. Additionally, and in the wake of *new historicism* and *new criticism*, the narrative structures of the biography as, for example, marked by its chronological sequencing have been questioned. Special emphasis is increasingly being placed on the narrative construction of both text and identities, but also the tension, interrelation and incongruence between individual and socio-historical context. Chronological approaches are giving way to thematic structures, closed unified images are surrendered for fragmentary sketches, and the interference of the representational means and forms of scholarly biographical accounts with the apprehension of the biographical subjects are taken into consideration.[11] Pierre Bourdieu's remarks on the "illusion of biography," which famously questioned the sense of trying to recreate a life without taking recourse to its many defining relations and structures by comparing it to a subway map,[12] serves here as a reminder,

---

[8] See, for example, Gradmann, "Geschichte."

[9] For an overview see Hamilton, *Biography*.

[10] See also Baratay, *Biographies animales*, 13–20.

[11] Klein and Schnicke, "20. Jahrhundert," 264.

[12] Bourdieu, "L'illusion biographique."

that the nature of biography is still to be regarded as undetermined. The question is whether this serves as an invitation to or a warning against trying to incorporate animals into these biographical frameworks.

Methodological Layouts

As such, animal biographies, like biographies in general, ultimately remain constructions that attempt to trace a more or less coherent image of the life of an individual, as Bourdieu pointed out. Within this framework, biographies come in a variety of shapes and forms. This might be truer for nonhuman animals still, who themselves most likely do not care much for casting their lives in terms of biographies. Biographies can be smooth and uneventful, but they can also be broken, fractured, fragmented and fragile. They can be collective and shared, yet they can also be deeply individual and isolated, distinct from any other biography. For some individuals or even groups of individuals, biographies can be comprehensively recoverable, but they can also be partial, interrupted and sketchy. As a consequence, within biographical writing, the real and the fictional always and necessarily pervade each other.[13] It is the task of the biographer to organize the remnants into a coherent story; it is he or she who creates meaning through the organization of fragments and sources. This, of course, is not peculiar to animal biographies, but rather the standard mode of operation for historians and literary scholars alike.

Following from these thoughts, one of the most challenging methodological problems of biographies, regardless of whether their subjects are animals or humans, remains the question of what constitutes an individual life and whether it is the individual life at all that is to be the focus of a biography, as some definitions still hold.[14] This stands in contrast to the many attempts at biographies that use the individual's life to offer a narrative background for illustrating specific socio-spatial contexts, or that are interested in a whole social group, which they try to capture by using the sum of the fragments provided by individual biographies.[15] These attempts have found their application in the writing of collective biographies, in which a group or a network is being portrayed by a comparative analysis of their lives. *Prosography*, as this approach is also called, is defined as the investigation of the common characteristics of an historical group, whose

---

[13] Pycior, "Public and Private," 177–178.
[14] See, for example, Hornung, "Anthropology."
[15] Schnicke, "Begriffsgeschichte."

individual biographies may be largely untraceable.[16] Methodologically, these approaches rely on the collection of large data sets, including key information such as education, place of birth, profession of parents and so forth, which are then read against the backdrop of historical developments. Lately, attention also has been directed at the encounter between humans and animals as a heuristic tool.[17] The question, to which this volume hopes to provide some answers, remains whether or not such methods are applicable to animals—or whether they can and maybe even must be enriched, for example, by ethological and ethnological approaches. Using collective biographies in the traditional human-centered way is also seen as a way to create situated subjectivities. Thus, by turning to telling and reframing animal lives through the method of biography, we also hope to remake animal identities.

More than the writing of human biographies, the writing of animal biographies then relies fundamentally on interdisciplinary efforts. Even though animals are present throughout the array of cultural documents and artifacts, at least within the last two or three centuries a lot of knowledge about animals has been collected within the natural sciences. So while there is much information available about animals and their lives, the task now, as has been argued by Erica Fudge among others,[18] is to submit this knowledge to new and critical analyses in order to perceive animals in new lights. This requires recalibrating the pairing of methods and sources by crossing disciplinary boundaries on both levels. As a consequence, the writing of animal biographies should remain open, in our view, to a wide range of data and sources. However, because we see this volume as an introduction to animal biography as a methodological as well as theoretical approach, we want to limit these methodological attempts and place them within the framework of a humanities scholarship. Hence, this volume focuses on reframing the animal biography in historical, cultural and literary studies.

THEORETICAL PROMISES

Narrowing in on the biography, this volume is not about animal *auto*-biographies. We are neither focusing on the self-expression of the animal, nor, as suggested earlier, do we turn to the animal biography as a way of

---

[16] See, for example, Booth, *How to Make it.*
[17] Davies and Gannon, "Collective Biography."
[18] Fudge, "Animal Lives."

rendering the animal's mind, thoughts and way of experiencing into speech, as DeMello does with her fine collection of essays *Speaking for Animals*.[19] Instead, we are interested in evaluating the constructing of animal biographies as a way of making visible and honoring animals as individuals externally, from historical sources, lived experiences, the bodies of animals. The two perspectives are closely related, of course, in that they share a desire to honor, capture and make noticeable the animal as an agent, who is individually self-determined, at least to some degree, and in taking seriously the parts animals play in society; likewise the two perspectives are not mutually exclusive (F. Middelhoff's and M. DeMello's contributions to this volume make this obvious). But whereas the autobiography approaches animal agency by trying to bring to light the self-experience of an animal other, the biography attempts to reveal agency through external markers and through the intertwinement with others and the historical, socio-cultural context. Through the biography, individuals and suppressed groups hence become visible as social, rather than cognitive actors.[20]

Yet, while biography and the individual are inseparably intertwined, they far from simply and unequivocally conform to each other. When the biographers of the nineteenth century approached their protagonists as personifications of the socio-political conditions of their time, both studying and writing history through the lives of a few powerful men, they tended to overwrite the individuality of their protagonists and identify them with the social realities of their times. As such, these biographies, while apparently making the life of one individual their principal material, really proved de-individualizing—even if it was not to the detriment of the perceived individual grandeur of their subjects. Thus simultaneously de- and hyper-individualizing, biography's relationship with the individual appears deeply ambiguous. The critique that formed against such biographical privileging and elevation of a few over the many during the first half of the twentieth century, in turn, did not necessarily elevate the individual more broadly through acknowledgment of a more widespread biography-worthiness of the individual as such. Rather, its main thrust was directed at the identification of the actions of some individuals with history itself that extended to these individuals near total stature over the course of societies by reducing everyone else to mere extras on the set of a 1960s epic film. More than on individuals, the door to democratization of the

---

[19] DeMello, "Introduction."
[20] Cf. Klein and Schnicke, "20. Jahrhundert," 259.

biography recoiled exemplarily, if opening on the individual nevertheless potentially thereby as well. The demolition of the nineteenth century biography then lent voice to the suffering of repressed groups—people of color, women, workers—while also highlighting the individual's fragility and fragmentation by emphasizing the limitation of its power. Thus, the relationship between biography and individual is precarious. As a consequence, the studying of biography today has moved away from the idea of a coherent narrative while also always reflecting upon the process of mediation that is inherent to the narration and production of the biography (and, indeed, all knowledge).

It is precisely this theoretical insight, however, that not only makes the biography a possible approach to the consideration of other lives, but places it as a competent voice within the conundrum of how one might be able to speak about and represent the individual experience of the other. One of the major critiques of a social and cultural reevaluation of animals that intends to recognize animals as autonomous, self-acting individuals is the anthropocentrism that is argued to be inherent in their every representation.[21] In the tension between the biographer on the one hand and the particular object of a biography on the other—that is, the challenge of reproducing and invoking the life and experiences of another individual subject—the biography as a scholarly genre has always been imbued with the same epistemological challenge, only in relation to other humans. Indeed, it is the mainstay of the biography to *give form* to the other. As such, the biographed is always also the product of the biographer, while the perspective of biographer and biographed cannot be neatly separated. Reframing animal lives through a biographical lens thus does not by itself lead to the envisioned emancipation of their protagonists by way of their individualization. Yet the alternative to a crude scientific objectivism that the biography represents, including its receptiveness to the anecdotal, its transgression of the delimitation between science and art, and the space it leaves for differentiation and deviance, holds specific promises for human-animal studies. Lurking ephemerally between the lines of the discursive aether of human-animal studies, the individuality of the animal breaks to the surface in spontaneous eruptions, before descending back into the ineffable. Biography might provide a footing for these notions of a life peculiar to animals and help to give it form. That Virginia Woolf, who

---

[21] On the last point, see, for example, the discussion of anthropocentrism in Prade, *Sprachoffenheit*, 35–43.

famously democratized the biography by claiming that "anyone who has lived a life, and left a record of that life, [is] worthy of a biography,"[22] chose to write a biography on behalf of an animal, thence seems little surprising.[23]

Needless to say, that significant theoretical and methodological questions remain. Is the focus on a few pronounced animal personalities (or even a few specific collectives of animals) not just shifting the perimeter of the collective, without any potential for moving beyond the anthropocentrism in our relation to animals? What about the vast number of individual animals who do not leave distinguished marks? Do they not become even more invisible than before? Can collective biographies compensate for such limitations? In allusion to Bourdieu, we might also ask if the concept of biography is at all useful for the recovering of individuality. Additionally, if we consider the concept of the biography limiting for humans, is the construction of animal biographies not counterproductive, especially if we want to honor the individuality and agency of animals? Do individuals even have biographies in the first place—or, coming from the opposite direction, is the construction of a biography a necessary precondition for subjectivity? And do animals in particular have biographies, or is their experience instead rather momentary, and the writing of animal biographies therefore entirely an anthropomorphic and anthropocentric construction? Would this extend to all species? Or are biographies peculiar to human, and maybe just a few other nonhuman species? The purpose of this volume is to pursue and think through some of these challenges.

For our opening part, titled "Explorations," we choose to trace the appearance of animal biography back to biographical, not historical, interspecies beginnings. Whether by studying the lives of animal ethologists and biologists and their passion for studying animals, by looking for animals in archival material and finding an intimate relationship between a man and a horse, or by questioning whether a fictional animal is based on a real life animal in contact to the text's author, animal biographies are discovered and explored through interlinkages with human caretakers, riders, keepers, feeders, admirers, observers. These explorations may be the result of a well-designed research program or a mere coincidental stumbling over a life influencing other lives. Matthew Chrulew's attempt to frame animal biographies is placed at the intersection of these poles. By sketching out

[22] Woolf, "Art of Biography," 226–227.
[23] Woolf, *Flush*.

how "charismatic or confounding creatures shape the life of the animal scientist, affect their interests and ideas, impel a drive to biological knowledge, [and] compel the writing of animal lives," he not only shows how biographies of scientists have been imprinted by the animals they encounter, but how animal biographies lie at the center of their descriptive framework. Using the narrative evidence of the scientist's encounters, especially those of the Swiss zoologist Heini Hediger and curator-emeritus of the Bronx zoo, Lee Crandall, as a source, he traces back the historical appreciation of animals as biographical subjects in the work of historian Eric Baratay and philosophical ethologist Dominique Lestel. Upon closer examination, autobiography, animal biography and zoo-biography become, as Chrulew argues, interwoven, opening up the chance to follow not only the famous but the common animals into their dens, cages and enclosures. In her take on working as an animal historian in the archive, Hilda Kean shows that it is not only scientists' accounts through which these biographical glimpses can be retrieved. Although exploration is a routine endeavor of any archival work, it is unexpected discoveries while "filling gaps" in a story that lead to encounters with unexpected individuals. Arguing that these glimpses may be just part of a larger picture, she exemplifies how the relational and often emotional connections between humans and animals can provide a starting point for a biographical account that represents at least that side of an animal's existence that is shared with human beings. Frederike Middelhoff, in her chapter on literary autozoographies, questions the aim of finding an "actual," metaphorical meaning behind an animal's narrative voice. Instead proposing to utilize species-specific and indeed zoological readings when approaching and studying such texts, she highlights the role literature can play in coming to terms with the epistemological, cultural, socio-historical and esthetic complexities that animal selves present. Taking the German Romantic author E.T.A. Hoffman and his novel *The Life and Opinions of the Tomcat Murr* as an example, she suggests that animal traces within these texts need to be explored by taking apart the all too obvious relationship between narrator and author, and evaluating the empirical foundations of the text in search for the autobiographical selves.

The volume's second part turns to "Reflections" on the biography as an opening for a deeper conversation with socio-political as well as cultural contexts. Here, animal biographies serve as an entry point for providing a narration that goes far beyond the individual's life story, even if the individual life remains a focal point. The animal biographies in this section point beyond a narrow biological confinement to an interspecies social meta-level, without, however, depriving the protagonists of their individuality or making the animals disappear altogether. This holds true particularly for those animal individuals of whom a wide array of source material, including taxidermic evidence, is available. Reflecting upon what is, can and should be told beyond the limitation of reconstructing a life is at the heart of these chapters, which also entails reflecting on methodologies. Whether it is the contextual embedment within national or even nationalistic master narratives or the perceiving of primatologists' observations, they show how animal biographies might surpass the narration of the biological individual. Hachikō, the Akita dog of international fame and main character in Aaron Skabelund's contribution, makes this particularly obvious. Skabelund reflects on the challenges and possibilities of composing animal biographies, addressing especially the "subalternity" of animals as biographical agents, and intertwines these with questions of materiality (not only of the animal body but also of the source evidence that he relies upon) and temporality. Biographical discourses change after the death of the biographical subject and while this might be true also for humans, the culture of remembering animals seems to leave more room for instrumentalization, as Skabelund points out. He thus shows how the representation of the animal is highly adaptable to nationalistic idealization, and what can be gained by disentangling the individual life from the political agenda as well as by taking into account matters of breed. Breeding also takes center stage in Markus Krzsoka's evaluation of animals who are presumed "wild": in this case the European Bison, a species driven to near extinction at the turn of the twentieth century. Having a whole group of animals as object of a biographical account, the article reflects the possibility of writing a collective biography of the species based on the yearly pedigree book for all living specimens and their descendants. Krzoska asks whether these collective identities translate back into the possibility of tracing individuality, or not. Similar questions are raised in Mira Shah's chapter. While asserting that traditionally, scientific accounts of animals have worked toward an obscuring of individuality, she deduces that by reflecting on the popular scientific by-products of ethological fieldwork, in her case the biographies of primatologists, one cannot fail to note that it is individual animals that are being followed, observed, documented and described, sometimes for years, decades, even whole lives. She therefore suggests that autobiographical narratives and "research memoirs" of primatological fieldwork create textual animal subjects that endow the animals with literary agency. Reflecting both on the practice of primatological fieldwork as well as on the narrative structures of the texts, she stresses that subjectivity is created via animal biography.

Part III takes a look at what we have dubbed "Constructions" of animal biographies. Bearing in mind that all biographies are the result of an assemblage, an agglomeration and ordering of data, text, information, material and immaterial evidence, the means of construction—concretely, taxidermy and film—are discussed here. The production of certain biographies in visual media particularly and their ubiquity in popular culture generates icons that often seem to stand in for whole species and stereotyped animal-human relationships. A closer observation reveals, however, that this prioritization must not be the case, and that the construction of animals and their biographies instead comes in forms that bridge rather than conceal the difference between the whole and the individual. The interest in determining whether individuality is a precondition for constructing the historical subject lies behind Susan McHugh's reflection on the intersection of taxidermy and literary representations. The challenge for McHugh is that taxidermic displays adhere to a collective narrative of both the object itself and of its provenance. In a way similar to the case of Hachikō, the life after death inherent in the taxidermic display makes for a history different from the exhibit's previous life. McHugh therefore suggests a genealogical reading of both literary representations and historical accounts, in order to disentangle the constructions of life, death and afterlife, past, present and future as well as culture and biology. Using contemporary fiction about taxidermy and taxidermists as sources alongside taxidermied animals, she moreover reflects on animal biography as an esthetic formation. Esthetics come also into play in Daniel Wolf's dissection of the post-human dystopia represented by the rebooted *Planet of the Apes* franchise, and its main characters Caesar and Koba, apparently prime examples of animal biographies. Taking Deleuze and Guattari's as well as Haraway's concepts of *becoming* as foundation, this chapter describes the evolutionary process of constructing identities that are regarded as human or nonhuman. Surprisingly, the concepts of human and nonhuman are seldom interwoven despite the apes' anthropomorphized description. Wolf's detailed analysis of claims of anthropomorphism therefore asks for a disentanglement of categories of similarity and the construction of identities. An equally post-human perspective is presented in Dominic O'Key's chapter on the crocodile in the postscript to Werner Herzog's 3D documentary *Cave of Forgotten Dreams* from 2010. Herzog presents, in O'Key's reading, a speculative biography of animals depicted in the Chauvet cave in France who, in a postscript, are supposed to have outlived the human race. This framing of time then becomes one of the central questions in the construction of a biography. Drawing from George Bataille, Jacques Derrida and Bernhard Stiegler, O'Key suggests that matters of birth and death, beginning and collapse, technology and time create strange temporalities that impact upon the possibilities of writing biographies. Furthermore, the opening up of spaces by decentering the anthropos while creating a post-human context—a context, however, that is still inscribed by former human presences—to some extend confirms the ontological separation between humans and animals. By presenting a biography of the albino crocodiles of the cave, O'Key illustrates how, in their constructedness, animals are "always irrevocably marked" and simultaneously "mutated."

The final part of the volume offers "Experiments" in potential form, narration and embodied constitution of animal biographies. The three chapters address, each in their own way, the underlying human relationships that inform the presentation of biographies, through experimental fieldwork, concerns for animal rights, and the creating of profiles for one's beloved animal companion. Moreover, these chapters also show how creative writing processes and social media help to create particular forms of animal biographies that might trigger animal activism and concerns for animal well-being, historical interest as well as the literary imagination. By way of textual fragmentation, Radhika Subramaniam presents the animal, his human companion and the writer/researcher as three coordinates in the construction of the story, and the animal biography as result of their story-telling. Following the tracks and traces of the elephant Abu'l Abbas and his mahout from the court of the Caliph of Baghdad, Harun al Rashid, to Aachen, Germany, where he was given to Charlemagne, Subramaniam constructs a credible tale of this elephant's travels through considering the intertwined experiences of intimacy, isolation, confinement, migration and intelligibility, while also addressing the challenges of telling stories across species and time. By introducing human characters who accompany the elephant, she creates a "plausible fiction" that also questions the linearity of biographical projects and disassembles the composition of movement and time in an attempt to listen for and hear Abu'l Abbas' calls, the "elephant-like tricks that can travel over distances," both temporal and spatial, as one might add. An elephant also takes center stage in the account of Topsy presented in the following biographical eulogy by Kim Stallwood. Putting the life and (deplorable) death of Topsy in the framework of the building of the American industrial and entertainment empire, but also the history of zoos and circuses, this chapter calls for an empathic and compassionate reading of all sources available, moreover thickened by contemporary accounts on elephant behavior. The granting of rights to animals should thus include the right to a biographical narration that accepts the claim that animals are subjects, at the very least, of their lives. As such, Stallwood points out, writing animal biographies can help to give back to animals some of the autonomy they routinely are denied in a human-centered world. Margo DeMello, finally, takes up Stallwood's cue in her look at the creation of animal biographies on social media platforms like Twitter, Facebook and Instagram, as well as specialized animal sites, such as Catster, Dogster or Bunspace. Online animals, as DeMello shows, serve as more than the voice of a human writer who constructs fictional accounts of their pet(s), but can also be used to promote better treatment of animals beyond the digital sphere. While the very nature of online animal biographies may be anthropomorphic, DeMello argues, they may also create precedents for a new understanding of animal subjectivity and identity.

WORKS CITED

Baratay, Éric. *Biographies animales. Des vies retrouvées.* Paris: Seuil, 2017.

Bingley, William. *Animal Biography, or, Popular Zoology: Illustrated by Authentic Anecdotes of the Economy, Habits of Life, Instincts, and Sagacity of the Animal Creation.* 4 vols. London: Philips, 1829.

Booth, Alison. *How to Make it as a Woman: Collective Biographical History from Victoria to the Present.* Chicago: University of Chicago Press, 2004.

Bourdieu, Pierre. "L'illusion biographique". *Actes de la recherche en sciences sociales* 62.1 (1986): 69–72.

Davies, Bronwyn and Susanne Gannon. "Collective Biography and the Entangled Enlivening of Being". *International Review of Qualitative Research* 5.4 (2012): 357–377.

DeMello, Margo, ed. *Speaking for Animals: Animal Autobiographical Writing.* New York: Routledge, 2013.

———. "Introduction". In *Speaking for Animals: Animal Autobiographical Writing,* edited by Margo DeMello, 1–14. New York: Routledge, 2013.

Ferres, Kay. "Gender, Biography and the Public Sphere". In *Mapping Lives: The Uses of Biography,* edited by Peter France and William St Clair, 303–309. Oxford: Oxford University Press, 2002.

Fudge, Erica. "Animal Lives – Erica Fudge Asks If, and How, a Biography of an Animal Might Be Written." *History Today* 54.10 (2004): 21–26.

Gradmann, Christoph. "Geschichte, Fiktion und Erfahrung – kritische Anmerkungen zur neuerlichen Aktualität der historischen Biographie." *Internationales Archiv für Sozialgeschichte der deutschen Literatur (IASL)* 17.2 (1992): 1–16.

Hamilton, Nigel. *Biography*. Cambridge, MA: Harvard University Press, 2009.

Hornung, Alfred. "Anthropology and Life Writing." In *Encyclopedia of Life Writing: Autobiographical and Biographical Form*, edited by Margaretta Jolly, 38–41. London: Routledge, 2001.

Kean, Hilda. "Balto, the Alaskan Dog and His Statue in New Yorks Central Park: Animal Representation and National Heritage." *International Journal of Heritage Studies* 15.5 (2009): 413–430.

———. "An Exploration of the Sculptures of Greyfriars Bobby, Edinburgh, Scotland, and the Brown Dog, Battersea, South London, England." *Society and Animals* 11.4 (2003): 353–373.

Klein, Christian and Falko Schnicke. "20. Jahrhundert." In *Handbuch Biographie: Methoden, Traditionen, Theorien*, edited by Christian Klein, 251–264. Stuttgart: Metzler, 2009.

McHugh, Susan. *Animal Stories: Narrating Across Species Lines*. Minneapolis: University of Minnesota Press, 2011.

Prade, Juliane. *Sprachoffenheit: Mensch, Tier und Kind in der Autobiographie*. Königshausen & Neumann Würzburg, 2013.

Pycior, Helena. "The Public and Private Lives of 'First Dogs': Warren G. Harding's Laddie Boy and Franklin D. Roosevelt's Fala." In: *Beastly Natures: Animals, Humans, and the Study of History*, edited by Dorothee Brantz, 176–204. Charlottesville: University of Virginia Press, 2010.

———. "The Making of the 'First Dog': President Warren G. Harding and Laddie Boy." *Society and Animals* 13.2 (2005): 109–138.

Schnicke, Falko. "Begriffsgeschichte: Biographie und verwandte Termini." In *Handbuch Biographie: Methoden, Traditionen, Theorien*, edited by Christian Klein, 1–6. Stuttgart: Metzler, 2009.

White, Hayden V. *Tropics of Discourse. Essays in Cultural Criticism*. Baltimore: Johns Hopkins University Press, 1978.

Winkes, Rolf. "Boukephalas." In *Miscellanea Mediterranea (Archaeologia Transatlantica XVIII)*, edited by R. Ross Holloway, 101–107. Providence: Joukowsky Institute for Archaeology & the Ancient World, 2000.

Witz, Leslie. "The Making of an Animal Biography: Huberta's Journey into South African Natural History, 1928–1932." *Kronos* 30 (2004): 138–166.

Woolf, Virginia. "The Art of Biography." In *Collected Essays*, vol. 4, edited by Leonard Woolf, 221–228. London: Hogarth Press, 1967.

———. *Flush: A Biography*. London: Hogarth Press, 1933.

Zymner, Rüdiger. "Biographie als Gattung?" In *Handbuch Biographie: Methoden, Traditionen, Theorien*, edited by Christian Klein, 7–12. Stuttgart: Metzler, 2009.

PART I

Explorations

Living, Biting Monitors, a Morose Howler and Other Infamous Animals: Animal Biographies in Ethology and Zoo Biology

Matthew Chrulew

AUTOBIOGRAPHICAL ANIMALS

The early lives of biologists are often marked by transformative encounters with individual animals. The volume *Leaders in the Study of Animal Behavior: Autobiographical Perspectives*, a collection of first-person essays overviewing the lives and careers of foundational scientists in ethology and comparative psychology, is punctuated by such impactful experiences.[1] Curiosity about the natural world is a common characteristic averred in these accounts, many of which feature childhood menageries or experiences of awe and wonder in the wild. Common too are defining interactions with specific, singular creatures that solidify this interest and mark the author from a young age.

---

[1] Dewsbury, *Animal Behavior: Autobiographical Perspectives.* This volume was followed by a second over two decades later: Drickamer and Dewsbury, *Animal Behavior: Second Generation.*

M. Chrulew (✉)
Centre for Culture and Technology, Curtin University, Perth, WA, Australia

© The Author(s) 2018   19
A. Krebber, M. Roscher (eds.), *Animal Biography*,
Palgrave Studies in Animals and Literature,
https://doi.org/10.1007/978-3-319-98288-5_2

Entomologist Vincent G. Dethier writes evocatively of his fascinating "first acquaintance with a live butterfly [that] resulted entirely from the initiative of the butterfly."[2] Ethologist Irenäus Eibl-Eibesfeldt opens his autobiographical sketches with an early childhood memory of responding excitedly to a goldfish, and further "a mosaic of pictorial memories in my mind—like short film scenes—of anthills in our garden with ants transporting caterpillars, of spiders that I fed with flies, and of toads swimming in a nearby pond that I caught and released in our garden." He writes that "In every person's life, key experiences can be traced that in a decisive way direct the growth of one's individual interest, and one's outlook on the world," describing a memorable trip to the Alps with his father.[3] The pioneering cognitive ethologist Donald R. Griffin relates a "vivid memory [...] of a farmer's boy carrying home a dead possum he had trapped"[4] and of his yearning for trapping that, under stern encouragement, mutated into cave expeditions for the purposes of bat-banding. Eckhard H. Hess reflects on his childhood keeping of animals, "that commonplace activity so usual in those who later become ethologists." Indeed, he writes, "Konrad Lorenz once said that all of the ethologists he knew carried out this boyhood activity," which meant "taking on of a responsibility for providing an environment suitable for that particular animal and seeing to it that normal activities could take place in such a period of confinement" or else releasing the animal. This activity, he believes, "has something to do with the nature of the kind of research" he went on to perform, citing R.F. Ewer's remark that "Ethologists are scientists who love the animals which they use in their research."[5] John A. King, whose research focused on the behavioural impact of early life experiences on animals, writes in his piece titled "Those Critical Periods of Social Reinforcement" of a singular

> childhood realization: I like animals. Somewhere in the ontogeny of most people, there seems to be a switch that turns some, as children, onto animals and others away from animals. Rather than an on-off switch, the early experiences with animals resemble a throttle that is at rest in some children and pushed ever onward in others until their entire lives involve animals in some respect. My throttle is full speed ahead.[6]

[2] Dewsbury, *Animal Behavior: Autobiographical Perspectives*, 45.
[3] Ibid., 69.
[4] Ibid., 121.
[5] Ibid., 183.
[6] Ibid., 205–206.

The contribution of Heini Hediger, the influential Swiss zoo biologist, animal psychologist and zoo director, fits into this genre. He professes from a very early age an excessive curiosity about animals and a peculiar habit for collecting them. He jokes of having been "imprinted on zoos" (as a surrogate mother of sorts, it is implied) in early visits with nurses to the zoological garden in Basel that as an adult he would come to direct. "I wanted to be in contact with animals and, consequently, assembled an impressive menagerie" that expanded from plush toys to living creatures like snakes and owls.[7] This growing collection, which distracted from his schoolwork, grew into expeditions to forests and swamps and, from there, journeys to Morocco and the South Pacific, where he observed and wrote about animals, on to biological studies at university and, ultimately, a distinguished and eventful career in zoological gardens.

It is a set of encounters with individual monitor lizards that he describes most strikingly. In 1929, he travelled as an assistant on an 18-month ethnological expedition during which he collected many specimens for his own studies and others that he donated to the Basel Museum of Natural History, where for a short time he later became curator of zoology. But his true inclinations lay elsewhere: "something was missing; I was working exclusively with dead animals when I was oriented toward living animals."[8] He had captured and kept monitor lizards during his stays on various South Pacific islands. The aggressive animals, he writes, "were remarkable in that they soon became completely tame. At first, I chained them to a post beneath our bungalow. When I approached them, I was greeted with threats, lashing tails, and defecation. After just a few days, however, I could feed them crabs and mice by hand without any problems."[9] This tameness allowed him to observe many new facts about monitor behaviour, their prowess at climbing, running and swimming. It also resulted in a new relationship that profoundly affected him, as upon their departure, "when it was time to put it in the alcohol tank, I was unable to perform my duty. Instead, I declared him officially taboo in the presence of the local chieftain and turned him loose."[10] This aspiring zoo director, oriented towards living animals, could not bring himself, in the interests of museological collection, to kill and preserve and thus objectify as a "specimen" for scientific

[7] Hediger, "Lifelong Attempt," 145.
[8] Ibid., 152.
[9] Ibid., 148–149.
[10] Ibid., 149.

knowledge this specific, living monitor with whom, in the process of taming, he had developed a relationship—asymmetrical, certainly, but nonetheless social.

This was not the only monitor lizard to profoundly mark Hediger's life: "Strangely enough," he writes, "it was a monitor [...] a 1.6-meter-long specimen, that gave me my only serious work-related injury in a career that spanned thirty-five years. At a press conference in which everything was going wrong, as is sometimes the case, I was bitten above the wrist [...] an injury that has since hampered my writing and perplexed graphologists."[11] Hediger was exceedingly proud of his injury record, achieved, he argued, through careful attention to animal behaviour, knowledge of their psychological needs that enabled the expert mediation of all animal-environment and animal-human encounters in captivity. This rare misunderstanding fatefully punctures his writing about animals. It has indeed perplexed, if not stymied, my own archival research into Hediger's zoo biology.[12] With a defiant bite, this anonymous yet singular lizard left its trace and marked those of its keeper. It entered into Hediger's auto-zoobiography, and thus into the annals of animal behaviour science.

It is revealing that these records of scientific beginnings—offering insights into both the institutional development of a field, and the personal development of its protagonists—are so regularly marked by such formative face-to-face encounters with familiars.[13] Time and again, charismatic or confounding creatures shape the life of the animal scientist, affect their interests and ideas, impel a drive to biological knowledge and compel the writing of animal lives. Intriguingly, the researchers often use technical terms and concepts to frame these early encounters, whether speaking in Lorenzian terms of "imprinting" on the zoo as Hediger does, recounting their early memories as meaningful "engrams" or reflecting on the significance, in their own ontogenetic development, of their social experiences of nonhuman others. Their mature research into the nature of nurture and of learning in orienting an organism within its environment thus provides a

---

[11] Ibid.

[12] I would like to acknowledge the assistance of the Australian Academy of the Humanities (Ernst Keller European Travelling Fellowship, 2013), the Zürich Zoo and the Australian Research Council (Discovery Early Career Researcher Award, DE160101531) in making this research possible.

[13] On the developmental and pedagogical significance of encounters with animals, see, for example, Marchesini, "Zoomimesis."

lexicon with which to frame the early experiences that, they tell us, impelled that very research. Writing, life and biology are tightly interwoven in this distinctive genre of self-reflection. It is at the same time a genre through which the lives of individual animals come to be narrated. These are not objectified or quantified but singular beings who by virtue of their qualitative distinctness and particular entanglement become an impactful part of the development and narration of scientific lives. Though far from complete animal biographies, these anecdotal episodes nonetheless relate significant life-shaping experiences, whether based on chance encounter, purposeful pursuit or shared life in common, that are remembered and given meaning as setting the researchers on the path to foundational scientific endeavour, to a life devoted to understanding animals.

ANIMAL BIOGRAPHY

Even from the earliest stages of the discipline, these "autobiographical perspectives" speak to the development, in the twentieth century, of new possibilities for comprehending and narrating the lives of animals, and to their intricate and multifaceted discursive and practical underpinnings. They tell us that both the desire and the opportunity to understand and describe animal conduct come from encounter and from shared life, and that such relationships have been significant in inspiring new ethological models and theories. And these new scientific perspectives—not just those of the European and American men described above but, particularly, later innovations and discoveries achieved by a wider range of scientists—have themselves made possible new forms of animal biography: not just in the genre of decisive childhood encounters, but more comprehensively and zoocentrically, in stories centred on the lives and distinctive characteristics of individual animals themselves.

How have the discoveries about animal behaviour of the twentieth century enabled or required new ways of narrating animal lives? Dominique Lestel argues that ethology's breakthroughs constitute a legitimate scientific revolution with profound consequences for our understanding of animals, including human beings.[14] Its substantiation of heretofore unrecognised capabilities—whether in terms of cognition and tool-use, cultural transmission and variation, invention and creativity or subjectivity and individuality—challenges inherited ideas of human exceptionalism and

---

[14] Lestel, *Origines animales.* See further Chrulew, "Philosophical Ethology."

animal mechanism. Of particular importance is the recognition that animals have not only a phylogenetic (or species) history and a cultural (or group) history but also their own coherent individual (biographical) history, diverging from their conspecifics due to differences of personality, experience or otherwise.[15] Importantly, these developments not only teach us about commonality between humans and animals, but in many ways themselves resulted from hybrid communities or at least new forms of interspecies relationship. For example, the longitudinal field studies by pioneering women such as Jane Goodall (with chimpanzees), Shirley Strum (with baboons) and Joyce Poole (with elephants) involved forms of shared life, mutual understanding, ethnographic description and biographical narration.[16] More than as a science of nonhuman culture, it was practising ethology as a social science and cultural activity itself that enabled the comprehension of animal sociality and individuality.

A clear example of these dynamics is given by Vinciane Despret when she tracks the emergence of an anthropological approach in Amotz Zahavi's field research on Arabian babblers, the subject of substantial controversy among sociobiologists.[17] Significant events in the lives of the birds—births and deaths, pairings, arrivals and expulsions—were not only taken as data, but enabled the babblers to become the heroes of surprising narrative genres: warlike epics, soap operas, romantic adventures. Despret traces Zahavi's method of engaging with the birds in close proximity, through daily following and provisioning, through individual recognition and naming. The field site is thus structured as an anthropological space in which the researcher can engage with his subject. Moreover, it is not the deep time of evolutionary theory, nor the experimental laboratory time of manipulation and variation, but rather historical time, lived time, in which the birds participate in this research. Importantly, Despret emphasises that this is not simply a secondary effect of the scientist's method: "the narrative and anecdotal form is the result at once of the anthropological approach and of the creative and diversified behaviour of the birds,"[18] which itself demands more qualitative techniques.

Various, often minoritarian practices and theories within ethology have thus helped to open up a domain for better understanding animals as individuals. Experimenting with techniques for disclosing their subjects'

---

[15] Lestel, *Origines animales*, 376–377.
[16] Lestel, *L'animal singulier*, 70.
[17] Despret, *Théorie éthologique*. (Unless otherwise noted, all translations are my own.)
[18] Ibid., 173.

interior lives, they both demand and make possible animal biographies. Rather than the quantification of species behaviour through an ethogram, it became clear that certain animals at least could be properly understood only by recognising their individuality as subjects and persons.[19] While the Lorenzian approach identifies behavioural differences as abnormal deviations from the species norm, the following, more anthropological generation of field studies tracks the particularities of each of their subjects. Breaking with the orthodox assumptions of species homogeneity and mechanistic stimulation that restrict animal diversity and plasticity and refuse animal self-identity and cognitive responsiveness, these new approaches recognise the coherence and meaningfulness of an animal's individual history:

> One feature of long-term longitudinal studies is that they follow specific individuals in detail and thus draw up genuine biographies. We have not paid enough attention to the growing practice of characterizing an animal through its biography, which supposes a temporal consistency in the idiosyncratic behaviours and 'mental states' (preferences, dislikes, skill...) of a given animal.[20]

The reciprocal familiarity that comes from extended observation allows these distinctive lives and personalities to be meaningfully distinguished, grasped and described.

Importantly, animal biography emerged in the description not only of individual "wild" animals as autonomous subjects in field studies, but in particular of "singular animals"—those who, as a result of intensive and often passionate relationships in the company of humans, develop surprising capabilities not normally thought available to their species.[21] Lestel argues that in hybrid human-animal communities (such as the ape language experiments of the sixties and seventies) animals become subjectified as strong heteronomous subjects: "*Animal biography* (the story of the life of an animal) was invented in the twentieth century, and some animals, like Washoe the chimpanzee and Kanzi the bonobo, became truly renowned. The 'self' of an animal that has a relationship with a human is different from the self it would have had if it had never interacted with a human."[22] Lestel

---

[19] Lestel, *L'animal singulier*, 36.
[20] Lestel, "The Biosemiotics," 50.
[21] Lestel, *L'animal singulier*, 69–74.
[22] Ibid., 74. Translated by Hollis Taylor, in Lestel, "Question," 119.

takes up this question again in his book on animal friendship, contrasting "exterior" animal biographies (recounted by people speaking in place of the animal) to those recounted by those who live with and know the animal concerned.[23] This dimension of shared life is significant: friendship with animals, Lestel argues, stems from narrating their lives as our friends through "collective biographies." The emphasis is not on representation but mutual production and transformation: hybrid community does not just enable the description of animal lives but, through particular and personal (rather than general and abstract) relationships, through the mediation of processes of storytelling, interpretation and interaction, it actively produces animal personhood with more complex and dynamic forms of interiority and identity. Not only does ethology reveal that animals are biographical subjects; shared lives contagiously actualise latent potentialities and catalyse novel modes of conduct among biographable animals.

These approaches and analyses open up the space of a more philosophical ethology—an ethology of the singular, rather than the general, as Lestel puts it—that is both critical of mechanomorphism and aware of the simultaneous necessity and dangers of the "mirror game" of anthropomorphism, filled with metaphors and analogies and cultural projections (whether of gender norms or economic models) but not reducible to such reflections, requiring a careful, situated hermeneutics of the significance of animal behaviour.[24] Crucially, the animals are also recognised as capable of actively responding to the questions asked of them, as co-producing their identity and inventing new relations and ways of life. No longer cleaving to the great divide between nature and culture, but situated within what Despret calls a "space of equilibrium," a web of relations in which both epistemological questions and cosmopolitical negotiations between humans and animals are at stake, different sorts of stories about animals become possible. In this ethopolitical domain of animal subjectification and interspecies composition and diplomacy, the most pressing "animal question" legitimately becomes that of their contemporaneity and identity: not just "can they speak?" or "can they suffer" but in fact "*who* are they, these animals, today?"[25]

It is from within this space that Éric Baratay asserts the need to move on from the vain and false traditional division of the human from the animal,

[23] Lestel, *Les amis*, 154–157.
[24] Buchanan et al., "General Introduction"; Lestel et al., "The Phenomenology."
[25] Chrulew, "Biopolitical Subjects."

to consider animals as individuals and thus to write their lives.[26] Baratay distinguishes a number of different forms that animal biographies have taken, from the fictional and anthropomorphic literary genre to the biographies of real celebrity animals at the turn of the nineteenth century. It is after 1950, he writes, that under the influence of popularised ethology we see biographies of ordinary animals: "We first preferred heroes and then representatives of their species, and finally, atypical individualities, almost unbearable by their character and behaviour."[27] Alongside social science approaches that focused on relations of everyday life, play and work, on animals as agents in history, both ethology and animal philosophy recognised the richness of animal existence, the sharing of emotions, the variation within cultures and between diverse personalities, the capacity for coherent internal self-relation and for change relevant to others and over time: "The individual is also placed at the heart of encounters, interspecific companionships, hybrid communities."[28] Yet while Baratay recognises biographies of animals produced by some ethologists, from Lorenz and his birds to Goodall and her chimps, these do not quite comprise, he argues, an autonomous biographical genre, insofar as what is being shown through the individual animal is the species and its relations.

Building on such developments, Baratay proposes and himself attempts another approach, a form of animal biography in which one places oneself "on the animal's side" to relate its life: "to place oneself on the side of the animal in order to account for what he experiences, feels at a given moment, during a period or during his life."[29] While the idea of taking the animal's point of view has often been criticised as an impossible enterprise, Baratay defends the significance of limited, uncertain insight into the worlds of others. Alongside the Uexküllian approach mentioned, he points to the existence of an alternative zoocentric tradition of painting, writing and psychology since the second half of the nineteenth century in such figures as Jack London, Franz Kafka and Virginia Woolf—a mode that has much in common with the ethologists and field primatologists who successfully inserted themselves among animals, and one that has recently returned,

---

[26] Baratay, *Biographies animales*. His preamble on the conditions of possibility for such an endeavour emphasises the developments in twentieth-century ethology and their interpretation in the philosophy of animality of Lestel, Despret, Haraway and others as enabling new ways of narrating animal lives.

[27] Ibid., 17.

[28] Ibid., 20.

[29] Ibid., 21–22, see also Baratay, *Le point de vue*.

prizing the capacity to suggest the alterity and diversity of the animal point of view despite the risks of humanisation and reduction. Animal worlds can only be better understood and related to by overcoming ignorance and the obstacles to shared feeling, by glimpsing how they perceive human beings and taking this into account in our own perceptions.

New, interdisciplinary approaches to biography thus become possible: "For these purposes, it is necessary to revise history, to change the Western conception of animals, to eschew anthropocentrism, to control anthropomorphism, to broaden our concepts, to cross the natural and human sciences."[30] Drawing on the vocabulary of ethology, "the notions of individual, person and subject must be reconfigured"[31] beyond restricted ideas of nature as an exploitable object, instead incorporating the nonhuman. Baratay broaches the technical and methodological difficulties of this task, the restricted availability of documents and archives, emphasising the need to multiply sources and access as many facets as possible. "These biographies," he writes, "will inevitably be partial, covering only the aspects glimpsed by the sources, and biased, resting only on the faculties granted to animals [...] for the moment."[32] The challenging question of *how* to write animal biographies should be confronted as an opportunity and experimented with as a new genre: "To pass over to the side of other living beings, a way of writing must also be constructed, developed, gradually improved and gotten used to."[33] Of course, such biographical excavation is not possible for most animals, in the anonymity of their lives and deaths, with no traces left behind. Yet some definitively archived cases remain; and in other cases, those in between, the task remains to work out how to tell their stories and disclose their lives.

To this end, Baratay presents a range of different biographies—based on different materials and setting different aims—which he divides into four sections: the restitution of existences; feeling experiences; seizing an animal epoch; and thinking generations. The task of the restitution of existences is "to retrieve animal lives, to restore their existence, to show their singularity."[34] Yet it is also possible to capture from historical documents (albeit weakly, imperfectly) the feelings, sensations and images of lived experience—to understand ways of feeling in a psychological as well as geographical sense.

---

[30] Ibid., 24.
[31] Ibid., 26.
[32] Ibid., 30.
[33] Ibid., 29.
[34] Ibid., 31.

Even further, biographies can participate in understanding animal worlds. Historical phenomena of travel, commerce, capture and the attendant transformations of animal populations and environments make possible the demarcation of different periods for certain animal groups, different situations and ways of life and different epochs that can be characterised through biographical narrative (such as the humanised experience of chimpanzees in Europe from the sixteenth to eighteenth centuries, or the judiciously anthropomorphic biographies of the mid-nineteenth and twentieth centuries). To think generations, finally, means taking account of many dynamic epochs, not just biological but social generations, varying communities subjected to transformative historical dynamics, "characterized by changing environments, conditions, and thus behaviours."[35]

Baratay argues in conclusion that since animals are "no more 'natural' than humans," no more part of the "terrestrial décor" (in that they too adapt and evolve in relation to their environment, whether natural or artificial) there remains a significant task of attending to the ways animals adjust to ecological and anthropogenic conditions, to their fluctuating sociabilities: "A history of behaviours must be developed, of their construction, transmission, transformation and differentiation, in order to build a history of species, of their groups and their individuals."[36] If it can no longer be denied that animal societies have histories, then the historian has much to offer in partnership with the ethologist (and, one might insist, the philosopher). Importantly, Baratay asserts the exploratory significance of animal biography as a genre in this largely uncharted domain: "Biographies can be used as a way of approaching and testing, and thus as a mode of operation for questioning and experimenting, in order to make concrete the diversity of possibilities, to test the effects of environmental and genetic changes on behaviour."[37] This question achieves particular importance in the context of the history of animal captivity and its intensification in the anthropocene.

Zoo Biographies

Menageries and zoological gardens have been prominent sources of such histories and biographies. As colonial collecting and trade networks shipped innumerable creatures into urban contexts, where amateurs and

[35] Ibid., 175.
[36] Ibid., 270.
[37] Ibid., 270–271.

professionals lived in unprecedented proximities to exotic animals, new and often unexpected opportunities to disclose their lives arose. Of course, through most of zoo history animals have been understood as specimens, representatives of their species.[38] But anecdotes of individual animals have regularly been produced alongside the dominant descriptions. To the most famous and familiar stories like Jumbo the elephant and Knut the polar bear can be added the chimpanzee Consul of Manchester zoo, whose life Baratay narrates anew, and the remarkable elephant who lived in the Sun King's Versailles menagerie.[39] In their focus on the human dimensions of these burdened institutions, historical and cultural studies of zoological gardens have seldom paid sufficient attention to the individual and group lives of their nonhuman inhabitants, or to the distinctive forms of encounter, knowledge and writing produced within them.

Indeed, alongside ethology, the science of zoo biology has contributed to the development of knowledge about animal behaviour—particularly about its modification in the anthropogenic environments of captivity— and likewise given rise to new animal stories. In this segregated yet nonetheless permeable mode of living alongside animals, not only new forms of knowledge and practices of care, but also emergent animal subjectivities gave rise to new forms of animal biography. In particular, it was a process of biopolitical modernisation and professionalisation across the twentieth century that saw the keeping of captive animals become founded on scientific knowledge of optimal methods for nutrition, hygiene, enclosure, enrichment and propagation. As we saw in Hediger's autobiographical account of the tame monitor that he could not bring himself to preserve, zoo biology is oriented towards living animals or, more precisely, towards *making animals live*. And indeed Hediger was very influential in this regard: across his books and articles as well as professional interventions, he helped develop and articulate zoo biology as the science of human-animal interaction and animal subjectification in captivity. His Uexküllian

[38] See, for example, Velvin, *Portraits*, in which animals such as "the cheetah," "the lion" and "the bactrian camel" are evoked according to the distinctive characteristics of the species.

[39] Within his natural history, the French Academician Claude Perrault includes a set of intriguing and somewhat out-of-place anecdotes about this elephant sourced from the animal's keepers and repeated later in Loisel's history of zoos. This distinctive animal biography, based on living encounter, supplements and in some ways destabilises the extensive anatomical descriptions of elephants, based on autopsy, among which it is nestled "word for word." See Chrulew, "Biopolitical Thresholds," 135–138.

approach always began zoocentrically from the phenomenological world of the animal; by taking its point of view into account, by understanding how it perceives the different elements and agents of its new environment, the deleterious effects of captivity could be ameliorated. In order to properly care for any particular animal, its keepers must know not only its species-specific requirements but also its biographical life history, its traumas and attachments. Thus their familiarity, expert knowledge and everyday contact enabled zoo men and women (directors, curators, veterinarians, keepers and others) to become spokespersons for the ways of life and modes of interaction of certain animals, as species but also as individuals, articulating their preferences and needs, personality and interiority.

Zoo biography, the writing of captive animal lives, is thus intertwined with and enabled by not just *zoo biology*, the knowledge of captive animal life, but also *zoo biopower*—the techniques for the optimisation of animal life in captivity. And whatever may have been learned and refined of the production of life, the power exercised over animals in this apparatus has long had damaging effects. That is, the often pitiable relations constituted in the zoo—a site that Lestel calls the "degree zero" of hybrid community[40]—have most often produced bare or wounded lives, impoverished or pathologised or otherwise harmed animal bodies and souls. The tales that emerge from this tangle of domination and encounter, curiosity and custody, are those of capture and resistance, taming and refusal, adaptation and malformation.

Perhaps more revealing, then, are not the lives of famous zoo animals but rather the lives of *infamous* animals—not so much scandalous or notorious but, nonetheless, unsettling and deviant, whose brief clashes with the anthropocentric power of collection and management have left behind enigmatic traces. Of course, the vast majority of captured animals died during trapping or transit or endured poor, unremarked lives as subjects of spectacle and perhaps research but not narrative. Yet this anonymous multitude has also made its mark on the archive, pressed up against the weight of textual history with its tremors and cries. In "The Life of Infamous Men"—the introduction to a collection of records of notorious abnormals in their encounters with judicial and psychological authorities—Foucault captures the way such unprivileged, otherwise silenced people enter into the archive through clashes with the mechanisms of authority: "All these lives, which were destined to pass beneath all discourse and to disappear

---

[40] Lestel, *L'animalité*, 109–110.

without ever being spoken, have only been able to leave behind traces—brief, incisive, and often enigmatic—at the point of their instantaneous contact with power."[41] He thus models a historical method that eschews famous stories and dominant narratives, instead trawling for records of resistance, traces of violence and confrontation, moments of fury and capture.

The institutional archive of zoo biology indeed includes countless residues of animal lives thrown up against captivity over decades and generations: untameable beasts, uncharismatic creatures, those not amenable to captivity whether malnourished, panicked or morose. Numerous examples could be given—like Hediger's escapees or Meyer-Holzapfel's abnormals[42]—but I will take up Lee Crandall's 1964 *The Management of Wild Mammals in Captivity*, an essential record of the biopolitical modernisation of zoological gardens. As Crandall writes, "Within the present century great strides have been made in the development of maintenance methods that will satisfy the physical and psychological needs of the animals and at the same time allow them to be so shown that at least some segments of natural habitats and life cycles are illustrated."[43] Crandall's book catalogues precisely this development of the science of zoo biology and, at the same time, the uncountable animal lives spent on its achievement. An ornithologist and keeper at the New York Zoological Park in the first half of the twentieth century, Crandall continued to work through his retirement as Curator Emeritus, painstakingly compiling the data for this volume. The encyclopaedic tome includes over seven hundred pages of taxonomically organised information and advice resulting from innumerable encounters and experiments. Crandall drew on his own 50-year career of practice and observation, as well as on the records of that institution, supplementing this from correspondence with zoo keepers and directors around the world, as well as from the published scientific literature.

With imposing regularity, readers are informed of the experience with captive management of the multiplicity of the world's mammals collected for urban display. As well as general information on their description, distribution, status in the wild and even cultural symbolism, he relates their natural habits, whether climbing or jumping, feeding or fasting behaviours, periods of higher or lower activity, needs for seclusion or protection from

---

[41] Foucault, "Infamous Men," 79–80.

[42] See, for example, the chapter on "Cage Breakers" in Hediger, *Wild Animals*, 61–70; Meyer-Holzapfel, "Abnormal Behavior," 476–503.

[43] Crandall, *Wild Mammals*, vii.

bright light. He describes various difficulties particular to the way a species reacts, physically and psychologically, to captivity: calm or nervous temperaments, shy or eager responses to keepers' attention, tameability and tractability at various stages of ontogenetic development and any species-specific handling techniques necessary due to inherent dangers such as claws, quills, size or strength. He lists specialised dietary requirements and different feeding regimens and nutritional substitutes tried with varying levels of success. He describes architectural and logistical requirements (temperature, ventilation, light, dimensions, flooring, sanitation, sleeping or breakout areas) to ensure the security and welfare of the animal enclosed. Longevity records indicate how long members of a species have survived in captivity. Each species' captive breeding record is also given: whether it has in fact been brought to reproduce, what methods were used, what results obtained and relevant data such as gestation periods and appropriate group makeup—essential information for institutions increasingly reliant on reproducing their own stock.

Overall, Crandall describes the particular techniques of management necessary for each species: what worked, and what did not, as zoos went about their business of trying to keep them alive, to make them live. Some are readily adaptable to captivity; they acclimatise and breed well, are content to be observed, handled and exhibited. Others struggle for a range of reasons—sensitivity, specialisation, vulnerability—and thus often die, or live poorly, merely survive. His text is a record of wounded lives and premature deaths, of convulsions of resistance to the ordeals of captivity and the penetration and intensification of biopower. He describes problems encountered and solutions attempted, ignorance and learning, failures and renewed attempts. Nascent zoo biological techniques meet their limits in the refusals and intransigencies of their wards; the animals act out, break free, take ill, die, until conditions are changed to suit them, however minimally. And as these observations and experiences are noted, aggregated and compiled, these disposable lives and deaths become captured again as data, contributing to the development of knowledge, skill and expertise for the future improvement of care. Through experimentation with biopolitical conditions, emerging from and developing new forms of human-animal interaction and shared life, however damaged, whatever the cost of lives and generations—the apparatus learns.[44]

---

[44] On the ways such harms, and particularly deaths, due to captivity were operationalised in zoo biological knowledge, see Chrulew, "Death at the Zoo."

The focus of these captivity histories is thus still that of the species and specimen: knowledge accumulates around the characteristics, norms and limits of a natural kind. Yet individual animals, often given proper names, do still populate these records: as representatives, but also as pioneers, achieving novel events such as the first in captivity or the first captive birth, or when distinctive temperament, character or exploits demand an anecdote. Many turn out to be docile, tractable, well-adjusted, but more often we find failure or defiance: fights, injuries, maladjustments, mortalities, clashes between an unwilling body and the machinery of biological care. We read fragments on shy, stressed inmates, exposed and inescapably visible. There are tales of escapes, as the ingenuity of moat-swimmers, cage-breakers, tree-climbers and fence-jumpers forces their keepers to refine their calculations of glass strength, leap distance or antipathy to water or heights. We find many references to nervous, excitable, delicate or sullen animals. This captive multitude is morose, moribund, difficult, irritable, ill-tempered, quarrelsome, aggressive and dangerous—in short, unmanageable. There are "truculent and unresponsive"[45] Tasmanian devils, stone-throwing chimpanzees,[46] biting woodchucks[47] and rhinos,[48] swiping leopards,[49] defiant camels[50] and flighty deer.[51] There are tantrum-throwing tapirs[52] and convulsing weasels,[53] a "savage, nervous, and unapproachable"[54] wild ass and "a particularly obstreperous black rhinoceros bull."[55] "The single short-lived [fossa] specimen kept here was savage and intractable,"[56] whereas one lesser panda, "if actually touched, usually shows its resentment by emitting explosive coughing sounds."[57] As we read of their whines and cries, their creative escapes and flurries of refusal, the singular imposes itself among the general. Like Hediger's monitor, these animals have bite; the archive, in turn, is marked and marred.

[45] Crandall, *Wild Mammals*, 24.
[46] Ibid., 144.
[47] Ibid., 216.
[48] Ibid., 510.
[49] Ibid., 376.
[50] Ibid., 545.
[51] Ibid., 573.
[52] Ibid., 499.
[53] Ibid., 324.
[54] Ibid., 492.
[55] Ibid., 509.
[56] Ibid., 355.
[57] Ibid., 316.

Death stretches all through the book. Of those who survive capture, a great many die in transit (due to stress, lack of food or poor conditions) or soon after. Crandall describes a flying lemur who "was greatly weakened on arrival in New York and refused a wide variety of fruits and leaves [...] Two or three days later the flying lemur succumbed, bringing to a dismal end what was probably the most determined attempt that has been made to keep this intriguing creature in captivity."[58] Some cases are spectacular: "On September 26, 1960, a giraffe that had just been unloaded from a ship at a New York dock, escaped from its crate, ran to the end of the pier, and fell into the water. Observers reported that the animal sank from sight almost at once without making effective efforts to swim."[59] But this passage on anteaters is more typical: "Specimens received here in 1917 and 1936 lived only 3 and 2 days, respectively."[60] Most died simply due to poor condition on arrival or inability to acclimatise. For every longevity record meant to indicate lifespan achievements there are countless examples of short-lived internees' deaths in captivity, due to drownings and falls, impaction and poisoning, disease and malnutrition. Even when accommodation and eventually breeding success are achieved, many of the young die soon after birth (whether devoured or neglected by their parents due to disturbance or lacking critical survival skills and anyone to teach them). Tales of successful sexual but not cultural reproduction are unfortunately common: "A pair of newly imported klipspringers was added to our collection on August 27, 1940. The female gave birth to a single youngster soon after arrival but failed to rear it."[61] Of course, when breeding finally becomes regularised, it often leads to surplus animals, the problem now one of disposal.

Even among those who manage to survive and endure, their lives are often impoverished or impaired. Crandall writes that few howler monkeys were imported or kept "due to the temperamental inability to adapt to captivity conditions, commonly known as 'moroseness,' as well as to the specialization of feeding habits."[62] He relates the tale of one particularly morose individual: "On July 20, 1950, Charles Cordier [the zoo's collector] returned from Ecuador with an infant male mantled howling monkey

---

[58] Ibid., 57–58.
[59] Ibid., 608.
[60] Ibid., 186.
[61] Ibid., 673.
[62] Ibid., 91–92.

[...] bearing the fairly descriptive name of 'Ugly.' This tiny creature was still being bottle-fed, a system that was continued in our Animal Nursery."[63] In these conditions Ugly's attachments were somewhat disturbed:

> Ugly grew rapidly and at an early age was provided with a small rough towel, changed daily. Like most young primates he became deeply attached to this bit of cloth, using it not only as a cape but as a means of retirement, sometimes covering himself completely. Eventually it had to be removed, following a period of several days during which Ugly refused to leave his shelter even for food. Prompt return to normal followed, and the towel was never returned.[64]

After describing Ugly's dietary schedule, Crandall details the shifts in Ugly's responses to the world:

> Up to the age of two years Ugly welcomed visitors by creeping forward in a crawling position, growling softly. He then sought the proffered finger or knuckle, upon which he chewed frantically but gently. After passing this age his temper became more uncertain, except toward his keeper. He had acquired the ability to roar, too, and did so on frequent occasions.[65]

While he managed to share his cage with another monkey without either fighting or becoming friends,

> By the time Ugly was three years old, he had become so irascible that he was considered unsafe even by his keeper, Mrs. Helen Martini, a woman of great sympathy and feeling.[66] He was therefore removed to a cage in the Small Mammal House [...] Here he lived until May 18, 1954, establishing a record of 3 years, 9 months, 28 days. At the time of death Ugly was quite black throughout and weighed 11.44 pounds or 5.2 kilograms.[67]

But as a post mortem confirmed no parasites, "The card on which the results were recorded gives the cause of death as acute pulmonary edema. An added line reads: 'Spasmodic inappetence for three to four weeks

---

[63] Ibid., 92, see also Crandall and Bridges, *Zoo Man's*, 28–30.

[64] Ibid., 92–93.

[65] Ibid., 93.

[66] The wife of the Lion House keeper, Mrs Martini, acted as surrogate mother for a range of animals, particularly big cats, in Crandall's accounts.

[67] Crandall, *Wild Mammals*, 93.

prior to death.'"[68] It seems, that is, that Ugly died of loneliness. Yet his life remains a lesson:

> Summing up, there appears to be at least one serious obstacle to keeping howlers for lengthy periods. Taken young enough, the animals' basic temperamental resistance can be overcome. Also, food requirements can then be reconciled to a diet that can readily be supplied [...] But the psychological necessity for companionship, apparently especially strong in howlers, was no longer satisfied in the case of Ugly, when his changing nature blocked established human contacts and he would accept no other. It may be the case that the solution lies in rearing a pair of infants together. If so, this remains to be done.[69]

Indeed, if this brief biography of Ugly's wretched life in captivity teaches us anything, it is that there has always been much work to be done, and much that remains to be done, when it comes to attaching well.

This tome on the management of mammals in captivity, then, is another "anthology of existences. Lives of a few lines or of a few pages, countless misfortunes and adventures, gathered together in a handful of words"[70] in which the otherwise unrecorded experiences of innumerable zoo animals howl their stories of disrupted generations and lives cut short by the trauma of capture. This professional volume of Crandall's was followed, two years later, by another work—*A Zoo Man's Notebook*—that retold a selection of these stories for a more popular audience.[71] What had been zoo biological records for specialists became interesting anecdotes and charming tales of life and work in the zoo. In the foreword, Crandall says that he looks upon this book "as a leisurely stroll through a garden where I have spent my life—a zoological garden." In his retirement, he can now leave that work for "the men and women who now have the cares and responsibilities I had for so long"—he can pass on his accumulated knowledge to the next generation of zoo professionals. For Crandall, this coauthored abridgement of the earlier scientific volume more satisfactorily evokes the "too lively a subject"[72] of animals and zoos "with the addition of such comments and anecdotes as seemed necessary to round out the accounts of certain animals."[73] Yet even distilled and tidied, these

---

[68] Ibid., 94.
[69] Ibid.
[70] Foucault, "Infamous Men," 76.
[71] Crandall and Bridges, *Zoo Man's*.
[72] Ibid., v.
[73] Ibid., vi.

"fragments of discourse" still markedly trail, with all their ugliness and pain, "the fragments of a reality in which they take part."[74]

Crandall opens the notebook with some brief autobiographical reflections that echo those of other ethologists and zoo biologists. As a child he had his own "private zoo" filled with "all the owls, turtles, and snakes I could find in the immediate neighborhood."[75] He did not last long in medical school, for "What I really wanted was something to do with animals—wild animals. This feeling was very real and ever present, but I didn't know what I could do about it."[76] So he found his way to William T. Hornaday, director of the New York Zoological Park, where he became a student keeper, was apprenticed into the arcane knowledge and "everyday practicalities"[77] of gamekeeping, and set off on the path of learning that would constitute his career and culminate in these career-summing books. But as this volume's final section suggests, "A Notebook Never Ends." Having collected observations of animals and squirrelled them away on index cards for 60 years, "a grain-by-grain addition to the art and practice of zoo-keeping,"[78] he reflects on the motivations and rewards of his career:

> I must admit that the deepest satisfactions of a long life in the zoo are not those set down in notebooks. How can you—or why should you?—make a few penciled notes to record how you feel as you await the return of a collecting expedition? Or the quiet, glowing joy of staring for the first time at an animal rarity you never expected to see alive?[79]

If it is experiences such as these that are the height of work with zoo animals, "the mainspring of all those years of work, worry, success, failure, accomplishment [...] was acceptance of the challenge that every captive wild animal presents" to care for it in an environment not its own. While admitting to failures at this task, yet maintaining some progress, it is this challenge that "sustains and motivates a zoo man—the coming ever closer to understanding the nature and needs of the wild animals under his care, devising ways of satisfying them, seeing the animals respond to his perceptions and

[74] Foucault, "Infamous Men," 79.
[75] Crandall and Bridges, *Zoo Man's*, 1.
[76] Ibid., 2.
[77] Ibid., 4.
[78] Ibid., 215.
[79] Ibid., 215–216.

ingenuity."[80] One's passionate curiosity about animals is satisfied in this fraught daily task of learning how better to live with them. As in other autobiographies, such practical knowledge and the animal biographies it makes possible—communicated in notebooks such as these—has its fount in the relational, interspecies crucibles of experience.

Works Cited

Baratay, Éric. *Biographies animales: Des vies retrouvées*. Paris: Seuil, 2017.

———. *Le point de vue animal: Une autre version de l'histoire*. Paris: Seuil, 2012.

Buchanan, Brett, Jeffrey Bussolini, and Matthew Chrulew. "General Introduction: Philosophical Ethology." *Angelaki* 19.3 (2014): 1–3.

Chrulew, Matthew. "'An Art of Both Caring and Locking Up': Biopolitical Thresholds in the Zoological Garden." *SubStance* 43.2 (2014a): 124–147.

———. "Animals as Biopolitical Subjects." In *Foucault and Animals*, edited by Matthew Chrulew and Dinesh Wadiwel, 222–238. Leiden: Brill, 2016.

———. "The Philosophical Ethology of Dominique Lestel." *Angelaki* 19.3 (2014b): 17–44.

———. "Preventing and Giving Death at the Zoo: Heini Hediger's 'Death Due to Behaviour'." In *Animal Death*, edited by Fiona Probyn-Rapsey and Jay Johnston, 221–238. Sydney: Sydney University Press, 2013.

Crandall, Lee S. *The Management of Wild Mammals in Captivity*. Chicago and London: The University of Chicago Press, 1964.

Crandall, Lee S. and William Bridges. *A Zoo Man's Notebook*. Chicago and London: The University of Chicago Press, 1966.

Despret, Vinciane. *Naissance d'une théorie éthologique: La danse du cratérope écaillé*. Paris: Les Empêcheurs de Penser En Rond, 1996.

Dewsbury, Donald A., ed. *Leaders in the Study of Animal Behavior: Autobiographical Perspectives*. Lewisburg: Bucknell University Press, 1985.

Drickamer, Lee C. and Donald A. Dewsbury, ed. *Leaders in Animal Behavior: The Second Generation*. Cambridge: Cambridge University Press, 2009.

Foucault, Michel. "The Life of Infamous Men." Translated by Paul Foss and Meaghan Morris. In *Power, Truth, Strategy*, edited by Meaghan Morris and Paul Patton, 76–91. Sydney: Feral Publications, 1979.

Hediger, Heini. "A Lifelong Attempt to Understand Animals." In *Leaders in the Study of Animal Behavior: Autobiographical Perspectives*, edited by Donald A. Dewsbury, 144–181. Lewisburg: Bucknell University Press, 1985.

———. *Ein Leben mit Tieren: Im Zoo und in aller Welt*. Zurich: Werd, 1990.

———. *Wild Animals in Captivity: An Outline of the Biology of Zoological Gardens*. Translated by G. Sircom. New York: Dover, 1964.

---

[80] Ibid., 216.

Lestel, Dominique. *Les Amis de mes amis.* Paris: Seuil, 2007a.

———. *L'Animal singulier.* Paris: Seuil, 2004.

———. *L'Animalité: Essai sur le statut de l'humain.* Paris: L'Herne, 2007b [1996].

———. "The Biosemiotics and Phylogenesis of Culture." *Social Science Information* 41.1 (2002): 35–68.

———. *Les Origines animales de la culture.* Paris: Flammarion, 2003 [2001].

———. "The Question of the Animal Subject." Trans. Hollis Taylor. *Angelaki* 19:3 (2014): 113–125.

Lestel, Dominique, Jeffrey Bussolini, and Matthew Chrulew. "The Phenomenology of Animal Life." *Environmental Humanities* 5 (2014): 125–148.

Marchesini, Roberto. "Zoomimesis." Trans. Jeffrey Bussolini. *Angelaki* 21:1 (2016): 175–197.

Meyer-Holzapfel, Monica. "Abnormal Behavior in Zoo Animals." In *Abnormal Behavior in Animals,* edited by M.W. Fox, 476–503. Philadelphia: W.B. Saunders, 1968.

Velvin, Ellen. *Portraits at the Zoo.* London: Hodder and Stoughton, 1915.

CHAPTER 3

Finding a Man and his Horse in the Archive?

Hilda Kean

INTRODUCTION

I was not looking for a man in the archive but an animal, who most preferably would be a cat or dog. I had asked Camden Archives in central London whether they had any diaries of people possessing animals living in the area during the Second World War. I was researching the animal-human relationship at that time and longed for as much material as possible. I was presented with a large box containing several diaries dating from 1937 to 1950 and was told that there were no acquisition details and that the only information was the name of the writer, Laurance Holman. Although I had previously found some accounts of cats and dogs in diaries, for example, in the Imperial War Museum archive, I had not seen any account of the lives of horses. It has been very unusual to see extensive examples of people's diaries, including animals,[1] in relation to the Second World War especially because—apart from occasional cats and dogs—they are rarely highlighting

---

[1] Kean, *The Great Cat and Dog Massacre.*

H. Kean (✉)
University of Greenwich, London, UK

University College London, London, UK

41
A. Krebber, M. Roscher (eds.), *Animal Biography*,
Palgrave Studies in Animals and Literature,
https://doi.org/10.1007/978-3-319-98288-5_3

upon the life of a horse within the family. So the diary becomes unusual both in focusing upon an individual horse but also incorporating this story within London. The archivists (and I) knew nothing of the diarist, not even his address or who had deposited the materials—and nothing about any horse![2] This diary would turn out to be very different.

The first diary was on hunting during 1937 when, as I would discover, the writer lived at Bestbeech St Mary near Wadhurst on the Kent and also Sussex borders and rode to horse with the local fox hunt. He had come to hunting—and horse riding—only in middle age being introduced through a close friend. Accounts of fox hunting were not what I was looking for but I thought it only polite to at least dip into these archives. However, my interest was quickly aroused by this following diary entry, for in it is described the start of a relationship with a horse called Mariana who was borrowed from a (nameless) friend. Laurance and Mariana first went riding together on 4 December 1937. Later in that December the friend explained to Laurance "I could have 'Mariana' for as long as I liked ... (sic) for ever if wished, provided I didn't part with her."[3]

Although I was a long-standing researcher and like many historians had spent many hours visiting archives, my experience had often been akin to that described by the historian Carolyn Steedman of undertaking research in a rush with insufficient time to engage in leisurely note-taking. But on the occasion of first encountering Mariana and Holman I had recently left my former place of employment, Ruskin College, Oxford, and was engaged with others in a largely unsuccessful campaign to save important historic records of former students.[4] Accordingly, I was extremely diligent about valuing and engaging with this material as extensively as possible. I was both ensuring that no copies were being destroyed—as had happened at Ruskin College—but that I was also looking in much detail at the small written contents of the diary.

I was also aware of the analysis described by Walter Benjamin. In *The Arcades Project*—as his translators describe—Benjamin's central concern

---

[2] Holman, *Diaries*. (Despite much searching of alternative proposals nothing has been found on the reasons for the deposition of the diary.)

[3] Ibid., Friday 17 December 1937.

[4] Kean, "Whose Archive?" (Despite the huge opposition to the destruction of former students' files more of the adults' materials from the early twentieth century and later twentieth century were totally destroyed.)

was "for the historical object of interpretation."[5] When he wrote of the "consideration of great things from the past" he was also drawing out this view to explain how "[w]e don't displace our being into theirs; they step into our life."[6] I found Benjamin's approach of importance for how he relates to his own position, as well as for what it suggests to those of recent historians exploring different approaches from the past in present writing. There is a key relationship between the past and the present. Thus, although I was concerned with the diary material, which was intended to reveal material on the nature of horses, I also became very aware of the male experience of life when war took place from 1939 to 1945. That is, the diarist was revealing accounts of his relationship with Mariana but was also showing his own experience of life at the time in written circumstances that I had not encountered. In the past, I have read other diaries and archival material and tended to identify with certain writers because of their actions. I had primarily heard of the wartime from my dead father or grandfather but I had been fascinated by Holman's own past in London. The words being used by Holman employed the initials of out of date slang such as TG or NBG (Thank God or No Bloody Good) or revealed that he went to the *Studio* (a long-closed news cinema in Oxford Street) or the specific cost of food.[7] This emphasis helped also to draw me in to the approaches of Walter Benjamin on how the past is made relevant in the present. His argument ensured that particular events of an earlier time were not forgotten but made relevant in a certain contemporary moment.

My attention was drawn not only to the activity of general horses during the war but also the man himself living in London during the same period. I was delighted to find an overlooked scrap of paper giving a 'clue' to the man's address—subsequently in Bedford Square in central London behind the British Museum. I had no connection whatsoever with Laurance Holman (or Mariana) and so initially I used the diaries as a starting point for 'facts' about the man's life and times. As Carolyn Steedman has wryly commented, "Perhaps gap-filling is a puerile thing—no justification for a book—but historians do love doing it."[8] Having previously explored the writing and historiography of family history I was also aware of the range of materials I might employ to construct Holman's life (as

---

[5] Benjamin, *Arcades Project*, xii.
[6] Ibid., 206.
[7] Holman, *Diaries*, 6 April 1949; Benjamin, *Arcades Project*, 206.
[8] Steedman, *Everyday Life*, 32.

well as the caveats attached to such a project).[9] But, as I was to find, there was also much about the horse who Holman rode upon daily and the human-equine relationship they both experienced. That is, while I am cautious about how much I 'discovered' about Mariana my cautiousness also has extended to my perceptions of Holman.

Although the diaries about a middle-aged, middle-class man living in London at the height of the war and the nature of horse riding at the time were interesting, as a historiographical exploration the key, however, was not so much the material but my role of approach as a historian.[10] I had the hypothesis (confirmed in reading many other contemporary materials) that there would be extant material about animal-human relationships if I looked for it and that I could probably use it in writing a history of the war that privileged nonhuman animals.[11] I realise that this seems a different stance to some other animal studies researchers who are dismissive of human-produced materials believing that these are incapable of being used to create nonhuman centred histories. Some of those who have been most critical of the possibility of history embracing animals tend, like Cary Wolfe, to work outside this specific field. As he has argued:

> So even though—to return to our historian example—your concept of the discipline's *external* relations to its larger environment is post humanist in taking seriously the existence of nonhuman subjects and the consequent compulsion to make the discipline respond to the question of nonhuman animals foisted on it by changes in the discipline's environment, your *internal* disciplinarity may remain humanist through and through.[12]

In order to create *human*-centred histories, historians initiate a task of imagining, of thinking about what was it like to be alive in another time and place, in order to bring that past into the present in some way. Those who think about such questions realise, however, that completion and success in such an endeavour is impossible since, amongst other things, there will only ever be traces existing in the present from the past. In her insightful work, *Dust*, Carolyn Steedman has also explored what historians do when they go to "the archive," the commonplace location of paper-based

---

[9] Kean, *London Stories*.

[10] For further discussion of this approach see Kean, "Challenges for Historians."

[11] Although my recent book, *The Great Cat and Dog Massacre*, focuses on the survival (and also death) of cats and dogs during the war there is also brief coverage of horses at that time.

[12] Wolfe, *Posthumanism*, 123–124 (original emphases).

materials that conventional historians use. It is, she says: "[to] do with longing and appropriation. It is to do with wanting things that are put together, collected, collated, named in lists and indices; a place where a whole world, a social order, may be *imagined* by the recurrence of a name in a register, through a scrap of paper, or some other little piece of flotsam."[13] Many historians realise the rational impossibility of re-creating experiences from the past, but there is always the hope that it is possible to do this particularly if one thinks it worthwhile to validate past lives. Indeed, if historians did not think it valuable to even attempt this task, then clearly we would not write "history." This is what historians do: we find material, often created in different times, with which to imagine a past and bring it alive in the present. So while I certainly recognise the particular issues relating to the writing of animal biography—the problem of representation and agency not being the least of these—nevertheless I think it is valid to draw analogies with the writing of history about humans. Too often a conventional approach to history-writing is assumed whereas many of the imaginative approaches being adopted nowadays might also be explored in relation to animal-human histories.

BIOGRAPHICAL MATERIAL ON MARIANA

I now turn to material about Mariana garnered from just this one 'source,' the diaries of Laurance Holman. This does not mean that I am simply looking at these diaries, but I realise that personal coverage of companion *horses* in *diaries* is not found routinely, particularly during the 1940s. Thus drawing on his general analysis of horses in the 1940s, Pegasus, a horse organiser, emphasised the need for balance as what became the "sine qua non" of riding. He argued that a horse needed to move in a controlled way at the required pace but the rider had to adapt his or her movement and adjust their weight in relation to the horse's behaviour. Acting both independently and in response to each other was what was required.[14] However, this form of an account of horses was not seen in the conventional writing of diaries. Holman's diaries were unusual for their time in that *every* day Holman recorded his ride and other observations relating to the behaviour and well-being of Mariana. Initially the diaries record that Mariana was born in the late 1920s, then owned by a well-off man

---

[13] Steedman, *Dust*, 81 (emphasis added).
[14] Pegasus, *Horse Talks*, 25, 30.

living in Hampstead in North London. By 1937 Mariana was living with Laurance Holman, then a man in his 50s, who was new to riding. Laurance Holman was an advertising businessman, who owned his own company (as well as living in accommodation) near the back of the British Museum.

The first time in early December 1937 that Mariana went out with Laurance she was much admired and seen as "a joy to ride."[15] Mariana also started to ride for the first time on Holman's hunt where he was admired for two jumps while kicking another horse while she got "ticked off."[16] By 17 December she was transferred unofficially to Holman by his friend, as mentioned above.[17] Thus from the beginning of the equine-human encounter a relationship between horse and man is being constructed as a framework for Holman's future recording in his diary. She was a horse who liked to gallop: "full gallop up the hill: she evidently is too vigorous and need to be given less corn." Compared to another horse, Security, Holman opined, "but in comparison—Mariana's alive...."[18]

By 1940 both Holman and Mariana were living permanently in London within daily riding access of both Regent's Park and Hyde Park, including fashionable Rotten Row, where the two rode for around two hours a day. She continued to be lively and apparently knowing her own mind: "Took M for a walk in Regent's Park: she sumped down with me on her and was walked back: nothing wrong said Angell: she just wanted a roll in the sand!"[19] Both man and horse lived through and survived the Blitz and wartime in central London. That is, the lives of both of them were both disrupted and changed because of the war. However, the total war was a concept that can be applied to the writing of their circumstances, which we can access to some extent—if we choose to acknowledge interest in an animal existence—through diaries.

Indeed, Mariana became part of Holman's own wartime topography for actually visiting where bombs had fallen in the night: "...last night my 'M.G' was within 100 yds of a house demolished in Woburn Sq and 'Mariana' was about the same distance from a crater made in Wimpole Street."[20] The war itself had not made Holman aware of where Mariana lived—he obviously

[15] Holman, *Diaries*, Wednesday 8 December 1937.
[16] Ibid., Wednesday 15 December 1937.
[17] Ibid., Friday 17 December 1937.
[18] Ibid., Wednesday 15 December 1937; Saturday 12 November 1938; Saturday 2 January 1938.
[19] Ibid., Saturday 1 June 1940.
[20] Ibid., Thursday 19 September 1940.

knew that very well. However, the nature of topography in a war context, identifying places by the falling of bombs in this example, served to highlight the different spaces inhabited by man and horse and the way they were united by the experience of war. The diaries are rather different, for example, to male enthusiasts particularly because these accounts from Holman are normally just seven small inches long per page and the main emphasis is almost exclusively upon personal existence rather than upon military activity outside Britain.[21] Due to paper rationing the wartime diaries were very small, Letts type diaries, which allowed just a few lines of writing per day.[22] After major bombardment in central London, Holman and Mariana would often jointly view the damage. For example, Holman noted, "Last night was the worst 'Blitz' so far: went 11 to 1 for a ride around the damage: saw John Lewis, D.H. Evans, Selfridges but not Peter Robinsons."[23] Their joint experience of war was also evident when they sheltered in the Horse Guards' barracks—that housed soldiers and horses alike alongside Hyde Park. As Holman noted in his diary on 30 September 1940, "Said a little prayer of thanks for another night of safety: midday ride with raid shelter in L*[ife]*. G*[uard]*. Barracks on the way back. Mariana went home so walked her from the Victoria Gate."[24] Even when there had been heavy bombardment on the previous night, Holman and Mariana would still cross Hyde Park, albeit on occasion they "went into [the] Life Guards anticipating the all clear."[25] Apparently both man and horse shared a calm approach towards air raids, as indicated by this entry: "rode in H Park: on way back saw first aerial barrage attack from Horseback: about 12 of them with shells 'puffing' all around: M took no heed and was quite quiet."[26] Thus in his written diary comments on the Blitz there are frequent references to Mariana such as a bombing, "within 100 yards of Mariana" or while jointly Holman and Mariana "passed" Whitehall while "all these spots in my ride" had been attacked.[27]

Throughout the early years of the war Mariana and Laurance rode most days and this was routinely briefly recorded, for example: "Mariana is a bit

[21] See, for example, Foster, *The Real Dad's Army*, or: Millgate, *Mr Brown's War*.

[22] Once the war ends, the size of Holman's diaries—usually containing daily *Punch* cartoons—offer a different form of writing. There is a large page every day. There are no longer end-of-week areas leading to additional space and comment.

[23] Holman, *Diaries*, Thursday 19 September 1940.

[24] Ibid., Monday 30 September 1940.

[25] Ibid., Friday 27 September 1940.

[26] Ibid.

[27] Ibid., Wednesday 16 October 1940, Friday 18 October 1940.

'frisky' these days; in Season I suspect."[28] When there was snow or frost Mariana stayed in the stables but in January 1941 after several days of poor weather Holman, "Took M for first ride in 9 days: she slipped down crossing the Edgware Rd: I fell very gently on my left side: no harm done."[29] The absent reference to injury suggests no harm was done to Mariana either.

Man and horse also both experienced the effects of rationing. As Holman wrote of his own experience, in her own way Mariana also demonstrated the effect of a diet in which although hay and chaff was not rationed, oats, beans and bran were for those living or working in towns. (It was assumed in parliament that certain non-rationed feeding stuff was available on farms.) Moreover some horses were employed by the government on transport duties; 300 other horses were bought by the French government in the first months of the war. Horse dealers were approached to register their horses with the War Office. Light draught horses which were capable of pulling a big weight were particularly in demand.[30] Both "working" horses as well as those kept for riding were initially included within the rationing—with higher quotas being allocated for animals working in transport and haulage.[31] This was later amended, so that horses who were not "performing useful work" were expected to be fed on food grown by their owners.[32] "Too much hay and too little corn" resulted in a horse such as Mariana being "all springs."[33]

Although such problems would have affected all horses kept for riding purposes in London, unfortunately Mariana was beset with specific problems of mobility and lameness for a period of some two years. This is observed very closely by Holman since he was a newcomer to horse riding and he had never previously seen incapacity in a horse. (He was also aware of his *own* problems of ill health.) Holman's lack of previous experience apparently led him to try many alternative treatments and to defer euthanasia to Mariana, despite the encouragement of his more experienced friends. For example, Holman took Mariana out for a walk declaring "but she's so lame I daren't take her out for a ride to-morrow. I'm grieved about

[28] Ibid., Friday 6 December 1940.
[29] Ibid., Thursday 22 January 1941.
[30] Kean, *The Great Cat and Dog Massacre*, 69, 91.
[31] *Hansard*. House of Commons Debates, 6 February 1941: Vol. 368 cc1108–10W. Question from Colonel Carver to Major Lloyd George, Parliamentary Secretary to the Board of Trade.
[32] *Hansard*. House of Commons Debates, 11 November 1941: Vol. 374 c2088W. Mr. Rostron Duckworth to Mr. Hutton, Minister of Agriculture.
[33] Holman, *Diaries*, Wednesday 12 August 1942.

her: am afraid she'll have to be put down."[34] Instead treatment followed from the Royal Veterinary College and a period of convalescence, where Mariana was visited on a number of occasions by the concerned Holman: "horseless, went out to see 'Mariana' at 'the Home of Rest'; nice crisp cold day ... the mare is no worse but not appreciably better."[35] As Holman returned to the stables in February 1942, the stable manager declared that Mariana was "sounder than she has been for 2 years" and subsequently she was "stepping out" well and without any show of lameness. As Holman noted, "I dared not hope for such a good result."[36] But the lameness returned, rubber heels did no good and it was clear that little could have been done to improve her condition.

Echoing the practice of nineteenth century sculptors commissioned to create lifelike images of companion animals to act as memorials after their own death Holman, who was also an artist and sculptor and leading member of the London Sketch Club, spent months sculpting Mariana's face including modelling in her stall. Thus he described "M nuzzling me all the time,"[37] and they spent time together in the stables even when they were not riding. But decline was inevitable and Mariana became in affectionate anthropomorphic vein "the old dear."[38] Although there was still apparently joint enjoyment of some rides, such as the following: "Today's ride was crisp and clear, enjoyed by M and LH," but her "last ride to HP [Hyde Park]: to Lancaster Gate (Victoria G[ate]) and back; poor dear, she's done." Holman also remarked that "nearly 5 years since I got the mare. Hope I get another as good natured and as good looking if such there be. I'm doubtful."[39]

During the next three days Holman noted that he had requested his friend "to see to the funeral [sic] of Mariana" and regretted that he had not done this sooner "instead of keeping on, living in hope" for the "Poor old thing."[40] Apart from referring to the horse's condition Holman also criticised himself over the past years saying, "I can see, now, that I ought to have sanctioned it sooner, instead of keeping on, living on hope. Poor

[34] Ibid., Saturday 18 October 1941.
[35] Ibid., Saturday 13 December 1941.
[36] Ibid., Monday 2 March 1942.
[37] Ibid., Monday 21 September 1942.
[38] Ibid., Saturday 26 September 1942.
[39] Ibid., Sunday 25 October 1942.
[40] Ibid., Sunday 25 October 1942.

darling: I shall be glad to know it is all over."[41] By the end of the week Holman's friend rang him quickly to confirm Mariana's "zero hour of 9 a.m." He added in his statement that, "It's all over, instantaneously and without pain...." Reflecting also on the previous week, as he was customed to do in his diary Holman explained that, "This week has been wet, dismal, and weary. Mariana was part of my life, how much I didn't fully know until this week."[42] Over the next weeks Holman mourned Mariana and also noted the physical impact on his own body of her death: "Had a bad head all day: emotional aftermath I supposed."[43] In the remaining eight years of his life Holman rode with other horses, including Trump, of whom he declared, "I've shed more tears over 'Trump' than I've done over many humans."[44] Yet none would compare to the relationship enjoyed with his first horse, Mariana. Importantly his emotional response to Mariana was far more important than his expression towards humans' lives.

Clearly this biographical account of Mariana is drawn from just one type of material, the contemporary diary of her rider. There are, of course, particular characteristics of the genre that influence the type of information included at that time. Holman saw riding and developing expertise in the recreation as a key part of his own existence—even though doctors had often cautioned him against such strenuous exercise. Perhaps because of his relatively new hobby it was important for Holman to record daily details of both his own riding and aspects of Mariana's behaviour. By noting daily events these points inevitably include the mundane. It is, of course, an account of what Holman notices, or is told about Mariana, and it includes his own emotional response. Nevertheless, there is material here about the horse, her "agency" in relation to Holman and, to some extent, the relationship *between* them—not simply Holman's emotions, although those are obviously there. It sheds light on an equine-human relationship at that particular time for which there is scant contemporary material.

Writing about his own important work on "The Great Diary Project" Irving Finkel has suggested:

People in all walks of life have confided and often still confide their thoughts and experiences to the written page, and the result is a unique record of

---

[41] Ibid., Wednesday 28 October 1942.
[42] Ibid., Saturday 31 October 1942.
[43] Ibid., Wednesday 4 November 1942.
[44] Ibid., Friday 9 May 1947.

what happens to an individual over months, or even years, as seen through their eyes. No other kind of document offers such a wealth of information about daily life and the ups and downs of human existence.[45]

Within Holman's diary, dates are a feature. The form is itself one that is framed by time: discrete spaces into which to put events of the day and of Mariana's experience. It also included space for end-of-week reflections. Thus Holman continues to reflect back upon his experiences at the end of the week, showing the extent of his memory during the seven-day procedure. Therefore, although Mariana's experience of her poor personal life is covered within the diary, Laurance's perception of his heart condition is also revealed.

Recently Stephen F. Eisenman in an article critical of animal studies work suggests that there are examples of mediated or dependent agency: "Animals, like humans, in short, have acted individually and collectively— that is, politically—to affirm their interests, but historians and critics associated with AS [*Animal Studies*] have mostly missed that fact."[46] However, the Holman diary practice considers his horse activity in rather different ways. It may be possible for historians not only to acknowledge, but more importantly to analyse, the affective agency of nonhuman animals in history. As Birke and Hockenhull demonstrate in analysing horses, "co-ordinating behaviour with another entails an emotional component, which both reflects and produces the relationship, and so does interspecies co-ordination, even if this behaviour is not identical." As they also argue, "A better understanding of how togetherness and partnership are built by humans and by companion animals, would surely benefit us all."[47] While such writers note the difficulty of obtaining the past practice of animals such as horses[48] the unusual approach exemplified by Laurance Holman not only illustrates the extent of horse experience—and death—but the relationship between the human and the animal. His experience of his own poor health, alongside his role in London during the Second World War, helped create his own perception of his horse's recent life.

---

[45] "The Great Diary Project."
[46] Eisenmann, "Swinish Multitude," 344.
[47] Birke and Hockenhull, "Journeys."
[48] See, for example, Andria Pooley-Ebert, "Species Agency."

The Diary Life of Laurance Holman

Reflecting on Holman's diary particularly during the Second World War and afterwards is significant. I read this not as a diary for personal publication, or for others to read, but am conscious he is writing for himself.[49] The audience for the diary seems to be for him rather than given to his second wife. Events were remembered but also they found a place in a chronologically ordered narrative around the physical form and structure of a diary. Importantly the tiny structure of the diary almost explicitly ensures that daily horse activity—or difficulty—can influence the diarist's own life approaches. While acknowledging that even the material on Mariana is not extensive little is known of the diarist. Apart from his own diary, I found different notions of his life through official documents.[50] That is there were terms of "factual" information, material such as that found in census returns, birth, marriage and death certificates and Post Office Directories and in some ways the diary was similar in composition to that discovered in family research.

Laurance Holman died suddenly in April 1950, from a heart attack, having completed his last diary entry just two days before and also on the same day as his last ride on a horse.[51] Although relatively well-off, Holman was not seen as a financially important man in society. I am not suggesting that the factual data tells us much significantly about the man, but I am not at all convinced that the diary entries really tell us that much either about the relationship between man and horse. I obviously learnt about his relationship with Mariana (and later Trump), and what food Holman himself ate, when he went to bed, his overdraft, his health and his attitude towards his growing age, new contracts and his ambiguous relationship with Wendy (who was his mistress and then wife). With reference to Mariana her own details include her daily routines, her health, her temperament, her reaction to the noise of bombing, the date and circumstances of her death—not dissimilar sorts of

---

[49] Kean, "The Home Front," 163.

[50] Human materials came from census returns, birth, marriage and death certificates, archive of the London Sketch Club, Post Office directories, electoral registers, local newspapers, maps and books and periodicals in British Library, Colindale, and the Camden Archives.

[51] This broad material is also drawn from the plethora of abstract archival material. Holman left £80,000.

material to that we know of Holman. I became, however, more convinced that the diary also told me little when I was contacted by two
men through the notes on my website. One had been working as a
young man in the Holman advertising workshop and another had been
a young relative. Interestingly they gave me different perspectives on
their memory of this self-made man.[52] They also did acknowledge
Holman's daily interest in his horses.

I am now obliged to acknowledge that the diary was related to the
experience of one man and was only one facet of his existence. I was aware
that the diary carried a very particular narrative but I was also recognisant
of the content of his official documents. The diarist is only one face of
Laurance Holman's existence: his identity as a writer and that which
engaged with his horses. But I suggest we should not regard such material
too critically and then be forgetful of drawing parallels with the accounts
of Mariana—and her apparent engagement with Holman.

This is a partial account of a horse: but it is also a partial account of a
man. In particular Holman's emotional response to Mariana's death is an
important influence on the man's life. Significantly too the relationship
with Mariana also reads far more important than his experience of living in
London during the Second World War. I never intended to try to publish
the diary for a printed publication. Holman is not really in the public eye
and the audience for the diary seems to be him: he refers back to earlier
years to evaluate current physical and financial health. The plethora of
figures exists—numbers of cheques written, fluctuations in the stock market, sales and purchase of shares, amount of time riding and when, food
purchase on a Saturday on the way back from the stables, and even the
time he goes to bed. Such comments are surely all indicators of someone
seeking to create some control over his own life.

If we are interested in acknowledging the identity of individual animals,
even those that were living during the Second World War, it also means
recognising the traces and relationships that did exist between the animal
and the human. I had not found a man *as such* in the archives but I *had
found* traces of his existence and also those of Mariana and her later horse
companions.

---

[52] "As a young man I worked for L.H. at his advertising agency in Bedford Square. First
from Easter 1944 to June 1946 then conscription and again on leaving the army in 1948
until shortly before his death in 1950." See Graham Lewis, "As written to my website."

Acknowledgement Thanks to Russell Burrows, Kim Stallwood, André Krebber and Mieke Roscher for their support.

WORKS CITED

Benjamin, Walter. *The Arcades Project*. Translated by H. Eiland and K. McLaughlin. Cambridge: Harvard University Press, 2002.

Birke, Lynda and Jo Hockenhull. "Journeys Together: Horses and Humans in Partnership." *Society and Animals* 23.1 (2015): 81–100.

Eisenman, Stephen. "The Real 'Swinish Multitude'." *Critical Inquiry* 42.2 (2016): 339–373.

Foster, Rodney. *The Real Dad's Army: The War Diaries of Col.Rodney Foster*. Edited by Ronnie Scott. London: Pensions, 2011.

Hansard. House of Commons Debates, February 6, 1941a: Vol. 368 cc1108–10W. Question from Colonel Carver to Major Lloyd George, Parliamentary Secretary to the Board of Trade.

———. House of Commons Debates, November 11, 1941b: Vol. 374 c2088W. Mr. Rostron Duckworth to Mr. Hutton, Minister of Agriculture.

Holman, Laurence. *Diaries*. London: Borough of Camden Archives.

Kean, Hilda. "Whose Archive? Whose History? Destruction of Archives at Ruskin College, Oxford." http://www.historyworkshop.org.uk/whose-archive-whose-history-destruction-of-archives-at-ruskin-college-oxford/. Accessed July 19, 2017.

———. *London Stories: Personal Lives: Public Histories*. London: Rivers Oram Press, 2004.

———. "Challenges for Historians Writing Animal-Human History: What is Really Enough?" *Anthrozoös* 25, Suppl. 1 (2012): 57–72.

———. "The Home Front as a 'Moment' for Animals and Humans: Exploring the Animal-Human Relationship in Contemporary Diaries and Letters." In *The Home Front in Britain. Images, Myths and Forgotten Experiences Since 1914*, edited by Maggie Andrews and Janis Lomas, 152–169. Basingstoke: Palgrave Macmillan, 2014.

———. *The Great Cat and Dog Massacre. The Real Story of World War 11's Unknown Tragedy*. Chicago: University of Chicago Press, 2017.

Lewis, Graham. "As Written to My Website." http://hildakean.com/?p=1672. Accessed August 2, 2017.

Milligate, Helen D. *Mr. Brown's War: A Diary of the Second World War*. Stroud: Sutton, 1998.

Pegasus. *Horse Talks: A Vade Mecum for Young Riders*. London: Collins, 1948.

Pooley-Ebert, Andria. "Species Agency: Comparative Study of Horse-Human Relations in Chicago and Rural Illinois." In *The Historical Animal*, edited by Susan Nance, 148–165. New York: Syracuse University Press, 2015.

Steedman, Carolyn. *Dust*. Manchester: Manchester University Press, 2001.

———. *An Everyday Life of the English Working Class: Work, Self and Sociability in the Early Nineteenth Century*. Cambridge: Cambridge University Press, 2013.

The Great Diary Project. http://www.thegreatdiaryproject.co.uk/. Accessed October 1, 2017.

Wolfe, Cary. *What is Posthumanism?* Minneapolis: University of Minnesota Press, 2009.

CHAPTER 4

Recovering and Reconstructing Animal Selves in Literary Autozoographies

Frederike Middelhoff

Introduction: Autobiographical Animals

Animal quasi-autobiographical stories have been distributed for more than 200 years.[1] The genre stages animals as the narrators, or even writers, of their lives, retrospectively engaging with their upbringing, educational training, memorable developments, and experiences from a first-person perspective. The autobiographical animal narrator comprehensively and anthropomorphically narrates his or her life, while the animal protagonist, that is, the experiencing subject of the story, behaves "naturally," neither metamorphosing nor using human language, as is the case in many fables, parables, or fairy tales. This chapter discusses animal autobiographies as "literary autozoographies." The neologism, as I have stated elsewhere,[2] hinges on the assertion that representations of (autobiographical) animals can only be grasped adequately in their

[1] DeMello, "Introduction."
[2] Middelhoff, "Literary Autozoographies."

F. Middelhoff (✉)
Julius-Maximilians-University, Würzburg, Germany

© The Author(s) 2018
A. Krebber, M. Roscher (eds.), *Animal Biography*,
Palgrave Studies in Animals and Literature,
https://doi.org/10.1007/978-3-319-98288-5_4

57

epistemological, cultural, socio-historical, and esthetic complexity, if zoological and zoographical[3] contexts, scientific and popular discourses on what distinguishes a specific animal species, are taken into consideration. Minding and "self-ing" animal individuals in autobiographical narratives, literary autozoographies indeed have zoology in mind: they reflect, negotiate, co-produce, and affect zoological knowledge, cultural imaginations, and social practices concerning animal species. The term thus takes both the methodological and theoretical perspectives as well as the object of its own investigation into account. Apart from the inquiry into the genre's epistemology and contexts, it can make sense to pin these texts down with regard to the lives of "real" (referential) animals reconfigured and immortalized in autozoographical accounts.

Conventionally, studies on animal life writing have applied what Susan McHugh aptly denotes as the "disappearing animal trick."[4] As soon as literary autozoographies are read as satire, parody, allegory, parable, and so on, self-narrating animals vanish in exchange for what is alleged to be their "actual" meaning. Considered as human representatives or "mere" literary motifs, animal narrator-protagonists become nonhuman signifiers for alleged signified human concerns. Only recently literary scholars have begun to inquire into the meanings of autozoographical animals *as* animals.[5] This chapter is interested in the epistemological and (auto)biographical aspects of literary autozoographies. Following preliminary thoughts on the genre, it investigates how literary representations of autozoographical selves relate to and take part in zoological, historical discourse. If natural history created "biographies of species,"[6] how did literary autozoography, imagining and narrating individual animal lives, challenge and contribute to species knowledge? The chapter then examines the material semiotics[7] and interrelations of "real" and "fictional" animals. Can autozoographical writings actually be considered a means of recovering animal lives? Taking the German Romantic E.T.A. Hoffmann

---

[3] Zoography refers to the "description of the forms, nature, and properties of animals"; zoology figures as "[a] treatise concerning living creatures" (Sheridan, *Complete Dictionary*, n.p.).

[4] McHugh, "Animal Farm's," 24.

[5] I.a., Keenleyside, "Introduction"; Smith, "Representing Animal," For an overview of recent scholarship on animal autobiography, see Herman, "Animal Autobiography," 2–4.

[6] Toepfer, *Historisches Wörterbuch*, 497. All following translations from German are my own.

[7] Haraway, *Staying with*, 4.

(1776–1822) and his feline autozoography *The Life and Opinions of the Tomcat Murr* (1819/21) as a case in point, the chapter shows that literary autozoographies not only negotiate and shape zoological knowledge on a species but may also incorporate and reflect extra-textual human-animal relationships, and thus point us at traces as well as acknowledgments of animal selves.

TRACKING ANIMAL SELVES IN AND BEYOND LITERARY AUTOZOOGRAPHIES

Ever since the genre's inception, albeit for very different reasons and with different narrative approaches,[8] authors of literary autozoographies have projected what it might be like to smell, feel, see, and taste the world of animals by conceiving animal life and experiences in the mode of the first person.[9] Most importantly for the context of this chapter, however, these narratives hinge on the premise that animals "have a perspective on and interest in situations and events."[10] Animal narrators in these stories are conscious, feeling, self-aware agents, regardless both of how often this agency might be discursively accompanied and, at times, "thwarted" by inherent physiological needs or impeded by human interventions, and of how much these representations might be dismissed as (naïve) anthropomorphism.

Life-narrating animals can but do not always have referential counter-parts beyond the texts. Although it is likely that many an author was inspired to write the first-person account of an animal's life by a specific animal known to or even living with him or her—as can be seen in many contemporary literary autozoographies giving photographical "existential" evidence of the autobiographized animal individual[11]—for many narratives, especially those dating back to the eighteenth and nineteenth centuries, such a connection between "real" and "literary" animals cannot

---

[8] Cp. Keenleyside, "Introduction"; Armbruster, "What Do We Want."

[9] Well-known examples of the genre include *Life of the Tomcat Murr* (Hoffmann, *Life and Opinions*), *Black Beauty* (Sewell, *Black Beauty*), and *Beautiful Joe* (Saunders, *Beautiful Joe*). The genre may have had its origins in Western literary history; however, a text like Sōseki Natsume's *Wagahai wa Neko de aru* (1905/2002) proves its appeal to non-Western authors. Contemporary autozoographical books (on demand) are ubiquitous, as a random search on Google will tell you.

[10] Herman, "Animal Autobiography," 6.

[11] Glööckler, *Billy King*; Siebert, *Angus*.

be drawn. It remains unclear, if not highly doubtful, whether Amante[12] or Zoddel[13] existed beyond the realm of the texts. Nonetheless, in a number of cases the texts themselves, paratexts (foreword, epilogue, book cover, etc.), additional information on the human author, or historical contexts make evident a reference to a specific animal. Murr,[14] Joe,[15] Angus,[16] Timothy,[17] Tosca, and Knut[18] are genuinely material-semiotic animals: they are figuring as literary characters and narrative authorities whose material lives reach beyond the pages of autozoographical books.[19] These animals appear in but have also existed apart from the world of fiction. Why could this be important for our reading of literary autozoographies? First, it can enable us to question the unilateral, essentialist notion of authorship and instead allow for an idea "of trans-species co-authorship,"[20] assuming that a human co-author is motivated "to infer and co-articulate, on the basis of the animal's observed dispositions and behavioral tendencies,"[21] an animal co-author's interests and intentions. Second, recognizing and investigating the connections between "real" and autozoographical animal individuals presents us with a means to grasp the modes of autozoographical representations, the form of the narrative as well as the functions of a specific text.

At first glance, however, it might be presupposed that animals are "not 'in' on the composition and dissemination"[22] of autozoographical narratives. Humans write about, but not in cooperation with animals; animals are represented in, but not co-producers of life narratives. Nevertheless, some texts invite us to acknowledge that their authors have rigorously tried to put themselves "in the animal's position (zoomorphism) and

---

[12] Trichter, *Lebensgeschichte.*

[13] Ranzoni, *Zaddel.*

[14] Hoffmann, *Life and Opinions.*

[15] Saunders, *Beautiful Joe.*

[16] Siebert, *Angus.*

[17] Klinkenborg, *Timothy.*

[18] Tawada, *Memoirs.*

[19] It would be short-sighted, however, to regard only those fictional animals with extra-textual counterparts as material-semiotic. Animal representations and real animals are two flipsides of that which we conceive of and attribute meaning to as "animals," with literary representations reflecting and shaping the cultural meanings and lives of real animals (Borgards, "Tiere und Literatur," 226, 239–240).

[20] Herman, "Animal Autobiography," 9.

[21] Ibid.

[22] Huff and Haefner, "Master's Voice," 156.

imagine[d] other senses and the creative realms of those senses."[23] To be sure, none of the writers of literary autozoographies can eschew an inherent epistemological anthropocentrism.[24] Human knowledge and animal representations are always subject to and limited by strictly human-centric perspectives. In this respect, "anthropomorphism is inevitable."[25] As a matter of fact, any verbal rendition of animal minds finds itself mired in this fundamental paradox: how to narrate an individual experience that is wordless but certainly not world- or voiceless?

Throughout the recent decades, ethological research has come to acknowledge that narrative is crucial to investigate and describe nonhuman life, realizing that "each animal has its own story to tell."[26] Similarly, many autozoographical texts try to tell the story of an animal's life by empathetically aligning themselves to nonhuman experiences. It can be suggested that something akin to what Kenneth Shapiro describes as kinesthetic empathy shaped some of the poetics of literary autozoographies. As "an interpretive investigative posture,"[27] kinesthetic empathy in play and corporeal interspecies engagements aims to "move into the world of the animal"[28] not only observed but lived and interacted with. This empathetic engagement, Shapiro notes, effectively "develops a biographical account."[29] Moreover, it can be argued that some autozoographical writers, akin to constructivist ethology, not only "regard the subjectivity of animals and the situational emplacement of their human observers as living beings themselves [as axiomatic]"[30] but also aim to "construct the ways that animals construct their worlds."[31] Attentive to and actively engaging in the ways individual animals move, gesture, and interact, while simultaneously taking part in this interaction, some autozoographical writers venture to invent, imagine, and reconfigure the shared lives, spaces, and experiences from a nonhuman perspective. In such accounts, animals are not excluded from but actively participate in the making of the text as part of a multispecies

[23] Jevbratt, "Interspecies," 17.
[24] Borgards, "Animal Studies," 223.
[25] Cadman, "Reflections," 178.
[26] De Waal, *Inner Ape*, 146.
[27] Shapiro, "Understanding dogs," 33.
[28] Ibid.
[29] Ibid., 34.
[30] Lestel et al., "Phenomenology," 128.
[31] Ibid.

project, or zoopoetics.[32] When a writer "undergoes the making process of *poiesis* in harmony with the gestures and vocalizations of nonhuman animals, [...] [i]t is a co-making. A joint venture."[33] Furthermore, it is not only by way of paying close attention to but also holding deep affections for specific companion animals that animal agency becomes apparent in the *poiesis* of literary autozoographies, as the discussion of Hoffmann's feline autozoography in the next part of this chapter will show.

Analyzing the intricacies and interdependencies of autozoographical animals and their respective "real" counterparts may also reveal different functional aspects of the texts. Many such narratives can be read as memorial and relational accounts, on the one hand, as well as covert human autobiographies on the other. Some authors commemorate their companions as "good friends,"[34] whose lives are written down "in memory of them"[35]; some try to write history anew by imagining the perspective of individual historical animals, while simultaneously allowing a critical view on human involvement in and impact on animal lives[36]; some upstage animal life, using the animal to narrate their own lives and lifestyles.[37] Animals in these texts are represented as heavily depending on and influenced by their human owners, yet they are also significantly affecting these humans in return.[38]

(Auto)Biographical and Epistemological Entanglements: Hoffmann's Tomcat(s)

Investigations into the interdependencies between Murr's textual representation and zoological discourse on domestic cats around 1800 remain as sparse as the inquiry into the fact that Hoffmann actually had a tomcat,

---

[32] Moe, *Zoopoetics.*
[33] Moe, "Toward Zoopoetics," 2.
[34] Arensburg, *Hundeleben,* 5.
[35] Ibid.
[36] Klinkenborg, *Timothy;* Tawada, *Memoirs.*
[37] Bush, *Millie's Book;* Glööckler, *Billy King.*
[38] This is the case, for example, in Siebert, *Angus.* At the end of the book, Siebert addresses the readers, relating his emotional engagement with and the post-mortem omnipresence of Angus (Ibid., 162–163, 171–173). Nonetheless, it should not be denied that we find a number of literary autozoographies in which the animal narrator is predominantly instrumentalized for voyeuristic, ideological, and self-fashioning purposes (cf., e.g., O'Hagan, *Life and Opinions;* Bush, *Millie's Book*). Such narratives may be seen to "appropriate species subjectivities for political and rhetorical purposes" (Huff and Haefner, "Master's Voice," 157).

called Murr, living, interacting, and drawing[39] with Hoffmann in Berlin during the time he sat down to write *Tomcat Murr*.[40] Hoffmann's novel is extraordinary not only for its proto-modernist experimentality but also for its anti-Cartesian views, "assert[ing] a continuity between celestial spirit, human mind, animal being and mechanical substance."[41] The novel presents itself as a concoction of animal autobiography and human biography, intertwining human and animal life in the story as well as in the form.[42] Signing the foreword with "E.T.A. Hoffmann,"[43] the editor explains that the reason for this "oddly assorted hotchpotch"[44] lies in the fact that the autobiographical cat had used Kapellmeister Johannes Kreisler's biography as blotting and writing paper. The result is a text which has the cat's autobiographical account—"my life story before the world,"[45] being a retrospective and philosophical-literary reflection on the genesis of the poetic, autobiographical cat—interrupted again and again by extracts from Kreisler's biography and vice versa. Scholars have tended to read the text as a work of social satire and as a parody of autobiography and the *Bildungsroman*,[46] reluctant to conceive of the cat as a material-semiotic agent, a "zoological-literary hybrid"[47]: a cat with very special skills like reading and writing on the one hand, and with ethologically sound, feline behavior on the other; a cat growing up and interacting with humans, cats, and dogs. Why could the depiction of a cat like Murr living and communicating with humans be of any relevance from a historical as well as an animal studies point of view? First, Murr's representation and trans-species

[39] To the note which announced the death of his tomcat and which he sent to his friend Theodor Gottlieb von Hippel, Hoffmann added a piece of paper with an undecipherable ink drawing that he had signed "Kater Murr." Today, the library catalogue lists Murr as the "artist" of the sketch and assumes that "Hoffmann produced the paper in memory of or sympathetic testimony" probably by "dipping the cat's paw into the ink, brushing it across the paper" (Hoffmann, "Quartblatt").

[40] Steinecke, "Kommentar," 907. Notable exceptions to this include Segebrecht, *Autobiographie*, 208, 217–218; Kofman, *Autobiogriffures*; Schröter, *Figur*; Borgards, "Tiere," 314.

[41] Hoffmann, *Life and Opinions*, xxviii.

[42] Murr, for example, appears in Kreisler's biography where he interacts with the Kapellmeister (Ibid., 21).

[43] Ibid., 5.

[44] Ibid., i.

[45] Ibid., 7.

[46] I.a., Stone, "E. T. A. Hoffmann"; Beardsley, *Hoffmanns Tierfiguren*.

[47] Borgards, "Tiere," 313.

relations can be regarded as a response to the disparagement of cats and a denial of feline companionship value we find in the accounts of natural history around 1800. Murr, by contrast, is an integral part in and accepted member of the *oikos* he shares with the servants and the human character called Master Abraham, who has taken him in as a kitten. In this respect, *Tomcat Murr* also prefigures the re-assessment of cats in German popular zoology in the course of the nineteenth century—a movement exchanging the idea of cats as semi-domestics whose "disposition is marked by deceit, guile, and a fondness for sweet things"[48] for the belief in cats' potential to become "an entertaining friend whose attachment is voluntary."[49] Second, it forces the reader to question whether there is indeed such a thing as "the" cat. Murr is represented not as one of many, but as one of a kind, proposing a model of animal individuality beyond species paradigms as dictated by the tableau of natural history. And, third, the cat's representation is indicative of Hoffmann's emotional attachment to and interaction with his own cat with whom he shared his apartment in Berlin between 1818 and 1821. In this regard, *Tomcat Murr* becomes tangible as the (auto)biographical portrayal of Hoffmann's cat and the affection the poet held for his feline companion.

WRITING FELINE (AUTO)BIOGRAPHY

The European history of domestic cats as undisputed members of the household and companion animals is a rather young one.[50] In late eighteenth century, the *Economic Encyclopaedia* simply defined "Hauskatze" as "domestic cat kept in the houses in contrast to wild cats."[51] It is telling that the entry speaks of cats being "kept" in the houses, not living or dwelling in them. Around 1800, cats were not considered as co-habitants but rather as reluctantly tolerated, half-wild beneficiaries of human settlements, decimating mice and rats which populated pantries and granaries. When Hoffmann published the first volume of his feline autozoography in 1819, cats still had a "hermaphrodite status as farm animal and symbol of the devil."[52]

---

[48] Bechstein, *Naturgeschichte Deutschlands*, 255.
[49] Michel, *Buch der Katzen*, 170.
[50] Hengerer, "Die Katze."
[51] Krünitz, *Encyklopädie*, 390.
[52] Leggewie, "Die Katze," 207.

Cats were also regarded as devious and dishonest animals. While the dog was hailed for his loyalty and servitude, the cat was devalued as treacherous and unsociable. One of the most pertinent voices in the discourse attributing negative characteristics to cats was Georges-Louis Leclerc Comte de Buffon (1707–1788). In his canonical *Natural History*, Buffon condemns the cat as the most unpleasant and dangerous of all domestic animals:

> The cat is a faithless domestic, and only kept through necessity [...] for we pay no respect to those who, being fond of all beasts, keeps [*sic*] cats for amusement. [...] [T]hese animals [...] possess an innate cunning, and perverse disposition, which age increases [...]. They are naturally inclined to theft, and the best of education only converts them into servile and flattering robbers [...]. [M]ost of them are half wild, know not their masters, frequent other granaries and never visit the kitchens and offices belonging to the house.[53]

To Buffon and German natural history writing of the eighteenth and early nineteenth centuries, a cat's presence in the household was nothing but a nuisance. The biography of the domestic cat in natural history, therefore, was dominated by the vilification of "the" feline character. In Hoffmann's feline autozoography, however, the reader is confronted with a very different picture—a feline representation which responds to and redefines conventional, denigrating feline characteristics and which not only promotes the individuality and exceptionality of a specific cat but also illustrates the tomcat's nonverbal communicative capacities. The text takes up the zoological and popular notion of cats as crafty, scheming, and independent to give it an ironic twist, satirizing stereotypical notions by presenting a cat who is so clever and self-confident as to be able to read and write and therefore rival human exceptionality[54]; an individual who only feigns when having to fear for his life[55] and who is in love with himself and his poetic ingenuity.[56] Thus, the novel mimics popular ideas of cats as aloof, conceited loners, but simultaneously presents a counternarrative of a cat

---

[53] Buffon, *Barr's Buffon*, 1–2, 6. A critical German translation of the French was published in 1773.

[54] Kofman, *Autobiogriffures.*

[55] Hoffmann, *Life and Opinions*, 62.

[56] Ibid., for example, 7, 26, 49, 63.

attached to and interacting with human characters,[57] stealing nothing but quotations.[58] Ultimately, Murr turns out neither harmful nor the object of the reader's derision.[59]

In fact, looking at (re-)assessments of "the" cat in the second half of the nineteenth century, the representation of Hoffmann's feline character can be regarded as a prefiguration of a change in zoology's feline descriptions. By mid-nineteenth century, conventional ideas and derogatory accounts of domestic cats came to be regarded as unfairly biased and prejudiced—henceforth, cats tended to be promoted as affectionate companion animals and were extolled as underestimated and misinterpreted.[60] According to the cat's most prominent zoological advocate in Germany, Alfred Ludwig Brehm, the cat used to be a completely misunderstood creature. The cat, Brehm writes, "is nothing less than false but, on the contrary, very candid; the cat is just as little deceitful as the dog and never scratches while she's coaxing; rather, she is loyally devoted to her masters [...]. *What she lacks most of all is a loving education on the part of the human to make her an entirely amiable animal.*"[61] As can be gathered from the account of another "cat-panegyrist,"[62] Hoffmann's literary cat is even cited to support the argument that cats are cordial, clever animals. In Gustav Michel's opinion, Hoffman "knew how to put a lot of imagination into his tomcat Murr,"[63] whereas "Buffon's opinions," Michel declares, have to be regarded as "sufficiently refuted by new accounts of natural scientists."[64] Judging from Brehm and Michel, Hoffmann's autozoographical tomcat represents a more authentic, unprejudiced account of feline life and behavior than what can be found in the natural history books of Hoffmann's contemporaries. As a well-known text, *Tomcat Murr* might not only have been ahead of its time but can also be seen as an influential actor in the redefinition of cats, contributing to readers' more favorable view of feline qualities, while also imbuing Brehm's and Michel's arguments. Murr is proof that Buffon is wrong. So how does the literary cat do that?

---

[57] Ibid., for example, 62, 245.
[58] Ibid., for example, 254.
[59] Müller-Seidel, "Nachwort," 684.
[60] Michel, *Buch der Katzen*; Bungartz, *Katzenbuch*.
[61] Brehm, "Aus dem Leben," 513 (original emphasis).
[62] Michel, *Buch der Katzen*, 10.
[63] Ibid., 176.
[64] Ibid., 27.

In Buffon's generic account, "the" cat neither gets attached to humans nor does she ever frequent the social and working spaces within a house. Murr, however, who had been rescued from drowning and brought up by Master Abraham, tells a very different story. Not only does this cat roam around the house from cellar to attic, Murr also goes in and out of his master's study where he even partakes in Abraham's work. Murr tells us that Abraham "was even pleased if, when he himself was working, I jumped up and settled down among the papers before him"[65] and "if he was studying at his desk, he would let me sit behind him on his chair."[66] Moreover, this cat is pampered and groomed by Master Abraham, who—as Murr relates—"spared no pains in brushing me clean with a soft brush and then combing my fur with a little comb until it shone."[67] Murr sleeps on "a big cushion well stuffed with horsehair"[68] and is nourished by the housemaid's "tasty porridge made of flour, sweet milk and butter."[69] As becomes evident in the course of the narrative, Murr is a well-established member of the household and interactively engages, for example, with the housemaid whom he not only "often encountered in the cellar and whose kitchen [he] [...] used to visit," but with whom he also "never met without playing an agreeable game."[70]

Furthermore, looking at that kind of interspecies interaction happening between Master Abraham and his cat, we seem to be observing something akin to Buffon's nightmare of a cat-loving, mutually amusing, co-constitutive relationship. Abraham not only calls his cat "the companion of my hearth and home"[71] and "the cleverest, best, and indeed the wittiest creature of his kind ever beheld"[72] but also finds himself getting even more attached to Murr after the cat returns from an absence of several days which had been brought about by an accident taking Murr away in a carriage.[73] On the cat's return to the house, Abraham admits: "The good creature showed not only intelligence and understanding, but also the most faithful devotion to his master, so that I now love him more than

---

[65] Hoffmann, *Life and Opinions*, 26.
[66] Ibid., 268.
[67] Ibid., 227.
[68] Ibid., 169.
[69] Ibid.
[70] Ibid., 245.
[71] Ibid., 108.
[72] Ibid., 21.
[73] Ibid., 80.

ever."[74] Neither faithless, nor cunning, Hoffmann's literary cat renounces the conventional narrative of "the" cat, ringing in a new era of looking at and engaging with cats in the course of the nineteenth century in which it also became compelling to admit to the idiosyncrasies of and differences between feline individuals in relation to their upbringing.

Apart from engaging with each other in the study or by playing, for example, with a toy, which Abraham has constructed, consisting of a stick with feathers attached to it,[75] Murr and Abraham also define and develop their relationship by communicating with each other face to face. As a matter of fact, Abraham talks to Murr every time they meet, and Murr—in return and in his very own cat-ish register textually encoded either linguistically or onomatopoetically—does not fail to show that he is far from ignorant of what is being said and meant. Sometimes this ends in Abraham furiously trying to rid himself of Murr's dirty paws after the tomcat had tried to bring his understanding across by "utter[ing] a very clear and melodious 'Miaow!' and without more ado jump[ing] on [his] master's lap"[76]; sometimes this appears as an address and counteraddress, a mini dialogue: "'Murr! Murr!' cried Master Abraham. / 'Purr—purr!' *replied* the tomcat, quite distinctly,"[77] as can be read in a passage told by the narrator of Kreisler's biography, underscoring that it is not only Murr's supposedly biased self(indulgingly)-reflexive perception interpreting the scene as a communicative situation. In the mornings, Murr usually approaches Abraham "to roll at his feet, caper about and jump up on his lap when he r[i]se[s] [...] and call[s], 'Good morning, Murr!'"[78] Speaking to and addressing the tomcat, Abraham acknowledges Murr as an experiencing, basically apprehending subject, while Murr's response (not: reaction), in turn, denotes his acknowledgment of Master Abraham as a communicative significant other. To speak with Donna Haraway, Murr and Abraham seem to be "[s]ignificantly other to each other" and "training each other in acts of communication [they] barely understand."[79] Despite misunderstandings and situations involving miscommunication, Murr and Abraham negotiate their relationship and relate to each other in everyday acts of verbal and nonverbal interaction. In the "act of speaking-for that crosses

---

[74] Ibid., 108.
[75] Ibid., 168.
[76] Hoffmann, *Life and Opinions*, 227.
[77] Ibid., 21 (emphasis added).
[78] Ibid., 168.
[79] Haraway, *Companion Species*, 2–3.

species lines,"[80] the autozoographical text thus mediates knowledge on interspecies behavior and interaction, speaking out for a companion species relationship transgressing and refuting contemporary zoological feline life stories.

One of the several passages giving a good impression of these interspecies communicative attempts in the novel is the scene in which Murr encounters Abraham after he had been bruised in a fight with another tomcat. Murr recounts:

> I felt myself being gently carried away by someone. It was my kind master, who had heard me outside the door [...]. 'Poor Murr,' he cried, 'what on earth have they done to you? [...]' / 'Oh, Master,' I thought, 'if only you knew!' [...] My good master laid me on my bed, [...] prepared two plasters and put them on my ear and my paw. I let him do all this calmly and patiently, only letting out a little 'Mrrr!' when the first plaster hurt me slightly. / 'You're a clever cat, Murr!' said my master. '[...] Keep quiet now, and when it's time for you to lick your wounded paw better you'll get the plaster off yourself. [...]' / I promised my master I would, offering him my sound paw in token of my satisfaction and my gratitude for his aid. *As usual*, he took it and shook it slightly without applying the least pressure.[81]

Although Murr cannot tell Abraham what has actually happened, he does not only comprehend Abraham's advice but also communicates his understanding nonverbally to Abraham who, in turn, acknowledges the cat's grasp and heed of advice by shaking Murr's offered paw—a silent communicative act the two characters have developed to express mutual consent. Getting in touch and being in touch via voice and body, Murr and Abraham seem to have cultivated their very own routine of shaping their encounters, that is, a mode of interaction building upon affect and mutual affection, reaching out across species lines.

WRITING MURR'S (AUTO)BIOGRAPHY

Looking at the representation of Murr, and the relationship between Murr and Abraham, one starts wondering how E.T.A. Hoffmann and his own cat fit into the picture. As a matter of fact, Hoffmann's feline autozoography ends with the editor announcing the death of the autobiographical

---

[80] Herman, "Animal Autobiography," 7.
[81] Hoffmann, *Life and Opinions*, 209–10 (emphasis added).

tomcat and, therefore, declaring the autobiographical account a fragment—yet not a figment, as shall be seen shortly. In the postscript of the text, the editor records: "That clever, well-educated, philosophical, poetical tomcat Murr was snatched away by bitter Death in the midst of a fine career. He died in the night between the twenty-ninth and the thirtieth of November, after a short but severe illness, with the calm and composure of a wise man."[82] It was exactly during that night in the year 1821 when Hoffmann's very own tomcat, Murr, died. On the day after the cat's death, Hoffmann sent out obituaries to his closest friends, running as follows:

> On the night of the 29th to 30th November this year, after a short but severe illness, my beloved ward the tomcat Murr departed this life for a better world, dead in the fourth year of his promising career. Those who knew the deceased youth, who saw him tread the path of virtue and justice, will judge of my pain and honour it by silence.[83]

Evidently, the editor's postscript of the novel is nothing but a literary version of the real death note handed out by Hoffmann, indicative of what Wulf Segebrecht has rightly conceived of as the poet's "expression of a true pain"[84] in the aftermath of his loss. At the end of the novel, it seems, fact and fiction, real and literary cat, have become thoroughly entwined. But is it just Murr's death that has been fictionalized to become part of Hoffmann's text? The biographical information we can gather from Hoffmann's friends and acquaintances and, first and foremost, the novel itself suggests otherwise: the representation of Hoffmann's literary cat as a clever, unique specimen, communicating with and endearing himself to Master Abraham, one of Hoffmann's "alter ego[s],"[85] might rather be seen as mirroring Hoffmann's own attachment to and everyday encounter with his cat. The smart, loyal cat of the text becomes palpable as thoroughly materially-semiotically entangled with the "real" Murr, if we look at statements dealing with Hoffmann's relation to his cat companion.

In a letter to his friend Speyer dated May 1820, for example, Hoffmann revealed that "*'[a] real cat* whom I have brought up, a tomcat of great beauty (his likeness is very well caught on the cover of this book) and of even

---

[82] Ibid., 322.
[83] Ibid., 323.
[84] Segebrecht, *Autobiographie*, 208.
[85] Steinecke, "Kommentar," 936.

greater intellect"[86] had induced him to write his latest (and, in fact, his last) novel revolving around an autobiographical tomcat. In addition, Hoffmann's friend Hitzig affirms in his biography on Hoffmann that the poet was indeed "inexhaustible in relating stories about the cleverness of his darling who usually rested on the drawers of his master's desk which he opened with his paws all by himself."[87] The literary cat's regular "settl[ing] down"[88] on Master Abraham's desk (on which Murr "l[ies] down in the midst of the papers" producing "a sensation of indescribable delight" in him) can thus be regarded a fictionally enriched descriptive portrayal of what Hoffmann himself was accustomed to in his own Berlin study. Adding an interpretative layer to the descriptive depiction by empathetically explaining the cat's behavior as a feline experience of pleasure ("sensation of indescribable delight"), Hoffmann gives (narrative) voice to the cat's alleged thoughts and feelings—mental and emotional capacities he also ascribed to his own cat sprawled out before him on his desk. As he "discover[ed] innovative breakthroughs in form through an attentiveness to another species bodily *poiesis*,"[89] Hoffmann conceived a humanimal novel ripped up in form as well as with regard to feline epistemology, leaving scratch marks on both dogmatic anthropocentrism and stereotypical denunciation of cats. Interacting with and attending to the gestures, movements, and behavioral traits of his cat, and empathetically interpreting Murr's experiences, Hoffmann's zoopoetics "mirror [...] the practice of collaborative (inter-human) autobiography."[90] Conceiving of the tomcat as a forthcoming, intelligent individual, a genuine autobiographical self, *Tomcat Murr* presents itself both as an illustration of what Hoffmann might have regarded as his companion's feline self and an indication of his own attachment to the cat.

Just how attached the poet actually was can be inferred from what the dramatist August Friedrich Klingemann describes in his autobiography. When he was first introduced to Hoffmann in November 1821, Klingemann found a man distressed and worried about the exacerbating condition of his sick cat. Klingemann was surprised, unwilling to believe that a man like

---

[86] Ibid., 323, (original emphasis). One of the copperplate engravings of the first edition shows a cat on a rooftop, clad in a toga, holding a quill and standing on two legs behind a table. Hoffmann made the engraving himself (ibid., 9).

[87] Hitzig, *Hoffmann's Leben*, 114.

[88] Hoffmann, *Life and Opinions*, 26.

[89] Moe, *Zoopoetics*, 10 (original emphasis).

[90] Herman, "Animal Autobiography," 17.

Hoffmann could actually be afflicted by a cat's illness.[91] However, as a friend then told him, "Hoffmann takes the matter very seriously as the suffering animal with whom he communicates via magnetic rapport is no other than the well-known, poetic *Tomcat Murr!*"[92] Hoffmann's tomcat was much more to the poet than "just a cat" or a stooge to the novel. Rather, Hoffmann's intimate relation to, his emotional investment in, and his "more-than-human" interaction with the cat seem to have found their way into the text. Such a "magnetic rapport" may be found in the novel's representation of interspecies communication between Murr and Master Abraham. With his miaow, for example, Murr can "express [...] joy, pain, delight and rapture, terror and despair, in short, all feelings and passions in their every nuance"[93]—emotional states and subjective experiences Master Abraham has learned to understand appropriately. With "several dulcet miaows," for instance, Murr can indicate to Abraham "that [he] had eaten enough."[94] Abraham, in turn, not only speaks to his "dear cat,"[95] he also lectures Murr to be "a good, sensible cat," advising him "to be always quiet and friendly, and perform all your undertakings without any fuss."[96]

Read along these lines and with regard to Hoffmann's biography, *Tomcat Murr*, becomes legible as much more than just a novel with a cat narrator-protagonist whose death coincides with that of Hoffmann's "real" tomcat. It is a text which commemorates a feline companion, a biographical sketch, which, echoing Erica Fudge, "bear[s] witness to [an] individual's potential to construct a life-story of him- or herself" and "communicate[s] through language the subject's own self-understanding (or misunderstanding)."[97] Hoffmann acknowledged his cat as a special, agential, if somewhat megalomaniac, being, as an idiosyncratic self, reaching out and relating to him with gestures, sounds, and movements; a self whose experience and modes of interaction he imaginatively re-inscribed into language. Attending and attentive to Murr's being and behavior, the tomcat's life (and death), the trace of the autobiographical self, has become part of and can be traced within the text. Yet the novel is not meant to give

[91] Klingemann, *Kunst und Natur*, 328.
[92] Ibid. (original emphasis).
[93] Hoffmann, *Life and Opinions*, 11.
[94] Ibid., 110.
[95] Ibid., 108.
[96] Ibid., 226.
[97] Fudge, "Animal," 21.

an accurate, pseudo-mimetic portrayal of Hoffmann's tomcat but rather speaks of and for a cat's self and its "ipseity of being *able to be* or *able to do* 'I'"[98] which is acknowledged, appreciated and cherished in and beyond the scopes of the text. Consequently, *Tomcat Murr* is autobiographical not (only) in terms of Hoffmann's textual re-appearance as editor and character (Abraham, Kreisler) of the novel, but first and foremost insofar as it imaginatively probes and gives form (*graphein*) to what may be conceived as Murr's self (*autos*) and his individually experienced life (*bios*).

CODA: ANIMAL SELVES IN/AND LITERARY AUTOZOOGRAPHIES

Animals leave traces. Roaming through, and intricately linked to their respective *Umwelt*, "a section carved out of the environment which we see spread around it,"[99] they leave behind feathers, fur, footprints, excrements, blood, broken twigs, torn slippers, toys, ink,[100] and so on. As Diane Davis, rephrasing Derrida, explains, Western philosophy has always acknowledged that "an animal" "lives and therefore writes itself, leaving its zoographical traces."[101] Nevertheless, it has never recognized these traces as *autozoo*graphical: an animal "has no autodeictic capacity and so no I; it therefore does not and cannot refer to its 'own' traces, it cannot give an account of itself (cannot write its autozoography)."[102] In this sense, autobiography appears exclusively human. Consequently, the history of autobiography has been equated with "the history of *human* self-consciousness."[103] *Autos* and *bios*, in this respect, are conceived as synonymous with "a qualified life, a particular way of life"[104]—a human life.[105]

[98] Derrida, *Animal*, 92 (original emphasis).
[99] Uexküll, "Stroll through," 13.
[100] Imagining self-referentiality beyond the anthropologocentric notions of continental philosophy, Derrida ponders "which way to take hold of a cuttlefish or octopus without hurting it too much, [...] keeping it at a distance long enough to expel its ink. In order to displace its power without doing anybody too much harm. Its ink or power would here be the 'I', not necessarily *the power to say* 'I' but the ipseity of being *able to be* or *able to do* 'I' before any autoreferential reference in a language" (Derrida, *Animal*, 92, original emphasis).
[101] Davis, "Autozoography," 538.
[102] Ibid. Cp. Derrida, *Animal*, 49–50.
[103] Misch, "Einleitung," 11 (emphasis added).
[104] Agamben, *Homo Sacer*, 1.
[105] Hengel, "Zoegraphy," 2–3.

The history of literary autozoographies tells a different, "more-than-human" story. Traditional autobiography centers on the idea of an identity between writer and narrator.[106] Literary autozoographies, by contrast, not only dismiss this identity pattern, thereby rendering it subject to scrutiny and skepticism, but also underscore the fact that any autobiographical self is a composed entity made-up of linguistic discourse, a "word-self" in a world built by words.[107] Sampling autobiographical poetics, literary autozoographies underline autobiography's rhetorical and literary preconditions and constructions, and expose the fictional elements of the genre. Thus, seen as a meta-genre, literary autozoographies foreground the blind spots of (human) autobiography.

Moreover, nonverbal semiosis, rhetoricity, and auto-traces—"the trace of [...] self, of this auto-presentation of the living (thing), this autobiographical guarantee"[108]—can be said to precede language and the pronounced or spelled "I."[109] The identity as well as the presence of the autobiographical self is, as Derrida reminds us, no more than a hallucinatory illusion in the mode of an "as if," a "bereaved allegory."[110] Autobiography then, as Paul de Man suggests, is nothing but a rhetorical figure—*prosopopoeia*—which "posit[s] voice or face by means of language."[111] If *prosopopoeia* is used to give voice to animals narrating their lives, attending to and being affected by animal individuals might be one of the (auto)biographers ways to conceive a/n (auto)zoopoetics of trans-species life writing. In this respect, literary autozoographies may not only record an animal life imprinting authors and authorship alike but can also signify a trace of animal self, an autobiographical animal, as it is perceived and esteemed by some authors in opposition to the anthropocentric, rationalist paradigm of "depriving animal life of any autobiographical relation to the self."[112] Literary autozoographies can attest and give testimony to an animal self by transcribing it into an autobiographical account with the means of *prosopopoeia*, "the trope of autobiography, by which one's name [...] is made as intelligible and memorable as a face."[113]

[106] Lejune, "Autobiographical Pact."
[107] Middelhoff, "Literary Autozoographies," 11–12.
[108] Derrida, *Animal*, 56.
[109] Davis, "Autozoography," 546–548.
[110] Derrida, *Memoires*, 28.
[111] De Man, "Autobiography," 930.
[112] Derrida, *Animal*, 93.
[113] De Man, "Autobiography," 926.

Autozoographical research follows animals' *autos* beyond the texts by examining the zoological and epistemological horizons of animal life writing as well as the relations between (human) writers, narrating animals, and animal characters. Literary autozoographies reflect and partake in our cultural imaginations of animals but also give form and contribute to zoological discourse. This chapter has tried to give a glance at what might be gained by correlating zoological literature with literary autozoographies and by investigating the representation of animal selves in and beyond autozoographical discourse. *The Life and Opinions of the Tomcat Murr* gives its own revised *opinions* on feline nature in general, *the life* of a special individual in particular. Contradicting generic life writing in natural history, the novel pinpoints zoology's incapability to conceive of (forms of) life beyond species paradigms. Hoffmann not only presents us with a counternarrative to zoological and popular narratives on cats in Germany around 1800, affecting how nineteenth-century zoology engaged with and evaluated cats but also left the mark of his Berlin cat for posterity, transforming the traces of a tomcat's self into *prosopopoetic*, autozoographical discourse.

WORKS CITED

Agamben, Giorgio. *Homo Sacer: Sovereign Power and Bare Life*. Translated by Daniel Heller-Roazen. Stanford: Stanford University Press, 1998.

Arensburg, Christian. *So ein Hundeleben: Die Memoiren meines Hundes Piter*. Stuttgart: Bogen, 1959.

Armbruster, Karla. "What Do We Want from Talking Animals? Reflections on Literary Representations of Animal Voices and Minds." In *Speaking for Animals: Animal Autobiographical Writing*, edited by Margo DeMello, 17–34. New York: Routledge, 2013.

Beardsley, Christa-Maria. *E.T.A. Hoffmanns Tierfiguren im Kontext der Romantik: Die poetisch–ästhetische und die gesellschaftliche Funktion der Tiere bei Hoffmann und in der Romantik*. Bonn: Bouvier, 1985.

Bechstein, Johann Matthäus. *Gemeinnützige Naturgeschichte Deutschlands nach allen drey Reichen: Ein Handbuch zur deutlichern und vollständigern Selbstbelehrung besonders für Forstmänner, Jugendlehrer und Oekonomen*. Leipzig: Siegfried Lebrecht Crusius, 1789.

Borgards, Roland. "Animal Studies." In *Rethinking Nature: Challenging Disciplinary Boundaries*, edited by Aurélie Choné, Isabelle Hajek, and Philippe Hamman, 221–231. Abington and New York: Routledge, 2017.

————. "Tiere." In *E.T.A. Hoffmann: Leben – Werk – Wirkung*, edited by Christine Lubkoll and Harald Neumeyer, 311–315. Stuttgart: Metzler, 2015.

————. "Tiere und Literatur." In *Tiere. Kulturwissenschaftliches Handbuch*, edited by Roland Borgards, 225–244. Stuttgart: Metzler, 2016.

Brehm, Alfred E. "Aus dem Leben der Hauskatze." *Die Gartenlaube* 36 (1859): 513–515.

Buffon, George-Louis Leclerc de. *Barr's Buffon: Buffon's Natural History*. Translated by James Smith Barr. London: H.D. Symonds, 1807.

Bungartz, Jean. *Illustriertes Katzenbuch: Rassenbeschreibung, Zucht, Pflege, Fütterung und Krankheiten der Katzen*. Berlin: Paul Parey, 1886.

Bush, Barbara. *Millie's Book: As Dictated to Barbara Bush*. New York: William Morrow and Company, 1990.

Cadman, Sam. "Reflections on Anthropocentrism, Anthropomorphism and Impossible Fiction: Towards a Typological Spectrum of Fictional Animals." *Animal Studies Journal* 5.2 (2016): 161–182.

Davis, Diane. "Autozoography: Notes Toward a Rhetoricity of the Living." *Philosophy & Rhetoric* 47.4 (2014): 533–553.

DeMello, Margo. "Introduction." In *Speaking for Animals: Animal Autobiographical Writing*, edited by Margo DeMello, 1–14. New York: Routledge, 2013.

Derrida, Jacques. *Memoires: For Paul de Man*. Translated by Cecile Lindsay et al. New York: Columbia University Press, 1989.

————. *The Animal That Therefore I Am*, edited by Marie-Louise Mallet. Translated by David Wills. New York: Fordham University Press, 2008.

De Man, Paul. "Autobiography as De-Facement." *Modern Language Notes* 94.5 (1979): 919–930.

De Waal, Frans. *Our Inner Ape: A Leading Primatologist Explains Why We Are Who We Are*. New York: Penguin, 2005.

Fudge, Erica. "Animal Lives." *History Today* 54.10 (2004): 21–26.

Glööckler, Harald. *Billy King: Mein Leben mit Harald Glööckler*. Falkensee: Tierisch Verlegen Verlagsgesellschaft, 2013.

Haraway, Donna. *Staying with the Trouble: Making Kin in the Chthulucene*. Durham and London: Duke University Press, 2016.

————. *The Companion Species Manifesto: Dogs, People, and Significant Otherness*. Chicago: Prickly Paradigm Press, 2003.

Hengel, Louis van den. "Zoegraphy: Per/Forming Posthuman Lives." *Biography* 35.1 (2012): 1–20.

Hengerer, Mark. "Die Katze in der Frühe Neuzeit: Stationen auf dem Weg zur Seelenverwandten des Menschen." In *Von Katzen und Menschen: Sozialgeschichte auf leisen Sohlen*, edited by Clemens Wischermann, 53–88. Konstanz: UVK Verlagsgesellschaft, 2007.

Herman, David. "Animal Autobiography; Or, Narration Beyond the Human." In *Humanities* 5 (2016): 1–17.

Hitzig, Julius Eduard. *E. T. A. Hoffmann's Leben und Nachlaß*. Stuttgart: Fr. Brod'hogsche Buchhandlung, 1839.

Hoffmann, Ernst Theodor Amadeus. *The Life and Opinions of the Tomcat Murr*. Translated by Anthea Bell. London: Penguin, 2006.

———. *"Quartblatt mit den Schriftzügen des Katers Murr."* http://digital.bib-bvb.de/view/bvbmets/viewer.0.6.1.jsp?folder_id=0&dvs=1505818211801~343&pid=11590321&locale=de&usePid1=true&usePid2=true. Accessed June 22, 2017.

Huff, Cynthia and Joel Haefner. "His Master's Voice: Animalographies, Life Writing, and the Posthuman." *Biography* 35.1 (2012): 153–169.

Jevbratt, Lisa. *"Interspecies Collaboration – Making Art Together with Nonhuman Animals."* http://jevbratt.com/writing/jevbratt_interspecies_collaboration.pdf. Accessed June 20, 2017.

Keenleyside, Heather. "Introduction." In *Animals*, edited by Heather Keenleyside, ix–xxii. London: Pickering & Chatto, 2012.

Klinkenborg, Verlyn. *Timothy; or, Notes of an Abject Reptile*. New York: Knopf, 2006.

Klingemann, August Friedrich. *Kunst und Natur: Blätter aus meinem Reisetagebuche*. Braunschweig: G.C.E. Meyer, 1828.

Kofman, Sarah. *Autobiogriffures du «Chat Murr» d'Hoffmann*. Paris: Galilée, 1984.

Krünitz, Johann Georg, ed. *Oekonomisch-technologische Encyklopädie, oder allgemeines System der Staats– Stadt– Haus– und Landwirthschaft und der Kunstgeschichte*, edited by Heinrich Gustav Flörke. Berlin: Joachim Pauli, 1781.

Leggewie, Claus. "Die Katze." In *Zoologicon: Ein kulturhistorisches Wörterbuch der Tiere*, edited by Christian Kassung, Jasmin Mersmann, and Olaf B. Rader, 206–211. München: Fink, 2012.

Lejeune, Philippe. "The Autobiographical Pact". In *On Autobiography*, edited by Paul John Eakin, 3–30. Translated by Katherine Leary. Minneapolis: University of Minnesota Press, 1989.

Lestel, Dominique, Jereffrey Bussolini, and Matthew Chrulew. "The Phenomenology of Animal Life." *Environmental Humanities* 5 (2014): 125–148.

McHugh, Susan. "*Animal Farm*'s Lesson for Literary (and) Animal Studies." *Humanimalia* 1.1 (2009): 24–39.

Michel, Gustav. *Das Buch der Katzen*. Weimar: Hermann Weißbach, 1870.

Middelhoff, Frederike. "Literary Autozoographies – Contextualizing Species Life in German Animal Autobiography." *Humanities* 6.23 (2017): 1–26.

Misch, Georg. "Einleitung." In *Geschichte der Autobiographie*, edited by Georg Misch, 3–21. Frankfurt am Main: Schulte-Bulmke, 1949.

Moe, Aaron M. "Toward Zoopoetics: Rethinking Whitman's Original Energy." *Walt Whitman Quarterly Review* 31 (2013): 1–17.

———. *Zoopoetics: Animals and the Making of Poetry*. Lanham: Lexington Books, 2014.

Müller-Seidel, Walter. "Nachwort." In *E. T. A. Hoffmann: Sämtliche Werke in fünf Einzelbänden, vol. 2, Die Elixiere des Teufels. Lebens-Ansichten des Katers Murr*, edited by Walter Müller-Seidel and Wolfgang Kron, 667–689. München: Winkler, 1961.

Natsume, Sōseki. *I Am a Cat*. Translated by Aiko Ito. North Clarendon: Tuttle, 2002.

O'Hagan, Andrew. *The Life and Opinions of Maf the Dog, and of His Friend Marilyn Monroe*. London: Faber & Faber, 2010.

Ranzoni, Emmerich. *Zoddel: Lebensgeschichte eines Hundes*. Wien: R. v. Waldheim, 1879.

Saunders, Margaret Marshall. *Beautiful Joe: An Autobiography*. Toronto: Baptist Book Room, 1894.

Schmitz-Emans, Monika. "Lebens-Ansichten des Katers Murr nebst fragmentarischer Biographie des Kapellmeisters Johannes Kreisler in zufälligen Makulaturblättern." In *E. T. A. Hoffmann: Leben – Werk – Wirkung*, edited by Christine Lubkoll and Harald Neumeyer, 152–160. Stuttgart: Metzler, 2015.

Schröter, Julian. *Figur – Personalität – Verhaltenstheorien: Zu einer Theorie fiktiver Tiere in Erzählungen der Romantik*. Saarbrücken: Akademikerverlag, 2013.

Segebrecht, Wulf. *Autobiographie und Dichtung: Eine Studie zum Werk E. T. A. Hoffmanns*. Stuttgart: Metzler, 1967.

Sewell, Anna. *Black Beauty: His Grooms and Companions: The Autobiography of a Horse*. London: Harrold and Sons, 1877.

Shapiro, Kenneth. J. "Understanding Dogs Through Kinesthetic Empathy, Social Construction, and History." In *Social Creatures: A Human and Animal Studies Reader*, edited by Clifton P. Flynn, 31–48. New York: Lantern Books, 2008.

Siebert, Charles. *Angus: A Memoir*. New York: Random House, 2000.

Sheridan, Thomas. 1790. *A Complete Dictionary of the English Language, Both with Regard to Sound and Meaning: One Main Object of Which Is to Establish a Plain and Permanent Standard Pronunciation*. London: Charles Dilly, 1790.

Smith, Julie A. "Representing Animal Minds in Early Animal Autobiography: Charlotte Tucker's *The Rambles of a Rat* and Nineteenth-Century Natural History." *Victorian Literature and Culture* 43 (2015): 725–744.

Steinecke, Hartmut. "Kommentar." In *E. T. A. Hoffmann: Sämtliche Werke, vol. 2, Lebens-Ansichten des Katers Murr*, edited by Harmut Steinecke and Gerhard Allroggen, 887–1202. Frankfurt am Main: Deutscher Klassiker Verlag, 1992.

Stone, Diana. "E. T. A. Hoffmann: The Conciliatory Satirist." *Monatshefte* 66.1 (1974): 55–73.

Tawada, Yoko. *Memoirs of a Polar Bear*. Translated by Susan Bernofsky. London: Portobello Books, 2016.

Toepfer, Georg. *Historisches Wörterbuch der Biologie: Geschichte und Theorie der biologischen Grundbegriffe, vol. 2, Ge—O*. Stuttgart: Metzler, 2011.

Trichter, Valentin [Tenneker, Christian Ehrenfried Seifert von]. *Lebensgeschichte der Mecklenburgischen Stute Amante*. Leipzig: Theodor Seeger, 1804.

von Uexküll, Jakob. "A Stroll Through the Worlds of Animals and Men: A Picture Book of Invisible Worlds." In *Instinctive Behavior: The Development of a Modern Concept*, edited and translated by Claire H. Schiller, 5–80. New York: International Universities Press, 1957.

PART II

Reflections

CHAPTER 5

A Dog's Life: The Challenges and Possibilities of Animal Biography

Aaron Skabelund

INTRODUCTION

If one were to write a biography of a nonhuman animal, a compelling possibility is Hachikō (1923–1935). An Akita dog, Hachi, as he was sometimes called, was born on 10 November 1923 outside the town of Ōdate in the northern prefecture of Akita, the namesake of the breed. Two months later, his owner shipped him nearly 20 hours by rail to Ueno Eizaburō (1871–1925), a professor of agricultural engineering at Tokyo Imperial University. Ueno had conducted research in Ōdate and that connection led associates there, who knew he was fond of dogs, to send him the puppy in early 1924. For the next 16 months, Hachikō walked with Ueno to the nearby Shibuya railway station in the morning and apparently met him at the station each evening and accompanied him home until 21 May 1925, when Ueno had a stroke and died while at work. Soon thereafter Hachikō is said to have begun a vigil outside the station awaiting the return of Ueno.

A common sight near Shibuya Station for years, he became known as the "Loyal Dog" (Chūken) Hachikō in 1932 after a newspaper article

A. Skabelund (✉)
Brigham Young University, Provo, UT, USA

© The Author(s) 2018
A. Krebber, M. Roscher (eds.), *Animal Biography*,
Palgrave Studies in Animals and Literature,
https://doi.org/10.1007/978-3-319-98288-5_5

Fig. 5.1   An undated photograph of Hachikō likely lying on the ground near Shibuya Station (used with permission of Hayashi Masaharu)

made him famous throughout and beyond Japan (Fig. 5.1). By 1934, grade-school children across the country were reading about his supposed loyalty in a national textbook. That same year, his fans erected a statue of him outside the station's main exit. A replica of the statue that was recast in 1948 stands today in front of the station's "Hachikō Exit." (The original statue was melted down during the war.) Another likeness of Hachikō, preserved by taxidermy, has been on display at the National Science Museum in Tokyo's Ueno Park since his death in 1935. His is a story that almost anyone familiar with Japan and many dog lovers know. Hachikō is one of the world's most celebrated dogs.

In this chapter, I use primary sources, including two that allow some animals to participate in the formulation of their life story, to construct a brief biography of Hachikō. I titled one of my first publications that mentioned Hachikō "Can the Subaltern Bark?"[1] This rather flippant rephrasing of Spivak's famous query challenges us to try to hear the voices of nonhuman animals. Rarely can we hear any animal voices from the past.

[1] Skabelund, "Can the Subaltern Bark?" 194–243.

Animals leave almost no records, so how can we recover their history? It is important to remember that the difficulties of telling the history of animals is similar to those faced in trying to retrieve the largely silent and invisible past of certain subaltern people. At least two modern technologies, photography—still and motion picture—and taxidermy, produced sources that allow some animals to "speak" and play a more direct, collaborative role in telling their own life stories. Mediated though they may be, though perhaps less so than other human representations of animals, these sources allow some animals to contribute to and constrain human discussions about them. In short, they allow animals to talk back. Specifically these technologies allowed Hachikō to talk back, to participate in the telling of his biography, and they might help us hear his bark and other animal voices, and to give them a role in the telling of their life stories.

A biographer can find an extraordinary amount of source material about Hachikō that could be used to reconstruct his life. Many, many dozens of newspaper and magazine articles, a book, and songs about and photographs of him as well as the textbook story and the Shibuya statue were produced while Hachikō was still very much alive. Some of these primary sources are included in a collection self-published by Hayashi Masaharu, who as a youngster remembered being taken by his parents to see Hachikō and petting him outside Shibuya Station.[2] The station's office contains an archive of Hachikō-related materials. Among its holdings are business cards of those who made financial donations to build the statue, essays composed by grade-school children about Hachikō, and other ephemeral. In Ōdate, the Society for the Preservation of the Akita dog displays a letter describing Hachikō's birth and first two months of life written by the (human) family into which he was born. And of course at the National Science Museum is the stuffed Hachikō himself, wearing the same harness and collar he wore while alive. There is no shortage of artifacts and textual sources to document this dog's life.

A biographer of Hachikō can visit where he once lived. During his first two months of life in Ōdate, the farm on which Hachikō lived was probably buried in deep snow. The area has changed little since his birth nearly a century ago. The same family still owns the property, on which sits a rebuilt home and shed. Small wooded hills rise behind it, and land that was likely being cleared for cultivation in the 1920s stretches in rice pad-

---

[2] Hayashi, *Hachikō.*

dies across the valley. (A massive faded plaque about Hachikō sits in the corner of the property and a public bathroom for tourists, the "Hachikō Toilet," built in the shape of two Akita dogs, is conveniently located across a narrow road from the property.) In contrast to his birthplace, the Tokyo neighborhood where he spent the rest of his life has been transformed even more drastically. The one-mile distance to the station that Hachikō once walked with Ueno and the surrounding area he later wandered alone and with other dogs was characterized in the 1920s and 1930s by low-slung single family residences with gardens, groves of trees, and fields. Now multi-storied homes and high-rise business and apartments buildings are the rule. The broad open space of what was the nearby Yoyogi army base is now a park, dotted with a few aging venues from the 1964 Olympic Summer Games.

Secondary work about Hachikō, a point of reference for any biographer, is extensive but has been aimed at a popular audience. Authors have written a lot about Hachikō over the years, but have rarely taken advantage of the abundant primary sources available or aimed for scholarly biographical standards. Hachikō has been most popular in material, including many books, aimed at children. In 1987, the Shochiku-Fuji film studio released "Hachikō monogatari" (The Story of Hachikō), a family-friendly movie, and in 2009 director Lasse Hallström, best known for "My Life as a Dog" (1985), remade the film as "Hachi: A Dog's Tale," setting it in Rhode Island town with a commuter railway station. As a result of all this cultural production and appropriation, Hachikō, though long dead, lives on in popular memory, and such reincarnations are also part of his biography.

For these reasons, writing the history of Hachikō would not only be easier than writing about just any other individual animal but also easier than narrating the lives of many of his average human contemporaries in Japan or elsewhere. That said, there are many methodological and theoretical challenges to animal biography, no matter how famous the subject. Scientific and social scientific fields such as ethology, comparative psychology, and ethnography can be helpful, but these interdisciplinary approaches are not without problems.

Scientists and social scientists who study canine behavior now recognize that the temperament and behavior of dogs are the product of both nature and nurture. The ethologist Ádám Miklósi has observed that though the scientific study of canines began with Pavlov in the early twentieth century, until recently "dogs [...] received relatively scant attention from ethologists and comparative psychologists."[3] This may be in part because the task is so daunting. With over four hundred distinctive breeds, canines are the most phenotypically diverse mammal. These phenotypes include morphological and breed-specific behavioral differences. Faced with such tremendous diversity in form and personality—that is, behavioral consistency across time and space—researchers have generally not investigated individual breeds. Rather, they have usually focused on groups of dogs that were bred for common practical tasks such as herding and hunting with the aim of identifying temperament and certain behaviors that are at least partly genetically determined.[4] They have also conducted research that has confirmed differences among similar types of canines depending on their biological sex. What is more difficult for researchers to determine are personality characteristics that are derivative of social interactions and culture, with humans and other dogs.

Such scientific and social scientific studies can help us understand some things about an individual dog like Hachikō, but only so much. Researchers have found, for example, that similar dog types not only exhibit common morphological traits but share a comparable character in terms of their trainability, boldness, calmness, and sociability.[5] Thus Akita, which have been bred as hunting and guarding dogs, not only have a solid muscular build but also generally have an alert and fearless temperament and a strong territorial instinct. Researchers have also found that male Akita exhibit this temperament in slightly different ways than females. What is much more difficult to measure is the influence of various environmental factors—such as wider cultural attitudes about and the treatment of canines by society, the gender and age of keepers, traumatic experiences, and specific interactions that contribute to the formation of a particular dog's distinctive personality and character.[6] This research—though little of it is breed specific to the Akita—and actual interaction with Akita dogs today may give one a better sense of Hachikō's character, but they have limitations. Such research and interactions cannot account for how the breed has changed from a century ago and how changes in culture and other environment conditions that the Akita shares with humans have changed them. They can only offer generalizations about an individual

[3] Miklósi, *Dog Behavior*, 1.
[4] Miklósi et al., "Personality," 198–199.
[5] Ibid., 200.
[6] Ibid., 206–208.

dog like Hachikō and his particular lived experience. Hachikō was separated from his mother at two months when he left Ōdate, separated from
his new master the next year when Ueno died, and became a semi-stray
dog for years wandering about the environs of Shibuya Station and interacting with a variety of humans and canines. Perhaps ethnography, such as
in Alan Beck's study of the ecology of free-range urban dogs in Baltimore,[7]
could shed some light on that part of his life, but its application to
Hachikō's situation would be constrained by historical, cultural, and individual differences, in other words by many of the same problems as ethological and comparative psychological research. As with the writing of
human biography, science and social science may help establish some
broad parameters that are useful in writing an animal biography, particularly a collective biography, but it is the essential tools of history—primary
sources, including photography and taxidermy that allowed Hachikō to
play a role in the telling of his own story—that are most useful for the
composition of an individual animal biography.

HACHIKŌ'S STORY

In the 1930s, indigenous dogs in Japan were rediscovered and transformed into an icon of purity, loyalty, and bravery—of a distinctive and
superior Japanese identity. The celebration of native "Japanese" dogs was
part of a trend that had developed in Europe in the second half of the
nineteenth century and spread with imperialism and the global diffusion
of Western modes of dog keeping and the ideology of animal pure-
bloodism. Nevertheless, the extolling of native dogs in Japan was of no
small irony. Westerners and many local elites alike had from the mid-
nineteenth century regarded indigenous dogs as barbaric and savage,
aggressive but cowardly, and of mixed or wolfish breed, while praising
Western dogs as thoroughly domesticated but powerful, and esteemed
them as purebred. But by the 1930s, these same native canines came to be
cited as an example of what supposedly made Japan superior to the West.
For decades rounded up for elimination by dogcatchers in the government's employ, "Japanese" dogs became immensely popular, serving as a
status symbol for anyone with the means to acquire one. Once the target
of derision, they became a source of pride.

---

[7] Beck, *Ecology*.

No dog represented this transformation better than Hachikō, who as a representative of native dogs became an icon of purity, loyalty, and bravery. Beginning with that first newspaper article that introduced him to a wide audience, Hachikō was praised for his fidelity, for appearing each evening outside of a Tokyo train station day after day, month after month, year after year, to await the return of his master. The actual story of Hachikō is not so sweet and sentimental. In the context of the 1930s it had complex, even disturbing implications. Hachikō became famous precisely because dog enthusiasts and government bureaucrats cast the dog as an exemplar of the Japanese empire's canine ideal: Japanese in character, pure in blood, loyal to a single master, and a fearless fighter. In addition, as today, at the time Hachikō captivated people because his living, breathing reality amplified his incredible symbolic power.

The celebration of Hachikō, and the transformation of the despised native dog into the venerated Japanese dog depended on the joint efforts of private dog enthusiasts in the Society for the Preservation of the Japanese Dog, and government officials in the Ministry of Education. In 1928, Saitō Hirokichi (1900–1964), concerned that native dogs through interbreeding were headed for what he believed was tantamount to extinction, founded the society. He then spent much of the next several years traveling to remote highland regions throughout the archipelago to locate what he considered to be purebred dogs and to campaign for their protection. Returning to Tokyo from one of those trips, he encountered Hachikō near Shibuya Station. He found the dog impressive enough to feature him on the pages of a society newsletter in 1929. Several years later, he realized that Hachikō had a potentially wider appeal and proposed a story about the dog to a reporter for the *Asahi*, a major national daily newspaper. Although Saitō was upset that the resulting article stated that Hachikō was of "mixed breed" rather than a pureblooded Akita, he was surely pleased with its prominent placement and a photograph of a forlorn-looking Hachikō in the paper's morning edition of 4 October 1932. "The Story of a Lovable Old Dog: A Seven-Year Expectant Wait for the Return of a Master Who Is No Longer of This World" told of the dog's supposed unflagging fidelity and portrayed him as a righteous mediator of dogfights and a protective patron for smaller canines.[8] The article launched Hachikō's tremendous popularity, which probably escalated to a degree beyond what anyone, including Saitō, anticipated.

---

[8] "Itoshi ya rōken," 8.

Saito's timing could not have been better. There are good, historical reasons why this dog got his day in 1932. The Manchurian Incident, the invasion of the northeastern Chinese province by Japanese forces began in September 1931, marked the start of what was repeatedly proclaimed to be an extended "national emergency." The invasion, coupled with a series of assassinations of top government officials by military officers and right-wing radicals at home, led to an end to political party rule by mid-1932. Historians have noted that this began the country's descent into the long, dark valley of militarism and fascism. The sentimental tale of Hachikō surely brought release from such uncertainties, but its very appeal stemmed from the fact that its underlying message subtly reinforced the upsurge in patriotism.

Saitō repeatedly claimed that Japanese dogs were superior to Western breeds. His following declaration made during a radio address in 1937 is telling: "No other dog has been the recipient of the superior attributes of the Japanese national spirit—courage, composure, boldness, and loyalty—that have been ingrained and preserved through interacting and dwelling with the Japanese nation for thousands of years."[9] Government officials thoroughly agreed with Saito. During the 1930s, the Ministry of Education designated seven breeds, starting with the Akita in 1931, as "Japanese" natural treasures. Hachikō was of course the embodiment of Japan's newly nationalized dogs. At the first dog show for only Japanese Dogs, the Society awarded Hachikō with a commemorative collar as an honorary participant. This artifact, a band of leather still encircles the stuffed Hachikō today in the National Science Museum. In death, as in life, Hachikō was tagged as Japanese.

The extraordinary amount of source material about Hachikō, among which his stuffed body is perhaps the most prominent, highlights the challenges and promises of animal biography. Such sources make reconstructing Hachikō's life relatively easy to do, but because they were produced and preserved in large part because they lent themselves to a particular nationalist political agenda, they must be deconstructed and disentangled from that agenda.

*   *   *

---

[9] Saitō, *Nihon no inu*, 271.

The Society's breeding standards and the government's moves to preserve native dogs reflected the complex nature of Japanese attitudes about racial identity during the 1930s. The policies and rhetoric of dog enthusiasts and government preservationists betrayed a strident concern with the maintenance of unbroken and undefiled blood ties of the Japanese nation and the imperial line. Society officials considered and government bureaucrats recognized as "Japanese" only those groups of canines whose pedigree had been attested in the archipelago since the beginning of (Japanese) time. The primary threat driving "Japanese" dogs to extinction, they contended, were canines of Western and mixed breed. Their actions and statements mirrored wider societal anxieties about human purity of blood, the superiority of the Japanese race, and the specter of miscegenation. Such a milieu was mirrored elsewhere at the time, perhaps most prominently by the Nazi's application of animal breeding to their policies to improve human heredity.[10] In Japan, Hachikō, as the symbol of the ideal Japanese dog, became the focus of such discussions.

The most pressing task for Saitō in the late 1920s and early 1930s was to determine precisely what a "Japanese" dog was. Like other breeding associations elsewhere, the Society used genealogical pedigrees to establish the supposed and undefiled lineage of dogs considered to be purebred and full-blooded. The Society put an emphasis on the physical appearance of dogs. They decided, as Saitō explained in his 1937 radio speech, that a pure Japanese dog must have two physical traits: "small, triangular ears that stand erect" and a "large and powerful curled tail."[11] Any animal that did not show these features was immediately regarded as suspect. Some people suggested that based on this standard Hachikō was not purebred because his tail slumped down when he walked and, even more noticeable, because his left ear drooped.[12]

Questions about Hachikō's purity of blood initially arose, to Saitō's consternation, from the *Asahi* article, which mentioned that he was of "mixed breed," and the accompanying photograph. That photo—one of numerous extant photographs of the dog—shows an aging, large, double-coated, cream-colored canine, hunched back on his hind legs, his right ear erect and his left ear drooping to the side, facing and gazing directly at the camera. At the time, Hachikō, still strongly built, stood at slightly over 25 inches at his

---

[10] See Sax, *Animals.*
[11] Ibid., 271.
[12] Saitō, "Aiken monogatari," 12, 60–61.

shoulders and weighed about 90 to 95 pounds, fairly typical for an adult male Akita. Then, and repeatedly over the years, Saitō emphatically defended the integrity of Hachikō's bloodline. He argued that the tail dropped and the ear flopped as a result of skin disease and not because of foreign contamination of the dog's pedigree.[13] He produced other photographs of Hachikō, including one he claimed dated from 1925, as visual evidence that the dog's ear in his younger years did not droop.[14] Although supportive of Saitō's claims, these photographs do not provide definitive proof of Hachikō's pure breed or blood (which is an arbitrarily constructed human standard anyway), but they do reveal just how concerned Saitō and others were about this issue. The photos do, however, allow Hachikō to contribute material evidence to the debate and to shape the discussion about his purported purity. In an even more corporeal fashion, Hachikō's body lent itself to the debate, though its form was drastically manipulated by human hands. Fortunately for Saitō, and indeed because of his influence, taxidermists working for the National Science Museum mounted Hachikō with his tail curled and both ears standing erect, so that he emerged looking like a young, healthy, pureblooded "Japanese" dog (Fig. 5.2).[15]

Fig. 5.2 Photograph of the stuffed Hachikō in the National Science Museum in Ueno Park, Tokyo. Notice the Pochi Club tag hanging from his harness. Hayashi Masaharu, ed. *Hachikō bunken shū* (Tokyo: Hayashi Masaharu, 1991, used with permission of the author)

[13] Saitō, *Nihon no inu*, 334–335.
[14] Ibid., 332.
[15] Shiina, *Taishō*, 262–268.

If it had not been for Hachikō, or more accurately, photographs of Hachikō in his later years, Saito and the taxidermists may have largely been successful in their attempt to get people to remember Hachikō as a young, healthy, pureblooded "Japanese" dog. A number of historians of natural history and science museums have observed that taxidermy seeks to conceal its work by creating the illusion that the mounts taxidermists create are purely natural specimens, neutral, and objective. As the historian Samuel Alberti has put it, "after the labor of manufacture, still further efforts are expended to conceal this work" to make mounts appear "impartial," "authorless," and to hide "their constructedness."[16] Taxidermists might be able to pull this off for the innumerable mounts of anonymous biological specimens, but not so for an animal celebrity such as Hachikō, who had been photographed throughout his life and garnered so much attention. Older photographs of Hachikō's living, aging, and failing body (as seen in Fig. 5.1)—along with, as we shall see, the true-to-life statue of Hachikō—permitted the dog, even in death, to create doubt about the form in which he was resurrected.

* * *

Preservationists were not the only bureaucrats in the Ministry of Education who were concerned about native dogs. Educators within the ministry, too, realized that native dogs like Hachikō—and other dogs in the service of the empire—could be elevated as icons of loyalty in imperial and wartime Japan. They deployed Hachikō as a pedagogical tool to instill in imperial subjects, especially children, a strong sense of loyalty.

The metaphorical mobilization of "Japanese" canines to foster loyalty was probably unrivaled. Such discourses extended to military dogs of Western breed in the employ of the army, especially Shepherd dogs. However, "Japanese" dogs were singled out even more often for their unconditional devotion. Commentators repeatedly asserted that the fidelity of indigenous dogs was unique among canines in that it was directed exclusively and unendingly to a single master. They were said to pine away at the passing of a master, and to fight to the death in his or her defense. More than once, the faithfulness of Hachikō and other "Japanese" dogs was compared to the *bushidō* ethos that supposedly bound a samurai warrior to his lord and the allegiance that people felt for the emperor.

[16] Alberti, "Constructing Nature," 79, 81.

The Society for the Preservation of the Japanese Dog and its allies in the Ministry of Education reveled in the attention that Hachikō was generating. In early 1934, they asked Andō Shō (1892–1945) to sculpt a statue of Hachikō, but on one condition. Andō had already created a plaster model of Hachikō the previous fall for an annual show at the Imperial Gallery of Art and in that work faithfully depicted Hachikō with a floppy left ear.[17] Such a design, they decided—at Saitō's insistence—would not do: Andō must depict the dog with both ears erect. Saitō's wish went unfulfilled, however, when the exigency of quickly completing the statue forced the sculptor to use his original model for the cast, and for perpetuity Hachikō was cast in bronze as a dog with a suspect ear.

The statue was dedicated in an elaborate hour-long ceremony on 21 April 1934. Several newspapers reported that the crowd was so large that it was almost impossible to move. Photographic evidence seems to confirm the scale of the spectacle and the presence of many youngsters and Saitō at the center of the activities (Fig. 5.3). Hachikō was the guest of honor. In one photo, he is arrayed in white and red ribbons but beginning to show his age. A film crew, dispatched by the Ministry of Foreign Affairs, captured the scene for a talkie—a short film with a soundtrack—to be distributed overseas. Unfortunately, that footage and any other video of Hachikō does not appear to be extant.

Ministry intervention ensured that the focus on Hachikō would be about loyalty rather than some other virtue or cause. For a brief time, Hachikō was acclaimed as a symbol of peace. When his story attracted attention and monetary contributions from America to build the statue, some pundits optimistically hailed Hachikō as an omen of improved relations with the United States. Other observers attempted to mobilize the dog to improve the plight of Tokyo's stray dog population, among whose ranks Hachikō sometimes wandered. After his master's untimely death, Ueno's widow Yaeko moved from the family home near Shibuya Station and worried that she could not care for a large dog and entrusted Hachikō first to relatives in Asakusa about seven miles away on the other side of the city. After Hachikō repeatedly escaped and returned to the family home in Shibuya, where he at least once damaged some fields in the vicinity, Yaeko asked her former gardener, Kobayashi Kikuzaburō (1871–1954), who lived near the Ueno home in Shibuya, to take care of the dog. It was from Kobayashi's home that Hachikō was said to have frequented Shibuya sta-

[17] Saitō, *Nihon no inu*, 337; Nihon inu hozon kai, *Shadan hōjin*, 55–57.

Fig. 5.3   Hachikō next to his bronze statue near Shibuya Station, probably on the day of its dedication, 21 April 1934. On the side of the photograph someone, perhaps Kobayashi Kikuzaburō, the Ueno family's gardener to whom this photo once belonged, has written, "A bashful (?) Hachikō looking up at the statue of himself." Hayashi Masaharu, ed. *Hachikō bunken shū* (Tokyo: Hayashi Masaharu, 1991, used with permission of the author), 252

tion. Dogcatchers, in fact, nabbed Hachikō several times in the late 1920s and early 1930s, and on one occasion the dog may have come within hours of being eliminated by officers at the pound. Although Society and Ministry officials did not encourage the view of Hachikō as homeless, some people, initially at least, thought of him as a canine destitute. Early letters to the editor expressed pity for the dog, parents of children like Hayashi (who many years later compiled the primary source collection of Hachikō-related materials) brought their children to pet him, and youngsters sent money so that Hachikō and other strays could be given milk, kept warm, and treated kindly.[18] Animal-welfare activists, such as those in the Japanese branch of the Humane Society, attempted to take advantage of these perceptions to promote more compassionate conditions in the city's notorious dog pounds.[19] The Humane Society made Hachikō an honorary member of its Pochi kurabu (Pooch Club), a group of select dogs from around the world, and its constituents called for better treatment of canines. The group also attached an ornament adorned with the club's name to Hachikō's collar, which dangles from the museum manikin to this day. The message stressed by animal-welfare activists, however, was largely overwhelmed by official and private voices praising the dog's devotion.

In the same month that Ministry officials helped raise the dog's bronze likeness outside Shibuya station, they incorporated Hachikō into the school curriculum by including his story in a new national ethics textbook for second-year students issued in April 1934. The painter Ishii Hakutei (1882–1958) provided an illustration for the story, depicting Hachikō with both ears erect—much to Saitō's relief, no doubt—waiting vainly but alertly outside Shibuya Station. The tale, "On o wasureru na" (Don't Forget Your Debts of Gratitude), was rendered in the following manner.

> Hachikō was a cute dog. Soon after he was born, a person far away adopted Hachikō and cared tenderly for him just as if he were his own child. As a result, his weak body became very strong. Every day when Hachikō's master departed for work, the dog would see him off at the train station, and every evening when he would return, Hachikō was there waiting to greet him at the station. Then one day, Hachikō's master died. The dog, because he did not understand, searched for him daily. Hachikō would look for his master among all the people who got off at the station each time a train arrived. Many months passed in this manner.
>
> Even though one, two, three, ten years passed, Hachikō—grown old searching for his master—can be seen in front of the station every day.[20]

Hints of how the text—which was part of the ethics primer until 1940—may have been taught can be gleaned from instructors' manuals and educational magazines. The Ministry of Education's official teacher's manual,

[18] *Chūken Hachikō kiroku.*
[19] Imagawa, *Inu no gendai shi*, 163.
[20] Kaigo et al., *Nihon kyōkasho*, 245.

which provided a longer, more detailed version of the story and a historical overview of Hachikō's life and the dedication of the statue, simply stated that its objective was to teach children that they should "not ever forget the debts of gratitude they have received from people."[21] The author of another such column, Kobayashi Gen, asserted that although the episode was true, teachers should teach it as a fable and not explore the tale's veracity in the classroom. "Second-year students are meek," Kobayashi wrote, "and will meekly accept what you tell them." He challenged teachers to instill in youngsters a sense of their indebtedness because "for children not to forget their debts, they must first feel them." The debts that Kobayashi had in mind were made clear in the following paragraph. He suggested that the story be read in class on 6 March, the birthday of the Meiji empress. This day, he recommended, should be dedicated to the important task of encouraging children to "contemplate the magnanimity of the splendid virtues of the imperial throne and to nourish hearts that will repay this supreme debt."[22]

In the 1930s, stories of dogs were ideal material for the government's efforts to inculcate the entire population with messages about duty to and sacrifice for the nation. More than anything, what made the Hachikō story so effective was that the protagonist was a dog, a seemingly benign, non-ideological, commonplace companion to which nearly everyone could relate. This was also the case for Nachi and Kongō, two "German" Shepherd dogs employed by the Japanese military who became famous around the same time.[23] Because the heroes of the Hachikō narrative and other stories were canines, they were appealing to children as well as adults. Perhaps the belief that they could control the story prompted Ministry of Education bureaucrats to make an exception to guidelines that discouraged the inclusion in textbooks of any topics related to characters still alive and to events still in the process of unfolding. There was, after all, no chance that Hachikō might actually speak up and contradict the dominant explanation of his motivations for loitering around the station. But his physical presence as preserved in photographs and what emerged from his body left room for plenty of speculation that sometimes supported and at times undermined the official narrative.

---

[21] Monbushō, *Jinjō shōgaku*, 134–145.
[22] Kobayashi, "Sangatsu," 115–116.
[23] For more on Nachi and Kongō, see Skabelund, "Breeding Racism."

The image of Hachikō as a model of dutiful devotion was not without its complications or its detractors, even within the Society for the Preservation of the Japanese Dog. Saitō's fellow Society member and canine researcher Hiraiwa Yonekichi (1898–1986) harshly criticized the projection of human motivations onto Hachikō. In 1935, Hiraiwa wrote that the "devotion of dogs does not stem from a sense of obligation for kindness received, but is based entirely on pure love." Despite the "dumbfounding" fuss over his alleged commitment to his master, he noted, Hachikō was still an unhappy dog who had lost his master. What Hiraiwa objected to most sharply was the use of Hachikō for the edification of children:

> There have been many people who one after another appear to manipulate even Hachikō's name in a variety of ways. Now he is even being used as material to teach people's children. This is because from the standpoint of human morality, everyday occurrences in the world of dogs are seen as extraordinary acts of good that demonstrate immeasurable integrity. They clamor 'Don't Forget Your Debts of Gratitude.' However, because there are no debts of gratitude in the world of dogs, there can be no forgetfulness. It is pathetic that only now, 'man'—that ingrate animal—is kneeling down to worship and plead for guidance from the law of dogs.[24]

Hiraiwa's contention that "the devotion of dogs does not stem from a sense of obligation for kindness receive, but is based entirely on pure love" presaged recent work on the emotional lives of animals. Jeffrey Moussaiff Masson, for example, has observed that "the dog is faithful or loyal [...] not because he feels obligation but because he feels love" and "for dogs, loyalty is the desire to be together with the loved one, *to be where one belongs.*"[25] Saitō, for his part, did not see the deployment of the story as troubling. Although he conceded years later that Hachikō did not understand the concept of obligation, elsewhere, in reference to Hiraiwa's criticism, he countered that the "greatest result [...] was that children throughout the country became very fond of dogs."[26] Saitō's statement may have been true, but if so, it also bolsters the possibility that educators could make use of children's affinity for dogs to foster allegiance to the state and to the emperor.

[24] Hiraiwa, "Watakushi no inu," 9, 69–70.
[25] Masson, *Dogs Never Lie*, 53, 61 (original emphasis).
[26] Saitō, *Nihon no inu*, 338–339.

Inflated claims of Hachikō's fidelity could not help but invite criticism, if not cynicism, in certain quarters. A number of observers of Hachikō's behavior ventured that perhaps the dog was not waiting for his master at all. On the contrary, they deduced, the dog was merely hanging around the station and its surrounding shops waiting to be fed. Hachikō, it was rumored, was especially fond of chicken kebabs, or *yakitori*. Saitō and others, however, rejected any notion that Hachikō was a mere stray loitering in search of handouts. Even in death—or perhaps especially because of the circumstances of his death—the controversy about the actual motivations of Hachikō persisted. The official story is that Hachikō died due to the effects of filariasis and old age. However, according to a widely circulated rumor attributed to the attending taxidermist, several bamboo *yakitori* skewers were discovered in the dog's stomach during his autopsy, a factor that may quite easily have contributed to his demise.[27] In this manner, Hachikō spoke by disgorging from the depths of his body material artifacts that further complicated and constrained his metaphorical manipulation, which may have been Hachikō's attempt to have the last word. Perhaps in the absence of eyewitness (human) testimony or still or moving photographic images of Hachikō devouring *yakitori*, Hachikō speaking beyond the grave in this manner is one of the few ways for him to have any say in the matter and to shed any light on his motivations.

* * *

Enthusiasts of Japanese dogs insisted that they were courageous and that Hachikō was too. They tried to persuade the Japanese military to deploy the dogs as army dogs. Many government and private dog trainers considered native dogs unfit for military and police work because of their relatively small size (except for the Akita), and because of their difficulty in obeying the commands of anyone other than the person who had trained them. They also found that their hunting instinct was so strong that they often abandoned the task at hand to chase any game encountered. Military canine trainers worked with some Akita dogs but in the end found that they were not nearly as effective as other breeds such as German Shepherds.

And Hachikō? In a largely unresolved irony, just as his floppy left ear and appetite for kebabs undermined pronouncements about his purported purity and the breed's unrivaled fidelity, his temperament seems to have

---

[27] Hayashi, *Hachikō*, 300.

weakened claims about Japanese dogs' incomparable martial spirit and bravery. As was related in what might be called his first biography, *The Story of the Loyal Dog Hachikō*, which was aimed at grade-school readers, the canine who was touted as the model "Japanese" dog and a guardian of smaller dogs seems in fact to have been quite fainthearted. While taking walks, Hachikō was apparently unnerved by gunfire resounding from military exercises at the nearby Yoyogi army base and was even rattled by children shooting toy guns.[28]

CONCLUSION

So when can the subaltern bark? The answer is twofold. First, as illustrated by the transformation of Japanese dogs from the nineteenth century to the 1930s, the subaltern can bark when native dogs, once denigrated by Westerners and many Japanese alike as savage and indistinct breed, were transformed into a nationalized, recognized pure breed. Second, the subaltern can bark when we recognize sources, such as photography and taxidermy, that allow dogs and other creatures in the past a voice and some degree of agency. If we do this, we will better recognize that history and culture are not just the creation of humans, but are the joint, shared creations of humans and other creatures. The bark of the subaltern, and the neigh, growl, howl, and the meow, deserve to be heard and included in the histories and biographies we humans tell.

An attention to Hachikō's contributions to how this dog's life might be told highlights the challenges and possibilities of animal biography. The political usefulness of Hachikō for nationalist imperatives helped to produce the ample source material that make it possible to construct his biography, yet a biographer must avoid allowing that agenda from determining the narrative and dictating conclusions. As Hiraiwa argued, Hachikō's apparent devotion was not grounded in loyalty but in affection for his departed companion, Professor Ueno. An appetite for handouts like *yakitori*, which he may have acquired waiting at the station for Ueno's return, perhaps both before and after his master's death, and which he may have associated with Ueno, probably played a role. This behavior or, more appropriately, these *actions* may have been typical to an Akita dog but they were individualized, the product of Hachikō's upbringing, personality, and a particular set of historical and cultural

[28] Kishi, *Chūken Hachikō*, 46.

contexts in which he lived, though generalized observations derived from ethology, comparative psychology, and ecology offer useful insights. Hachikō took action and made choices, though like humans his motivations were unclear and are perhaps much less knowable.

As with the biographies of well-, little-, and unknown people, putting the animal subject in his or her broader context is the most important task of a biographer. Though photography and taxidermy do allow certain animals to have a say, ultimately good old historical context is even more vital and one cannot do this without a wide variety of sources from which to draw, as Helena Prycior concluded in her argument for the possibility of "canine biography," at least for the "first dogs" of American presidents.[29] Thinking back on the variety of nonhuman animals with whom I have associated over the course of my life, I would be hard pressed to write a biography of any of them because of a lack of sources that could be used to contextualize their lives. Clearly I need to write more faithfully in my diary and mention them more often. As it is, they exist mostly in photographs and in my family's memories. We have a few photos of the bird dogs we had when I was a youngster, Bell (1965–1979) and Christie (1976–1979); more of the cats, Sora (Sky) and Botan (Peony) my family adopted as kittens in 2007; fewer of the brood of hens we have kept since 2011; and now innumerable digital photos, videos and the @pochithepoodle Instagram account of the abandoned toy poodle-mix puppy we found on the street in 2014 and named Pochi (a Japanese variant of pooch, probably the most popular name for dogs in Japan in the late nineteenth century, and the name of the Humane Society club that made Hachikō an honorary member). We have not and don't plan to preserve any of these animals, even Pochi, through taxidermy. Although still and moving photography and taxidermy may give them some say in how their biographies might be told, an array of other primary sources—the raw material of history—are the most essential to a biographer, whether the subject is a human or nonhuman animal, famous or relatively unknown.

Works Cited

Alberti, Samuel J.M.M. "Constructing Nature Behind Glass." *Museum and Society* 6.2 (2008): 73–97.

Beck, Alan M. *The Ecology of Stray Dogs: A Study of Free-Ranging Urban Animals.* Baltimore: York Press, 1973.

[29] Pycior, "The Public and Private Lives of 'First Dogs'," 179.

Chūken Hachikō kiroku: Shōten hen, gekan. Eastern Japan Railways Shibuya Station Archive, Tokyo.

Hayashi, Masaharu, ed. *Hachikō bunken shū.* Tokyo: Hayashi Masaharu, 1991.

Hiraiwa, Yonekichi. "Watakushi no inu." In *Zenshū Nihon dōbutsu shi,* edited by Miki Akira, 5–112. Tokyo: Kōdansha, 1983.

Imagawa, Isao. *Inu no gendai shi.* Tokyo: Gendai shokan, 1996.

Kaigo, Tokiomi, Ishikawa Ken, and Ishikawa Matsutarō, eds. *Nihon kyōkasho taikei: Kindai hen, dai-2-kan: Shushin 2.* Tokyo: Kōdansha, 1962.

Kishi, Kazutoshi. *Chūken Hachikō monogatari.* Tokyo: Monasu, 1934.

Kobayashi, Gen. "Sangatsu no kakka gakushū shiryō." *Gakushū kenkyū* 15 (1936): 115–116.

Masson, Jeffrey Moussaieff. *Dogs Never Lie About Love: Reflections on the Emotional World of Dogs.* New York: Three Rivers Press, 1997.

Miklósi, Ádám. *Dog Behavior, Evolution, and Cognition.* Oxford: Oxford University Press, 2015.

Miklósi, Ádám, Borbála Turcsán, and Enikö Kubinyi. "The Personality of Dogs." In *The Social Dog: Behavior and Cognition,* edited by Juliane Kaminki and Sarah Marshall-Pescini, 191–221. Boston: Academic Press, 2014.

Monbushō. *Jinjō shōgaku shūshin sho, maki ni kyōshi yō.* Tokyo: Monbushō, 1935.

Nihon inu hozon kai, ed. *Shadan hōjin Nihon inu hozon kai sōritsu gojū shūnen shi.* Tokyo: Nihon inu hozon kai, 1978.

Pycior, Helena. "The Public and Private Lives of 'First Dogs': Warren G. Harding's Laddie Boy and Franklin D. Roosevelt's Fala." In *Beastly Natures: Animals, Humans, and the Study of History,* edited by Dorothee Brantz, 176–203. Charlottesville: University of Virginia Press, 2010.

Saitō, Hirokichi. *Nihon no inu to ōkami.* Tokyo: Sekkaisha, 1964.

———. "Aiken monogatari." In *Zenshū Nihon dōbutsu shi,* edited by Miki Akira, 5–102. Tokyo: Kōdansha, 1983.

Sax, Boria. *Animals in the Third Reich: Pets, Scapegoats, and the Holocaust.* New York: Continuum, 2000.

Shiina, Noritaka. *Taishō hakubutsukan hiwa.* Tokyo: Ronzōsha, 2002.

Skabelund, Aaron. "Can the Subaltern Bark? Imperialism, Civilization, and Canine Cultures in Nineteenth-Century Japan." In *JAPANimals: History and Culture in Japan's Animal Life,* edited by Gregory M. Pflugfelder and Brett L. Walker, 194–243. Ann Arbor: Center for Japanese Studies, University of Michigan, 2005.

———. "Breeding Racism: The Imperial Battlefields of the 'German' Shepherd Dog." *Society and Animals* 16 (2008): 354–371.

"Itoshi ya rōken monogatari: Ima wa yo ni naki shujin no kaeri o machikaneru nana nenkan." *Asahi shinbun,* October 4, 1932.

CHAPTER 6

"We Know Them All": Does It Make Sense to Create a Collective Biography of the European Bison?

Markus Krzoska

When we talk about animal biographies, we usually have in mind the life and death of individual specimens: animals that lived through very special situations, mostly heroes, sometimes villains, and that are anthropomorphized based on their supposed abilities, emotions, or behavior. In this chapter, I will ask whether it makes sense to transfer methodological experiences from social and everyday history to the world of nonhuman animals. As an example, I will refer to European bison that embody a manageable group of individuals and at the same time can be viewed as a collective. Their history within the twentieth century is very well documented. From the perspective of zoological research and global campaigns to save an endangered species, they are often treated as an amorphous mass of nameless animals but there are also numerous instances in which they appear as individuals. Using the sources we have at our disposal,

M. Krzoska (✉)
Justus-Liebig-University Giessen, Giessen, Germany

University of Siegen, Siegen, Germany

© The Author(s) 2018
A. Krebber, M. Roscher (eds.), *Animal Biography*,
Palgrave Studies in Animals and Literature,
https://doi.org/10.1007/978-3-319-98288-5_6

103

including statistics, descriptions, and photographs, I will discuss the possibilities, potentials, and risks of writing a collective biography of European bison.

In the first step, I will differentiate between three different ways of composing collective biographies: firstly, by using a prosopographic method; secondly, by employing approaches from historical social research; and thirdly, by taking what we might call a constructivist approach. In the second step, I will try to link these approaches to the research of bison. Taking a critical view of the practicality and innovative power of these approaches, I will try, in the third step, to develop an alternative model of writing animal biographies. I would like to call this new approach "entangled biographies," which take into account the rather temporary or potential interaction between human and nonhuman animals, or even objects.

MODELS OF COLLECTIVE BIOGRAPHY

When talking about collective biography, we first have to address its definition and the methods it implies. Harders and Lipphardt define the genre quite plausibly: "Collective biography can deliver a broader view of the history of mentalities, encompassing, for example, political views, influences of a certain milieu, of historic events, or career patterns."[1] And furthermore:

Collective biographies can also be linked to other approaches with encouraging results. It can be combined with methods of discourse analysis, intellectual history, historical and empirical social research, analyses of generations and cohorts, histories of migration, and network analysis.[2]

There are different approaches when it comes to writing collective biographies. According to Wilhelm-Heinz Schröder, the first approach corresponds to the model of prosopography stemming from the Anglo-Saxon context; the second one is typically drawn from historical social research with reference to the New Social History and sociology; and the third approach, which Schröder does not mention, has to do with pure-breed constructivism.

Within this context, by prosopography we mean the production of statistical-empirical studies, "whose method is the systematic quantitative collection and evaluation of well-chosen biographical data, which should

---

[1] Harders and Lipphardt, "Kollektivbiographie in der Wissenschaftsgeschichte."
[2] Harders, "Legitimizing Biography," 53.

be as comprehensive as possible."[3] Starting with the fact that we only have limited information about individuals, the available data must be collected in a standardized manner in order to find common characteristics of the examined group. Therefore, it is crucial for the research to determine exact criteria for choosing the study population and that this population is as homogeneously composed as possible. Its geographical, chronological, and thematic borders must be defined exactly. In dealing with human animals, the standardized survey or the use of questionnaires is central.

For historical social research the role of generation and genealogy was—and still is—at the heart of biography studies. Aspects of temporality and succession are applied to single persons, and likewise to collective biographies, for example, when a certain cohort is analyzed. In order to avoid the excessive presentation of individuals, according to the *Handbuch Biographie* (*Companion to Biography*) from 2009, it is necessary to provide "theoretically and methodologically reflected, empiric and especially quantitatively supported investigation of a historical collective of persons in its respective social context with the help of a comparative analysis of the individual life stories of the group members."[4] Examining the "untypical, divergent and individual" offers opportunities for the analysis of social change. This method is particularly suitable for the research of underprivileged groups such as workers, women or national minorities.

Representatives of historical social research prefer to choose collective biographies as a method of examining "history from below." They want to reconstruct the lives of people who normally did not write about themselves, lives that are genuinely difficult to reconstruct for historians using traditional sources. Collective biographies based on new technical possibilities, for instance processing large amounts of information contained in machine-readable records, offer remedy here. This procedure offers the prospect of generating the kind of "objective findings" that at the very least would show a way for further analyzing a large group of thousands of animals. Historical social sciences had admittedly passed its peak in the 1980s, even if Mieke Roscher recently tried to demonstrate their usefulness for human-animal studies.[5] Instead of the analysis of large-scale social processes, one can identify a return of the "great white men" on the one hand, and a boom of micro-history arising out of social questions on the other.

---

[3] Schröder, *Kollektivbiographie*, 119.
[4] Harders and Schweiger, "Kollektivbiographische Ansätze."
[5] Roscher, "Zwischen Wirkungsmacht."

A third way to research collective biographies could be termed "post-structuralist." In this approach, researchers are "subject-objects" who cooperate on behalf of a chosen topic. "Drawing on their own memories relevant to that topic, and through the shared work of telling, listening and writing" they come to a certain, imaginary point from where they develop an "embodied sense of what happened," thereby establishing different kinds of truths.[6] Therefore, following post-Foucauldian theory, the agential subject and its nature appear to be more important than an imagined (or real) object, even when both are, in a certain way, "the same."

THE SPECIAL CASE OF THE EUROPEAN BISON

In April 1919, the First World War had been over for several months. However, in Eastern Europe the balance of power remained quite unclear as concrete borders still had to be drawn. Civil War raged in Russia and the newly established Polish state rather poorly attempted to impose its institutions and structures on regions where various linguistic and religious groups lived. Mythical to its residents, the woods of Białowieża—once the hunting ground of the Polish-Lithuanian princes and kings, later of the Russian czars—were since 1915 the special field of economic and colonial experiments of the German occupying forces who pitilessly plundered the timber stock.[7] Before the beginning of the war, about 500 European bison lived in the Puszcza Białowieska, as the forest was called by the locals who spoke both Polish and the Eastern Slavic dialects. This accounted for the largest population of bison worldwide. Then, in 1919, rumors that chaos and destruction were taking over the game park-like area spread to Warsaw, from where a small group of scientists led by the biologist Władysław Szafer went East under risky conditions. They wanted to examine if there were any bison left roaming in the Białowieża forest, following rumors of poaching by the hungry civilian population in the war's aftermath. Unfortunately, their sense of foreboding was confirmed as fact, as they only bumped into the disemboweled body of a bison cow, its head cut off as a trophy.[8]

During the following years, an international community consisting of scientists, amateur breeders, hunters, journalists and animal painters adapted a model that had previously been employed successfully to rescue

---

[6] Davies and Gannon, "Practices of Collective," 3.
[7] Bohn et al., *Wisent-Wildnis*.
[8] Szafer, "Pierwsze."

the North-American buffalo in 1905. Their goal was to develop a plan to save the species from becoming extinct. The situation was by far more difficult, however, as European bison lived throughout zoos and enclosures in eight countries and existed in an even lower number than their North-American counterparts.[9] Instead of 1000 buffaloes, they had only 30 so-called pureblood specimens of bison. In August 1923, the activists joined forces in Berlin and founded the *International Society for the Protection of the European Bison*. As one of their first steps, the activists decided to record the stock of the animals meticulously. Some years passed before the so-called *Bison Pedigree Book* was published. Fierce discussions ensued about the way the bison were bred. At the beginning the records were kept in Germany but after the end of the Second World War the responsibility was handed over to Polish scientists.[10]

Listing all European bison individuals worldwide, the *European Pedigree Book* has been compiled and published every year until today at Białowieża National Park. It provides a comprehensive and careful cultivated proof of ancestry as well as reliable software for the registration of genealogical connections, offering research opportunities in various fields. In addition to names and dates of birth (the first issues contain information on the death of important specimens as well), the sex, parents, breeder, owners, as well as registration numbers were also noted. Various supplements provide surveys and diagrams of special bloodlines. In addition, there are photographs showing many of the animals. Whilst the number of "pureblood" bison was easily manageable at the beginning, the preservation efforts expanded the stock of the endangered species significantly. Today, more than 3000 specimens are listed in the pedigree book.[11]

WE KNOW THEM ALL, BUT DOES THIS HELP?

The information collected in the pedigree book can be helpful in providing a prosoprographic way of writing a collective biography of European bison. However, the study not only recorded accurately the concrete data concerning the animals but also provided genealogical graphics, family trees, and other illustrative data. While the bison world survey is relatively complete, its criteria are, of course, man-made. The way of breeding

---

[9] Sztolcman, *Żubr*, 87.
[10] Raczyński and Bołbot, "The European," 10.
[11] Raczyński, "Księga."

determines the mark of quality. The so-called pureblood breeding excludes many specimens from consideration. It is true that we possess some data of those animals which have been and still are considered to be valuable enough to reproduce. One could compare the pedigree book with genealogical records of noblemen, which have been popular as a primary source for historians for a long time. Indeed, we can learn quite a lot from these books about kinship, origin, or fertility. With the help of statistical and quantitative analyses, we can make statements about the total population, average life expectancy, number of births per cow, the frequency of certain breeding places, or causes of death. By doing so, we are able to obtain, above all, important insights for scientific research which might help rescue the species in the long term.

Nonetheless, in a certain way such a collective biography continues the tradition of positivist and normative research in the history of human animals. There is no chance to follow the traces of the subaltern. Hybrids, for instance, half-breed of bison and cow, produced no evidence in the sources; they even did not get individual names. The pedigree book essentially shows a top-down perspective of the exclusive field of the breeders and therefore offers no opportunities for classical historical social research although the sheer flood of data does enable a computer-based analysis.

At this point I want to briefly mention the third approach, the post-structuralist one, because it does not fit well into our deliberations of animals, although the roots of this method are closely connected with another subaltern group, namely women.[12]

The post-structuralist auto-ethnography depends very strongly on language and a semi-conscious production of knowledge. Even though a fully "semiotized model of textuality" in the tradition of Derrida is rather rejected in favor of the Deleuzian model of different linkages and new alignments which "saves" the existence of materiality,[13] it is difficult to imagine how such a system could work in the context of animals. Such an approach might be feasible within the classical framework of biographical studies—provided the research is done collectively by a group of people dealing with bison. But does it make sense within a post-human model that tends to reconcile structure and agency deconstruction, and materiality, respectively?

---

[12] Haug, *Female Sexualization*.
[13] Grosz, *Space*, 126–127.

TOWARD A NEW ENTANGLEMENT OF BIOGRAPHIES

So are there any possibilities at all to research bison biographies beyond the individual or the collective? The solution I would like to suggest, albeit not being the most original one, takes the term Human-Animal Studies seriously while at the same time being consistent with the concept of historical network research. I propose to develop a new concept of entanglement to create or discover connections between human and nonhuman animals, between flora and fauna, or between bison and any kind of object in a neo-materialistic way.

What does entanglement mean within such a discourse or a performative practice? And how can we avoid normativity? The approach I propose is not so much about the examination of historic power structures and their constitution in space in a whatsoever *longue durée*,[14] but rather about situationality and potentiality.[15] Entangled biographies of human and nonhuman animals accept the fact that both are subjects, and that the interactive possibilities are potentially unlimited in terms of Deleuze and Guattari's rhizome metaphor.[16] Of course, the biographies of two or more animals can also be entangled.

According to Thomas Etzemüller, biography always represents a reconstruction of an act of construction.[17] Entangled biographies therefore create a new human-animal or animal-animal actant, whose two components undoubtedly can be subsumed under the concept of agency.[18] While we do not have enough information and means to reconstruct classical networks of animals for a longer period, we still can register entanglement as a short-term or potential connection by researching the interweaving of biographies in the fields of family, organization, place, or cultural affinity.[19]

The term "collective biography" increasingly went out of fashion, and has been gradually replaced by a research method known as historical network analysis. Today, biographies—disregarding bestsellers filling the shelves of bookstores—are more than ever considered to be "historical."

[14] Bauck and Maier, "Entangled History."
[15] I will not discuss here the methodological premises of entanglements. See for this Werner and Zimmermann, "Vergleich, Transfer, Verflechtung," 618–619.
[16] Deleuze and Guattari, *A Thousand Plateaus*.
[17] Etzemüller, *Biographien*, 62.
[18] Cf. Latour, "On Actor-Network Theory."
[19] Peters, "Group Biographies," 41.

"Biography must be a serious exploration of the relations of individuals to their specific societies and must draw on both oral and written sources."[20]

However, collective biographies are not simply collections of single lives: If such a product was ever to emerge, it would probably take shape in an "Encyclopedia of Bison." In contrast to such an encyclopedia, in which the criteria of a lemma more or less demand a sort of equality of all listed animals, a collective biography may outline the main points of a special field of research by choosing and omitting some aspects resulting from the respective scientific context. Admittedly, though, post-modern encyclopedias tend to fulfill such a definition. Their editors highlight some topics and neglect others, avoiding normative principles.[21] "It is the task of the biographer," to quote David Nasaw, "to disentangle, to prioritise, to attempt to understand how, in a given time and place, a 'self' is organized and performed."[22]

The way Nasaw understands disentanglement does not contradict my proposal. I will not recreate a new, lifelong sense within a single or collective biography, but rather find temporal, performative, and even potential connections, which promise, in the end, to provide a new perspective on human-animal relations.

Due to the selectiveness of written sources, spectacular performances must replace a broader analysis of animal life. While this might not always satisfy us, historians are acquainted to such phenomena from our "normal" work. There is no alternative unless we present arguments by analogy or merely speculate. Capturing moments of entanglement between human and nonhuman animals as well as objects can create something similar to collective biographies without repeating their naturalistic mistakes.

Let me show three examples of such entanglements from the context of European bison history. In all of them we find combinations of short-term encounters at certain places with given structures and actors. At the center of our attention will be animal resistance or reluctance. That does not mean that human-animal entanglement is always determined by violence or that conflict is the most decisive part of animal biography. The problem is that only spectacular events are reported in the sources, thereby always presenting a distorted view of life. Nevertheless, there is no doubt that the

[20] Agirreazkuenaga and Urquijo, "Europe's Cultural Legacy," 379.

[21] A – sometimes annoying – example for such an encyclopedia is Ferrari and Petrus, *Lexikon*.

[22] Nasaw, "AHR Roundtable," 576.

breeding of European bison and the extensive heteronomy of its life constitute a high degree of human-animal entanglement. Despite their deep knowledge about the animals, human actors still underestimate a bison's free will and readiness to (re-)act.

Animals and Their Breeders

In 1928 the Polish government decided to bring European bison back to the Białowieża Forest. The campaign was more of a national project than a biological necessity. Many experts in Poland and abroad had doubts. The administration of the newly founded national park appeared to be too weak, infrastructure and health care underdeveloped, the risks of illegal hunting enormous. Besides, the concentration of almost the complete Polish bison population in one place was deemed to be too risky given the potential for highly contagious diseases. In defiance of such warnings, the state institutions promptly erected an open-air enclosure and bought some specimens on the open market. Within a couple of months, between September 1929 and August 1930, two bulls and four cows were brought to Białowieża. Transport was quite difficult—the bulls in particular proved to be very uncooperative. This was not the last act of animal resistance, though. The official plan to expand the range of bison breeding required putting another male specimen in the enclosure. In 1935, 6-year-old bull Björnson (Nr. M-186) was bought from the Stockholm Zoo. He was confronted with alpha-male Borusse (M-163) in order to share the cows. But the competitive behavior of the animals was much stronger than human bio-political tension. On 18 July 1935, Borusse killed Björnson. In the words of Foucault, against the *dispositif* of sexuality "the rallying point for the counterattack ought not to be sexual desire, but bodies and pleasures"—or physical urges of animals.[23] Although this animal-animal entanglement provides only a snapshot of a biography, we can look for similar situations or the possibility of them in order to obtain more insights over such contacts. Only two years later Borusse the winner turned into a loser, when his rival Plisch (M-229) was brought to Białowieża from Upper Silesia and won the physical confrontation. At least this time the humans intervened before he was killed: Borusse survived, cut off from the production of offspring for the rest of his life, until his traces disappeared in the stomachs of poachers shortly after the end of the Second World War.

---

[23] Foucault, *History of Sexuality*, 157.

Animals and Their Ideologists

Another example is the refusal of performance as described by an observer shortly before the outbreak of the Second World War. In 1938, the Austrian diplomat Johannes Schwarzenberg witnessed an unprecedented event. The premiere gamekeeper of the Third Reich, Reichsjägermeister Hermann Göring, took special pleasure in the rustic beasts, receiving as a present two animals of this species from Poland for his domicile in Schorfheide, 50 km outside of Berlin. The first mating of the two European bison was to be carried out quite officially in the presence of the diplomatic corps. For this purpose, a sort of bullring was built at his manor in Carinhall. Then the following occurred:

> On the fixed day, after the diplomats and their wives had taken a seat, Göring, dressed in a leather jerkin a spear clenched in his fist, strode into the arena and delivered a speech. The meaning of the day was made clear to the audience, consisting of representatives of countries sympathetic to the Third Reich: for the first time after centuries of decline and the eradication of the highest values, the prototype of strength, German aurochs were to populate again the German forests. 'You, my dear gentlemen ambassadors, will, together with your attractive wives, be witnesses to the first fertilisation of a bison's cow by a powerful primordial bull. May the seed bring fruit, bestow many little oxen and little cows on our forests, and may this event work as an exemplary model!' After slight applause, the Reichsjägermeister withdrew to the rostrum with spear, leather jerkin and slouch hat. Two gates opposite each other opened; from one of them a cow broke out, from the other, pushed by bars, the auer bull tottered out, tired, indignant. Both animals stared at each other: Nothing! They continue staring. Encouraging calls are expressed behind the palisades. Still nothing! Göring's angry voice shouts for increased application of the bars. Farmhands sneak up and start to push the animals. Obscene shouts should spur bride and groom. All in vain! The two just do not want! Because nothing is working and the couple keeps on striking, the disappointed Jägermeister with apologetic gesture invites to a cocktail.[24]

Even if the diplomat might have added something here and there, it is possible to explain the failure of this "animal porn" with the resistance of the actress and the actor. The nonhuman animals seem to be as tired as the voyeuristic ambassadors with their wives on the rostrum. As it turned out

---

[24] Schwarzenberg and Meran-Schwarzenberg, *Erinnerungen*, 137.

this was a bad omen for the Germanic breeding of bison or aurochs, characterized by a strange mixture of ideological will and amateurism in the field of biology.

Animals and Their Constructors

The third and final example can be found in the 1950s and has to do with the human level of expectations and the animal's passive resistance. The Polish pioneers of veterinary medicine, assigned to give treatment to bison, were confronted with situations they could not have learnt during their education. In 1957, the first operation of a bison under general anesthetic for test purposes took place in Warsaw. The bull Plato (M-575) was supposed to be killed afterward, his hide donated to the Polish Prime Minister Józef Cyrankiewicz. However, the socialist schedule did not work as expected. At first, the surgery had to be postponed for half a year because Plato decided to lose his winter coat some days earlier. When the operation finally took place and the carotid was to be exposed, it became evident that the scalpels normally used could penetrate the skin of the animal, 4 cm thick, only under considerable difficulties. To make matters worse, Plato, who was quite old and suffered from a rheumatic disease which made it almost impossible for him to get up, moved quickly to attack the vet who had touched him, doubtlessly alarmed by this unusual, really hazardous situation.[25] While in the end the vets got the situation under control, we can discern here a line of situational entanglements with different actors. It would be even possible to expand the range of agency to objects, given that the animal skin as well as the scalpel could be understood as "actants" in the sense proposed by Bruno Latour, or to examine the meaning of materiality in this context, but that would lead us too far away from the issue at hand.[26]

CONCLUSION

Struggle for survival, reproduction, and resistance are therefore three central elements of entangled biographies. Here we get to know the nonhuman animals in other roles than those attributed to them by humans. They almost have equal rights within a system of social practices, a typified, routine, and

---

[25] Gill, "Wspomnienia," 90–92, 102–103.
[26] Latour, "On Actor-Network Theory"; Sarasin, "Mapping the Body."

socially understandable range of activities in which the bodies—or more generally the materiality—play a decisive role as skilled performances.[27]

Without relinquishing the human perspective, which is impossible under any circumstances, the bison is at least temporarily taken seriously. Since our perspective is limited, it does not make sense to expand the theory of social practices to bison in such a way that each kind of acting would be first based on knowledge in the sense of having a special expertise. These are the intellectual, almost normative limits of Human-Animal Studies.

Nevertheless, we can argue that there is an intense interaction between animals and their environment, a "structure of functional circles," as Jakob von Uexküll called it a century ago.[28] We do not have to follow further his theory about specific worlds of each species, which animals cannot leave, but in such entangled activities between living beings we can see something more than in relationships between humans and non-living objects, although there are some parallels. It certainly makes sense to look at each kind of network-like relations in a post-human world because it changes our perspective as well as our empathy toward "things." Animals are more than just things both in a concrete, practical and ethical, philosophical way.

We know, of course, that our definition—or rather explanation—of a given situation is subjective. However, it is not "too normative" to set off animal behavior in an emancipatory way. We just have to admit that it is impossible to reconstruct the whole life and personality of an animal or a group of them. Nevertheless, it is not reprehensible to concentrate on some (important) actions in a special cultural context in order to interpret them. Such an approach corresponds rather to an ethnographic or ethnomethodological practice of research than to a strictly historical or philosophical method.[29] The only alternative would be a position that seems to be predominant in post-human philosophy, namely a phenomenological perspective. Praxeology and temporality, as integral parts of biographical research, can help reconstruct some aspects of interaction between human and nonhuman animals. In so doing we do not have to exclude the field

---

[27] Reckwitz, "Toward a Theory," 251; Pavese, "Skill in Epistemology."

[28] Uexküll, *Umwelt und Innenwelt*, 6.

[29] There are of course some similarities to the "biography of an object" (*biografija vešči*) Sergej Tret'jakov developed in the 1930s, especially concerning the accentuation of the process instead of an analysis of the personality. See Fore, "Gegen den 'lebendigen Menschen'."

of collectivity. By observing animal behavior under given stable circumstances, like living in an enclosure for a certain time, we possibly can get illuminating results about the species, or at least a peer group. Although for some observers the question of animal agency seems to be irrelevant, the discussion about abilities and capabilities might proceed.[30]

One could go even further. As post-human research has made room for new methodological approaches beyond living matter, we have the chance to take into account aspects of entanglement concerning animals and objects. Many sources show how different specimens of bison react to captivity, for instance, the existence of walls, fences, and other obstacles, by trying to overcome or to destroy them.[31] But that is already a different story.

WORKS CITED

Agirreazkuenaga, Joseba and Mikel Urquijo. "Collective Biography and Europe's Cultural Legacy." *The European Legacy* 20.4 (2015): 373–388.

Bauck, Sönke and Thomas Maier. "Entangled History." *InterAmerican Wiki: Terms – Concepts – Critical Perspectives* (2015). http://www.uni-bielefeld.de/cias/wiki/e_Entangled_History.html. Accessed December 2, 2016.

Bohn, Thomas, Aliaksandr Dalhouski, and Markus Krzoska. *Wisent-Wildnis und Welterbe: Die Geschichte des polnisch-weißrussischen Białowieża-Nationalparks.* Köln: Böhlau, 2017.

Davies, Bronwyn and Susanne Gannon. "The Practices of Collective Biography." In *Doing Collective Biography: Investigating the Production of Subjectivity*, edited by eidem, 1–15. Maidenhead: Open University Press, 2006.

Deleuze, Gilles and Félix Guattari. *A Thousand Plateaus: Capitalism and Schizophrenia.* London: Athlone Press, 1988.

Etzemüller, Thomas. *Biographien: Lesen – erforschen – erzählen.* Frankfurt a. M.: Campus, 2012.

Ferrari, Arianna and Klaus Petrus, ed. *Lexikon der Mensch-Tier-Beziehungen.* Bielefeld: transcript, 2015.

Fore, David. "Gegen den 'lebendigen Menschen': Experimentelle sowjetische Biographik der 1920er Jahre." In *Die Biographie – Zur Grundlegung ihrer Theorie*, edited by Bernhard Fetz, 353–381. Berlin (et al.): De Gruyter, 2009.

Foucault, Michel. *The History of Sexuality I: An Introduction.* New York: Random House, 1978.

---

[30] Wirth et al., *Das Handeln der Tiere*; Latour, "Agency."
[31] See Jabłońska, *Moje*, passim.

Gill, Janusz. "Wspomnienia z kontaktów z żubrami w Puszczy Białowieskiej." In *Moje spotkanie z żubrami*, edited by Elżbieta Jabłońska, 87–113. Białowieża: Białowieski Park Narodowy, 2004.

Grosz, Elizabeth. *Space, Time and Perversion*. New York: Routledge, 1995.

Harders, Levke. "Legitimizing Biography: Critical Approaches to Biographical Research." *Bulletin of the German Historical Institute* 55 (2014): 49–56.

Harders, Levke and Veronika Lipphardt. "Kollektivbiographie in der Wissenschaftsgeschichte als qualitative und problemorientierte Methode." *Traverse* 2 (2006): 81–91.

Harders, Levke and Hannes Schweiger. "Kollektivbiographische Ansätze." In *Handbuch Biographie. Methoden, Traditionen, Theorien*, edited by Christian Klein, 194–198. Stuttgart and Weimar: J.B. Metzler'sche Verlagsbuchhandlung und Carl Ernst Poeschel Verlag, 2009.

Haug, Frigga, et al. *Female Sexualization: A Collective Work of Memory*. London: Verso, 1987.

Hoskins, Janet. "Agency, Biography and Objects." In *Handbook of Material Culture*, edited by Christopher Y. Tilley, Webb Keane, Susanne Küchler, Michael Rowlands, and Patricia Spyer, 74–84. London: Sage, 2006.

Jabłońska, Elżbieta, ed. *Moje spotkanie z żubrami*. Białowieża: Białowieski Park Narodowy, 2004.

Klein, Christian, ed. *Handbuch Biographie. Methoden, Traditionen, Theorien*. Stuttgart and Weimar: J.B. Metzler'sche Verlagsbuchhandlung und Carl Ernst Poeschel Verlag, 2009.

Latour, Bruno. "On Actor-Network Theory: A Few Clarifications Plus More than a Few Complications." *Soziale Welt* 47 (1996): 369–381.

———. "Agency at the Time of Anthropocene." *New Literary History* 45 (2014): 1–18.

Nasaw, David. "AHR Roundtable: Historians and Biography. Introduction." *American Historical Review* 114.3 (2009): 573–578.

Pavese, Carlotta: "Skill in Epistemology I: Skill and Knowledge." *Philosophy Compass* 11.11 (2016): 642–649. http://onlinelibrary.wiley.com/doi/10.1111/phc3.12359/full#references. Accessed December 30, 2016.

Peters, Margot. "Group Biographies. Challenges and Methods." In *New Directions in Biography*, edited by Anthony M. Friedson, 41–51. Hawaii: Published for the Biographical Research Center by the University Press of Hawaii, 1981.

Raczyński, Jan. *Księga Rodowodowa Żubrów = European Bison Pedigree Book 2015*. Białowieża: Białowieski Park Narodowy, 2016.

Raczyński, Jan and Małgorzata Bołbot. *The European Bison Pedigree Book in History and Today*. Białowieża: Białowieski Park Narodowy, 2009.

Reckwitz, Andreas. "Toward a Theory of Social Practices: A Development in Culturalist Theorizing." *European Journal of Social Theory* 5.2 (2002): 243–263.

Roscher, Mieke. "Zwischen Wirkungsmacht und Handlungsmacht: Sozialge-schichtliche Perspektiven auf tierliche Agency." In *Das Handeln der Tiere: Tierliche Agency im Fokus der Human-Animal Studies*, edited by Sven Wirth, Anett Laue, Markus Kurth, Katharina Dornenzweig, Leonie Bossert, and Karsten Balgar, 43–66. Bielefeld: transcript, 2016.

Sarasin, Philipp. "Mapping the Body: Körpergeschichte zwischen Konstruktivismus, Politik und Erfahrung." *Historische Anthropologie* 7.3 (1999): 437–451.

Schröder, Wilhelm Heinz. "Kollektivbiographie: Spurensuche, Gegenstand, Forschungsstrategie." *Historical Social Research*, Supplement 23 (2011): 74–152.

Szafer, Władysław. "Pierwsze karty z historii Białowieskiego Parku Narodowego." *Kosmos, Seria A* 6 (1957): 469–475.

Sztolcman, Jan. *Żubr: Jego przeszłość i przyszłość*. Warszawa: nakładem Centralnego Związku Polskich Stowarzyszeń Łowieckich, 1927.

von Meran-Schwarzenberg, Colienne Gräfin, Marysia Miller-Aichholz, and Erkinger Schwarzenberg, ed. *Johannes E. Schwarzenberg: Erinnerungen und Gedanken eines Diplomaten im Zeitenwandel 1903–1978*. Wien: Böhlau, 2013.

von Uexküll, Jakob. *Umwelt und Innenwelt der Tiere*. Berlin: Springer, 1921.

Werner, Michael and Bénédicte Zimmermann. "Vergleich, Transfer, Verflechtung: der Ansatz der "Histoire croisée" und die Herausforderung des Transnationalen." *Geschichte und Gesellschaft* 28 (2002): 607–636.

Wirth, Sven, Anett Laue, Markus Kurth, Katharina Dornenzweig, Leonie Bossert, and Karsten Balgar, ed. *Das Handeln der Tiere: Tierliche Agency im Fokus der Human-Animal Studies*. Bielefeld: transcript, 2016.

CHAPTER 7

Animal Life Stories; or, the Making of Animal Subjects in Primatological Narratives of Fieldwork

Mira Shah

There are certain primate individuals that—without ever having met them—I know quite intimately: the chimpanzees Flo, David, and Evered, for example; or the baboon matriarch Peggy, the gorilla male Digit, and the baboon "oddball" Nick. I know these primates by name and I am able to recognize them by picture because not only have they been subjected to the exploration and documentation of their life and behavior by several primatologists over the years, but also because they are protagonists of elaborate *stories* about them. I know them nearly as well as I know the primatologists telling these stories: Jane Goodall, Dian Fossey, Biruté Galdikas, Shirley C. Strum, or Robert Sapolsky. As can be expected, given that these authors mostly work within the framework of the natural sciences, they tell their stories not so much in their research publications but in a genre that I call "primatological autobiographies" or "research memoirs." This genre is a hybrid form: it usually tells the story of a single primatologist's often lifelong career in the field; it gives an account of the

M. Shah (✉)
Goethe-University, Frankfurt, Germany

© The Author(s) 2018
A. Krebber, M. Roscher (eds.), *Animal Biography*,
Palgrave Studies in Animals and Literature,
https://doi.org/10.1007/978-3-319-98288-5_7

specific research done over that time and provides the authors with the opportunity to share the experience of "doing research in the field" with an audience. And quite prominently, these narratives transport knowledge about the animal species in consideration, about its habitat and its interaction with the human world.[1]

Traditionally, as Lynda Birke has suggested, scientific accounts about animals have worked toward an "obscuring of individuality."[2] Ironically, they do so mainly by practices of identification: The practice of scientific naming—for example, *pan troglodytes* (the chimpanzee) or *papio cynocephalus* (the yellow baboon)—categorizes animals and describes them as a species; yet, to quote Birke, "who or what they are as individuals matters little for these purposes."[3] In ethological fieldwork, too, the overall aim is to gather behavioral information about a species or a group.[4] Notwithstanding this overriding focus on the taxonomic or social *collective* of animals, in order to gain epistemological insight into the species, *individual* animals are followed, observed, documented, and described. This line of research therefore tends to have "side effects," mainly, that the autobiographical narratives of primatological fieldwork recognize animals as subjects.

These narratives do so, I suggest, in three ways: (1) as written narratives of fieldwork, they create textual subjects; (2) they often do so by applying a melodramatic mode, which endows animal individuals with a literary agency that challenges the narratives of evolutionary ethology or sociobiology; and (3) the fieldwork of Jane Goodall, Dian Fossey, Biruté Galdikas, Shirley C. Strum, and even Robert Sapolsky is based on a quasi-ethnological, empathic approach to the animals, as field studies from the 1950s onward mostly involved not only observation *of,* but also *among* primate groups. What the texts relay about this fieldwork points toward a

---

[1] Asquith therefore sees this "narrative primatology" as going "to the heart of the fieldwork experience" by providing "sustained reports on the fieldwork experience and hence very much richer examples about methodology, about the nature of the relationship between the observers and animals, and that among animals themselves" (Asquith, "Natural Homes," 243) than research papers are able to reveal.

[2] Birke, *Feminism,* 7.

[3] Ibid.

[4] From the 1990s on, there has been a noticeable shift in research toward the inter-group differentiation of forms of culture, especially among chimpanzees, cf. McGrew, *Chimpanzee Materials;* Boesch and Tomasello, "Chimpanzee and Human"; Whiten et al., "Cultures"; Boesch, *Wild Cultures.*

relationship between researcher and researched, between human and non-human animal, that can be understood by way of the concept of recognition as developed by Axel Honneth in *The Struggle for Recognition* (1995).[5]

In the following paragraphs I will first look at how research memoirs—Dian Fossey's *Gorillas in the Mist* (1985), Jane Goodall's *In the Shadow of Man* (1971) and *Through A Window* (1990), Shirley Strum's *Almost Human* (1987), and Robert Sapolsky's *A Primate's Memoir* (2001)—work toward presenting primate individuals as textual subjects. I will then, secondly, concern myself with the characteristics and role of a melodramatic mode in the narration of these textual subjects and look at their potential for literary agency; and, finally, I will connect the method of fieldwork practiced by the authors as related through their memoirs with the idea of intersubjective recognition in order to show how the actualization of subjectivity is fundamental to the production of ethological knowledge.

PRIMATE LIFE STORIES

Let us start with the basic formation of subjects on a linguistic and narrative level. As narratives, primatological memoirs produce individualized animals as subject-actors of sentences, of plots and as protagonists of exemplary life stories. The genre individualizes its animals by endowing them with gendered pronouns, rendering an animal no longer as an 'it' but rather as 'she' or 'he'. These animals are given proper names that are often derived from personal traits and are embedded within a framework of signification. Reminded of a relative, for example, Dian Fossey calls one of the male gorillas Uncle Bert.[6] Because of his gray beard the chimpanzee David is called David Graybeard by Jane Goodall.[7] Robert Sapolsky names the baboon personnel of his narrative after Old Testament figures: Solomon, Leah, Devorah, Aaron, Isaac, Naomi, Rachel, even Obadiah, or Ezekiel.[8] For his readers, he contextualizes this with his orthodox Jewish

---

[5] As this essay focuses on Western, anglophone primatology, the frame of reference for animal subjectivity in the following will also be derived from Western conceptions of subjectivity and individualism. For non-Western schools of primatology and animal ethology see, for example, Takasaki, "Traditions"; Haraway, *Primate Visions*, 244–260.

[6] Cf. Fossey, *Gorillas*, 168.

[7] Cf. Lawick-Goodall, *Shadow of Man*, 33.

[8] Sapolsky, *Primate's Memoir*, 14. Sapolsky speaks candidly about his naming practices in *A Primate's Memoir* and describes this part of fieldwork as almost organic process of significa-

upbringing and concedes, that "with some sort of perversity that I suspect powers a lot of what primatologists do, I couldn't wait for the inevitable day that I could record in my field notebook that Nebuchanezzar and Naomi were off screwing in the bushes."[9] He revels in his choice when the significant names turn out to fit the individuals' personalities. Nebuchanezzar, for example, is "mean, stupid, and untalented" and fittingly described as having "only one eye and a disturbing rotty socket," "a flinty face" and "bad posture."[10] A series of inexplicably aggressive behaviors on Nebuchanezzar's part finally leads Sapolsky to write: "At this stage, as a trained scientist, all I can conclude is that Nebuchanezzar was a shit on some fundamental level."[11]

Not only are primates thus named, endowed with physical descriptions, and evaluated according to their perceived personality, the relations between these individual primates are carefully reconstructed and documented. Goodall, for example, writes about two of her key female chimpanzee characters:

> Flo's personality will become more vivid if I contrast it with that of another old female, Olly [...]. Olly, with her long face and loose wobbling lips [...] was remarkably different. Flo for the most part was relaxed in her relations with the adult males [...]. Olly, on the other hand, was tense and nervous in her relations with others of her kind. She was particularly apprehensive when in close proximity to adult males, and her hoarse, frenzied pant-grunts rose to near hysteria if high-ranking Goliath approached her.[12]

As we see, the individuals' characteristic traits, their appearance as well as their comportment are differentiated and described in anthropomorphic

---

tion: "I didn't plan beforehand to give the baboons Old Testament names. It just happened. A new adult male, leaving the troop he grew up in, would transfer into the troop, and during the few weeks when he'd vacillate about joining permanently, I would hesitate about giving him a name. I'd just refer to him in my notes as the new adult transfer, or NAT, or Nat, or, by the time he decided to stay forever, Nathanial. Adam was first known as ATM, for adult transfer male. The small kid who was first abbreviated as the SML kid then turned into Samuel on me. At that point I just gave up and started handing out the prophets and matriarchs and judges left and right" (Ibid.).

[9] Ibid.
[10] Ibid., 99.
[11] Ibid., 101.
[12] Lawick-Goodall, *Shadow of Man*, 81.

character qualities that make them stand out in the narrative.[13] As narrative devices, these characterizations are also of extra-textual importance, since we are contextually and paratextually advised to read these texts as nonfictional accounts of real-life events. The research memoirs are marketed to their audience as exactly that: accounts of real research conducted over years, sometimes decades, by the authors themselves. Prefaces and forewords as well as additional material (pedigrees, graphs, and lists) assure us of the factuality of the report and deliver reality markers for the mentioned simian personnel. In Jane Goodall's case, the chimpanzee protagonists even reappear throughout a number of different publications from the research memoirs *In the Shadow of Man* (1971), *Through a Window* (1990), and *Reason for Hope* (1999), across more strictly scientific publications as, for example, *The Chimpanzees of Gombe* (1986), up to her two-part *Autobiography in Letters, Africa in My Blood* (2001) and *Beyond Innocence* (2002). Therefore, the textual characterizations fashion not only intra- and intertextual characters but also relatable persons that can be traced beyond the text(s) in question.

Furthermore, the observations and data are arranged in such a manner as to form plots and life stories, that is, biographical narratives of individual animals. When female researchers endeavored into the field of primatology from the 1950s onward, the research focus started to shift from male hierarchies to female reproductive life in connection with group structure.[14] Most of the prominent primate researchers of that period emphasized the importance of female biographies and a denser form of scientific observation that was inspired by ethnographical or socioanthropological fieldwork and methodologically based on moderate participant observation.[15] As a result, the memoirs contain whole chapters concerned

---

[13] For a comprehensive linguistic analysis of the National Geographic articles by primatologists and the way that wordings "make it clear that the authors [...] establish the monkeys and apes as individual personalities with idiosyncratic traits, emotions, likes, dislikes, wishes and thoughts," see Sommer, *Foremost in Creation*, 193.

[14] Cf. Strum and Fedigan, "Changing Views"; Haraway, "Morphing."

[15] DeWalt et al., "Participant Observation." DeWalt et al. differentiate "moderate participation" from other forms of observation ("nonparticipation" and "active participation") and describe it as a form of engagement in fieldwork "when the ethnographer is present at the scene of the action but doesn't actively participate or interact, or only occasionally interacts" (Ibid., 262). This is a very fitting description of the primatologist's day-to-day situation of observation, where active interaction with the observed group of primates is not intended but occasional interaction cannot entirely be avoided, see also Sommer, "Anthropologist." Asquith therefore embraces anthropology as primatology's "natural home," but nevertheless

with the single life stories of their eponymous primates: "Flo and Her Family," "Melissa," "Beth," "Cara," "Georgina," and "Peggy."[16] In the structure of the whole narrative these chapters often complement or contrast biographical information about the human protagonists. Jane Goodall, for example, alludes to Flo's mothering style when she herself becomes a mother and takes her infant son with her to do fieldwork.[17] This strategy has prevailed, as even more recent primatological memoirs make use of this narrative arrangement to bring order to the collected empirical data and make it relatable to the reader. Robert Sapolsky's *A Primate's Memoir*, for example, lists chapters such as "Saul in the Wilderness" or "Nick."[18] Sapolsky starts his narrative with a repeating formula: "I joined the baboon troop during my twenty-first year"[19]; "I joined the troop in the last year of the reign of Solomon."[20] Rhetorically, he likens himself to a young immigrating male baboon, and he soon finds a baboon stand-in, Benjamin, to relate the experience of trying to habituate the baboon troop to his presence:

> Benjamin came from the troop on the Tanzanian border. Still just emerging from my own festering adolescent insecurities, I had a difficult time not identifying utterly with Benjamin and his foibles. His hair was berserko. Unkempt, shocks of it sticking out all over his head, weird clumps on his shoulders instead of a manly cape that is supposed to intimidate your rivals. He stumbled over his feet a lot, always sat on the stinging ants. [...] One day, early in that first year in the troop, I was observing Benjamin. [...] It was midday, and two minutes into the sample, Benjamin took a nap under a bush. An hour later, at the end of that riveting sample, everyone had moved off. When he awoke, he didn't know where the troop was, and neither did I. We were lost together. I stood on the roof of the Jeep and scanned with my binoculars. We looked at each other. I finally spotted them [...]. I drove

emphasizes that there are certain differences between the ethnological and the primatological interpretation of participant observation: "The ethnographer attempts to become a participant observer, to gain an 'emic' (insider's) view as does the primatologist, but the means differ. The ethnographer participates in the lives of the society s/he studies; the primatologist does his best not to participate so as not to influence the animals' 'natural' lives" (Asquith, "Natural Homes," 252).

[16] Cf. Lawick-Goodall, *Shadow of Man*, 101–103; Goodall, *Window*, 136–138; Galdikas, *Reflections*, 92–94, 109–111, 164–166; Strum, *Almost Human*, 38–40.

[17] Cf. Lawick-Goodall, *Shadow of Man*, 236–237.

[18] Cf. Sapolsky, *Primate's Memoir*, 95–97, 233–235.

[19] Ibid., 13.

[20] Ibid., 14.

off slowly, he ran after me, happy ending. After that, he would sit next to me when I worked on foot, sit on the bonnet of the Jeep when I worked out of the vehicle. It was around then that I decided he was my favorite baboon and bestowed upon him my favorite name, and everything he ever did subsequently reinforced that feeling.[21]

Benjamin here functions as a totem animal for Sapolsky's field experience *and* is portrayed as a specific, individual baboon that Sapolsky sympathizes with as a young, awkward male himself.

The commonness of the sum of the abovementioned rhetorical and narrative devices leads Gillian Whitlock therefore to conclude that such research memoirs individualize, classify, and characterize their nonhuman personnel, and render them in the gendered, sexed terms of western individualism as "biographical subjects."[22]

MELODRAMAS OF PRIMATE REPRODUCTION; OR, THE STRANGE CASE OF PRIMATE SEXUALITY

Instrumental to the process of the creation of biographical subjects in the primatological memoirs treated here is a mode of perception and of narration that can be called melodramatic. Various studies concerned with melodrama in theater, literature, and film have suggested that Anglo-Saxon cultural narration is inclined to use melodramatic modes to relay democratic and emotional educational intentions.[23] And primatological memoirs are nothing if not intended to educate politically and emotionally in respect of the vanishing primates they narrate.[24] It is therefore advisable to look at the role that a melodramatic mode plays in constituting animal biographies in this genre.

In part due to this inclination of primatological memoirs to prevailing literary and cultural forms of narration, the work of female primatologists in the 1960s to 1980s was met with skepticism in the name of "rational

---

[21] Ibid., 20–21.

[22] Whitlock, "Gorilla Girl," 478.

[23] See, for example, Tompkins, *Sensational Designs*; Williams, "Melodrama"; Brooks, *Melodramatic Imagination*; Decker, *Kritischer Blick*.

[24] That this mode even transpires into the literature about and analysis of these narratives is exemplified by Pollock, *Storytelling*. Pollock perceptibly shifts her focus from an analysis of fieldwork narratives to warning declamations of the threat of extinction and ecological destruction portrayed within these narratives.

science" conducted by contemporaries.[25] Female primatologists of that generation encountered academic rejection as well as immense publicity. Both were owed to the methodical and thematic shift to an emphasis on empathic observation of female primate experiences and a place for emotionality in scientific fieldwork and its evaluation. Dian Fossey's memoir *Gorillas in the Mist* can be regarded as "a radical life narrative project, using memoir to contest speciesism and renegotiate the terms of relational biography."[26] Yet, as a result of the peculiarly ideological contemporary reception and media-driven heroization of "women in the field" as bearers of NatureCulture, the public image of Fossey is still overwhelmingly determined by the rather soppy melodrama film treatment of her book that followed her murder. The 1988 movie *Gorillas in the Mist* does not focus so much on the gorillas, whose well-being Fossey put above all, even above a sense of self preservation, but, as Dennis Bingham has shown, on a sentimental interpretation of the researcher: a constantly affectively overwhelmed Fossey is situated in a love triangle with National Geographic photographer Bob Campell and her favorite male gorilla Digit. Thereby her scientific and conservational work among and for the gorillas is effectively devaluated in favor of a romantic 'biopic'.[27]

In a way though, the treatment of the female primatologist's fieldwork in the film takes part in primatology's own system of the ordering of perception through narration. Peter Brooks' seminal study calls the melodrama "a form of conception and expression," "a certain fiction system for making sense of experience, [...] a semantic field of force," even "a sense-making system."[28] For Eric Bentley, the melodramatic mode is based not only on a conception of the dramatic as the ability to both perceive elements of conflict and to respond emotionally to these elements of conflict, but also on the introduction of narrative and plot to the recounting of these elements, that is "a rearrangement of the incidents in the order most

---

[25] Most of the authors relate these adverse responses to their field research and discourse. Strum makes an especially valiant point in explaining how the research traditions and academic hierarchy sabotaged an unprejudiced discussion of her new findings, cf. Strum, *Almost Human*, 157–159. For the specifically gendered conundrum of primatological research paradigms see Haraway, *Primate Visions*, 244–246, 279; and for a contemporary continuance of this prejudicial devaluation of early field research as "verandah primatology," compare Sommer, *Anthropologist*, 35.

[26] Whitlock, "Gorilla Girl," 478.

[27] Cf. Bingham, *Whose Lives*, 296–298.

[28] Brooks, *Melodramatic Imagination*, xvii.

calculated to have the right effect."[29] Primatological autobiographies do exactly this: They condense decades of fieldwork experience and biographical incidents into a narrative, that is—in conforming to the goals of rhetoric—intended not only to delectate but to move and instruct at the same time. Research memoirs use the melodramatic mode as a sense-making system and a device within a framework of humanist and conservationist educational aims. This becomes all the more significant when texts employ melodramatic plot themes like the Disneyesque Mother-and-Child-topic, that is of obvious interest for primatological research, or the power struggle within primate groups which can easily be reshaped by captions like "Figan's Rise,"[30] Sapolsky's chronological ordering of fieldwork episodes as "reign of"[31] or similar rise-and-decline plots.

Even more pervasive is the melodramatic mode when it engages with another key primatologist topic: sex. One of Jane Goodall's chapters in *In the Shadow of Man* is aptly titled "Flo's Sex Life."[32] While, as Birke calls to mind, science often constructs animals and their bodies as lacking sexuality and desire, reducing their actions to "sex" and "reproduction,"[33] Goodall actively wonders about the intricacies of chimpanzee sex appeal when she states: "Old Flo, bulbous-nosed and ragged-eared, incredibly ugly by human standards, undoubtedly has more than her fair share of it."[34] What she witnesses in that chapter is an estrus cycle of a weathered female chimpanzee that leads to countless sexual encounters with various sexual partners. Although Goodall's narrative puts Flo at the center of this story—it is *her* sexual success that is documented and used as a foil to speculate about chimpanzee sex and reproduction –, this is a narrative mostly of what is done *to* her. She is approached, courted, threatened, mated, and followed. Goodall's choice of language as well as of information challenges the "rational" narrative of scientific observation, when she writes: "It was impossible for her to sit up or lie down without several pairs of eyes instantly swivelling in her direction, and if she got up to move on, the males were on their feet in no time. Every time there was any sort of excitement in the group […] then, one after the other, all the adult males

---

[29] Bentley, *The Life*, 14–15.
[30] Goodall, *Window*, 45–47.
[31] Cf Sapolsky, *Primate's Memoir*, 14, 95, 169.
[32] Lawick-Goodall, *Shadow of Man*, 79–81.
[33] Cf. Birke, *Feminism*, 124–126.
[34] Lawick-Goodall, *Shadow of Man*, 79.

mated Flo [...], each male simply took his turn."[35] Goodall's account climaxes with Flo arriving at Goodall's camp, "with a torn and bleeding bottom [...] somewhat tattered and exhausted by then,"[36] and shortly after "[s]he looked worn out, faded, incredibly tattered after her strenuous five weeks. There were two extra pieces torn from her ears and a variety of cuts and scrapes all over her body. That day she just lay around camp for several hours, looking utterly exhausted."[37]

Two decades later, in *Through a Window*, Goodall recounts another "successful" sexual encounter: Formerly expelled from the group, the male Evered returns as a successful wooer of females in estrus. While this story starts off as a hero's way to redemption, there is a subversive element here again: it is the violence which Evered applies to bring the females to heel. If the branch shaking doesn't "do its magic," and Wilkie refuses to "obey his summoning"—all this is Goodall's vocabulary—he pounds her repeatedly until she does: "Now at last, when he stopped his pounding and summoned her to approach she responded instantly. Hastening to crouch before him, with nervous panting grunts, she pressed her mouth to his thigh, kissing him."[38] Goodall tries to mollify the reader with the assurance that this is "the way of male chimpanzees after aggression" and by saying that "[o]nce punishment has been handed out, then it is time to make amends, to restore social harmony."[39] But on the next page she relates how Wilkie's son shares her nest that night and "surely the contact with his small, familiar body gave her some comfort after the bruisings and batterings of the long day."[40]

Within a chimpanzee world of reproductive behavior, this ordering of the narrative to a plot rich with comments and allusions to domestic violence narratives subversively reveals female suffering in the not yet fully sociobiologist world of ethological field research.[41] It turns the incidents

[35] Ibid., 85.
[36] Ibid.
[37] Ibid., 87.
[38] Goodall, *Window*, 74.
[39] Ibid.
[40] Ibid., 75.
[41] As I argue in my current research project "Ape and Affect. The Research Memoirs of Primatology," the language and plots of primatology change with its paradigms. For example, once Richard Dawkins's "selfish gene"-theory and the underlying sociobiologist models were popularized enough within the research field, melodramatic plots gave way to stories of reproductive investment originating rhetorically in market processes and strategies.

and events into a succession and arranges them into a plot that culminates in a repertoire of melodramatic topics of female victimhood. These topics are intricately connected to the establishing of selfhood by recognizing and identifying with victimhood, as Linda Williams has argued in her revision of melodrama. With its central feature of "pathos," the melodramatic mode offers not only "a complex negotiation between emotions and between emotion and thought"[42] but an epistemological tool to represent and expose challenging observations and experiences within comprehensible cultural models.[43] Ironically, the melodramatic mode thereby enables the recognition of individuals as such through their close fit to well-known cultural molds and the empathic identification with these individuals within a thusly preordained explanatory field.

FIELDWORK AS PARTICIPANT OBSERVATION AND RECOGNITION OF THE ANIMAL AS SUBJECT

Individualization through recognition is also found to be the bedrock of the research relationship and methods in primatological fieldwork and can be perceived of with the help of a socio-philosophical concept: Axel Honneth's critical theory of recognition is, as Zurn puts it, "an intersubjectivist theory of how individuals develop a practical identity, a sense of themselves as interacting, moral beings with unique characteristics and distinctive places in the social world."[44] It is built upon the hypothesis that personhood is constituted intersubjectively. Through intersubjective recognition, entities are engaged in the process of self-realization, or as Zurn writes: "we only become who we are through the interaction with others."[45] Going back to the early Hegel, the philosopher and social psychologist George Mead, and the psychoanalyst Donald Winnicott, Honneth identifies in *Struggle for Recognition* three forms of intersubjective recognition: love, under which he subsumes all primary relationships insofar as they are constituted by strong emotional attachments among a small number of people; legal relations; and solidarity.[46] Through these forms of intersubjective recognition the individual gains self-confidence,

---

[42] Williams, "Melodrama," 49.
[43] Ibid., 50.
[44] Zurn, *Axel Honneth*, 24.
[45] Ibid.
[46] Cf. Honneth, *Struggle*, 92–94.

self-respect, and self-esteem. If recognition is not established or is revoked, reification looms.[47]

How do primatology's animal habituation[48] and moderate participant observation, two cornerstones of fieldwork, fit into this socio-philosophical concept, then? I do not intend to imply that Honneth's recognition theory is per se extendable to include human-animal relations.[49] Rather I would like to use parts of Honneth's model for the conditions and emergence of identity to explain how primatological narratives produce animal subjects when they describe research methods and processes.

First and foremost, it is Dian Fossey's research memoir *Gorillas in the Mist*, which amply delivers examples of this "subject-production": In the field, Fossey and her team not only observe one specific group over time (as Goodall and Sapolsky do, for example), they encounter a range of discriminable gorilla individuals that are organized in different groups. These groups are variously constituted and unstable; behavior is therefore diverse within and without the group. As proven by violent encounters, these groups normally perceive humans as perilous intruders. Intruders are charged at and threatened, sometimes injured or killed. It is essential for a human researcher, then, to overcome this gorilla preconception and to be accepted as someone harmless, whose presence can be tolerated. In *Gorillas in the Mist*, Fossey identifies a three-part course of action as condition for fieldwork: the inconspicuousness of the observers, the attention to the needs of the animals, and as a result the habituation of the gorilla groups and individuals to the constant presence of human observers. These goals are achieved through a slow process of identifying and recognizing each other. For Fossey, the responsibility for this process lies solely in human hands. If somebody is attacked, surely the human person has trespassed into the safe zone of the animal. A charge directed at her, then, "was really my fault for having climbed the steep slope to approach directly beneath the animal *without first identifying myself.*"[50] This appropriation of responsibility could be read as a negation of animal agency, because the animal is

---

[47] Cf. Honneth, "Reification," 124–126.

[48] Habituation is the process of familiarizing animals to the researcher's presence in their habitat so that the animals eventually tolerate the observer and do not flee or behave abnormally when she or he is present.

[49] Although recent primatological arguing is opening the door to this kind of transference by conferring evolutionary history to sociocultural concepts; see, for example, Michael Tomasello's recent *A Natural History of Human Morality.*

[50] Fossey, *Gorillas*, 56 (emphasis added).

only shown to *react* to a human action in accordance with its behavioral "programming." But quite on the contrary, I argue, the animal is here read as an *interacting* Other, since *"upon recognizing me*, the group's dominant silverback swiftly braked to a stop three feet away."[51] Not only is the silverback here clearly an actor in the encounter—identification is also important for recognition, which in turn changes the course of action.

In the case of gorilla habituation, recognition is a two-way process. As the researchers learn to differentiate between the gorillas and identify individuals by their appearance and behavior, but also learn to recognize their needs, the gorillas appear to learn just as much about their observers and they learn how to differentiate between them as well. Slowly, this process of accumulated knowledge through personal identification turns into an affective relationship of trust. Only this trust—the confidence in not being hurt by the other—guarantees the long-term and close range observation necessary to collect data. Furthermore, this observation turns from "obscured contacts"[52] into (moderate) participation, when the gorillas recognize the human others not as inanimate objects like trees or stones but as opportunity for social interaction. Once habituation is established, Fossey not only observes uninhibited play behavior but realizes, that "when the group members knew I was present, a great part of the immatures' play behavior involved response reactions such as chestbeating, foliage whacking, or strutting. Each individual seemed to be trying to outdo the other in attention-getting actions."[53] Humans are not only recognized as person X or Y, male or female, they are also acknowledged as play partners, as entertainment and audience. Thereby it is the gorillas that realize a form of social self-awareness *for the humans*.[54] As Honneth claims, it is by acknowledging what significance the own actions have for the other that the subject is able to see itself as a social object in the actions of his or her

---

[51] Ibid. (emphasis added).

[52] Ibid., 172.

[53] Ibid.

[54] Or, as Mark Payne puts it: "To see oneself seen is to become aware of oneself as an object of another animal's perception, then as one object among others in this perception, and then, finally, as a participant in an intersubjective encounter as it is experienced by the other subject." In accord with Derridaen thinking, this self-awareness as participant in an intersubjective encounter with the animal other enables epistemological insights, when "understandings proliferate, knowledge is gained, imagination is unconstrained and generative" (Payne, *Animal Part*, 8).

interaction partner.[55] Much like in ethnological fieldwork, where the anthropologist has to integrate him- or herself into the studied community up to a level where he or she can participate in the communal and social life and thereby observe much more closely, the primatologists, too, have to learn the needs of individuals and the rules of gorilla social life. They find themselves once again in the role of an adolescent yet unaccustomed but slowly made familiar with a society's rules and rights.[56] The researchers thereby rise to having an identity as a socially tolerated member of a primate community, in which they henceforth can more or less participate.

This is not without complication, as Shirley Strum realizes when she is at the same time moved and alarmed by the intentional touch of juvenile baboon Robin:

> I was drawn further into the social network of the baboons than I had ever intended to go, I realized this one day [...]. I sat down at baboon level to watch them as they became engrossed in grooming. [...] Suddenly I felt a gentle touch at my back, too light to be an insect crawling inside it. I turned around quickly—and startled little Robin, Naomi's juvenile daughter, who was a few inches behind me. She retreated quickly, and I, just as quickly, figured out what had happened. Robin was very relaxed with me because I always seemed to be around her mother, and she approached me quietly and tentatively began to groom the lower part of my back. It was a gesture so intimate that it touched and thrilled me. But I was also upset that I had let it happen, worried that it might permanently change my relation to the troop and ruin my stand against interaction. At the same time it seemed to me incredible that a baboon had trusted me enough to cross the many barriers between us.[57]

Strum knows that once she has been identified and fully recognized as a social interaction partner she will also be subjected to baboon social life, which consists in a significant part of intersubjective aggression:

> It was always tempting to reach out across the species chasm to touch and communicate with the baboons, but I knew that if I did so, there would be a time when it would be dangerous even simply to observe them. Should they view me as another baboon, one with whom they could exchange touches and greetings, they would also see me as being able to accept their aggression which I could not do.[58]

[55] Cf. Honneth, *Struggle*, 74.
[56] Ibid., 78–79.
[57] Strum, *Almost Human*, 57–58.
[58] Ibid., 54–55.

The primatologist holds, in Strum's words, a privileged position "of being part of a group while remaining outside it, receiving many rewards without paying the price."[59]

All in all, this outline of a research relationship might seem to be too much about the human researcher's quest for identity, then. So let me suggest the following: The process of the emergence of practical identity, that sense of self as interacting, moral being with unique characteristics and distinctive places in the social world, as Zurn put it, is delivered in these primatological narratives as an *inter*-action between two living, moving, acting, *socializing* entities. The animal other is always presupposed to have, if not the status then the function of another subject. This important process stands at the beginning of field research—and beyond that it enables the gathering of specified and even paradigm shifting knowledge. The primatologists therefore feel indebted to their animal research subjects, as Shirley Strum realizes, when she writes: "Peggy, her family and friends were changing my image of baboons. Through them I developed a growing feeling about each individual as a unique character, one whose personality was molded by his or her individual history as well as by biological makeup."[60] It is the growing affective attachment to these individual animal personalities that furthers research as much as it—through the intersubjective individualizing ability of emotions—lends subjectivity to animal individuals.[61]

If Honneth's road to full practical identity leads from intersubjective recognition in forms of affective attachment, via legal recognition in the community to mutual solidarity, the primatological field research provides a mostly analogous pattern: As Fossey's and Strum's examples (among many others) show, the integration leads from the necessary relationship of cooperation between humans and, for example, gorillas, which is built on interindividual recognition and trust as well as the habituation to the human presence and the other primates' social rules, to the individual affective bond between specific researchers and the individuals they pursue

---

[59] Ibid., 55.

[60] Ibid., 52.

[61] I see here a realization of Susan McHugh's insightful demand of a "narrative ethology" (McHugh, *Animal Stories*, 5), which offers an engagement of ethology with narrative that may "configure people and animals as working together to do things that [...] invite more precise considerations of agency and narrative form" (Ibid.). Ethology and fiction alike, McHugh proposes, "proceed from the complicated operations of affect" and build the foundation for an "ethics premised on feelings" (Ibid., 211).

their research on. And it results in a strong concern for the welfare of the primates as individuals and as a species. Therefore, in the end, they, too, become an object of solidarity.

FINISHING REMARKS

The primatological autobiographies I looked at here all work toward recovering individual animals from the oblivion to which the production of knowledge often assigns them. Being set apart from the same authors' scientific publications, the autobiographical texts as *memoirs* carry the license to *elaborate* what the research itself *abstracts from*. They do so by showing in detail and mostly with a sense of literary prowess how ethological data and theories are generated: What is it like to be "in the field"? How is data gathered? More importantly, who does the gathering and whom is the data gathered from?

Strictly "scientific" research papers or textbooks convey a semiotics of ethology, in which individual animals and their behavior are merely more than a sign of an underlying evolutionary pattern. The primatological autobiographies, however, reveal how this semiotic relies on a methodology of participant and even empathic observation as well as processes of ordering through narration. In fact, narration is key in the recovering of any biography, human or nonhuman. If (auto-)biographical accounts order dates and events in meaningful sequences that attest to the relevance of a certain life, the ethology here discussed can likewise be described as being founded on narrative processes. Ethological field observation is transformed into narratives, first, in a process of data ordering, secondly, in the formation of theoretical conclusions, and thirdly, in narratives of autobiographical reports of research. As I argued, the primatological memoirs not only elaborate on forms of intersubjective recognition as a foundational means of fieldwork but they also make narrative processes in research and in the relating of that research more transparent. They do so by focusing on individual animals as named and gendered characters of an account, by recording their behavior, their family relations, and their interactions with animals and humans alike. These texts enrich the ontogenetic stages of infancy, adolescence, adulthood and old age with specific events, individual character traits and illustrative anecdotes: In retelling their own biography "in the field" and paralleling it with the life stories of their research subjects, researchers like Dian Fossey, Jane Goodall, Shirley Strum, or Robert Sapolsky not only recover animal biographies but also highlight their epistemic as well as their narrative function. Since these research memoirs are deeply embedded in cultural literary traditions that rely on the ordering of perception through narration, animal biographical subjectivity is shaped by the melodramatic as narrative mode, rhetorical device, and epistemological tool. From the arrangement of behavior in specific comprehensible plots to the subversive potential of allusions to female victimhood in ethology, the melodramatic mode delivers a sense-making system to primatology's memoirs, which brings about not only animal life stories but a grasp of what *animal personhood* might mean.

In these memoirs, the individual animal gains recognition as a (textual) subject of a primatologist's biographical and/or research narrative and as the (factual) subject of his or her individual animal life story. Furthermore, though, the openness with which these primatological research memoirs discuss the methodological but also personal emotional details of field research endows the animals these primatologists have known and narrated with the agency to potentially lend practical identity to the human author of that story. As such, as agents in a methodologically necessary process that can be understood with the concept of intersubjective recognition, they effectively *become* animal subjects in their own right by means of the textual representation.

In conclusion, one might suggest that because the animals populating primatological memoirs are firmly based on factual, well-documented animal individuals, the genre itself is *a* if not *the* medium of not only 'real-life' animal biographies but also animal subjectivity.

Works Cited

Asquith, Pamela J. "Natural Homes: Primate Fieldwork and the Anthropological Method." In *Centralizing Fieldwork: Critical Perspectives from Primatology and Biological Anthropology in the Lens of Social Anthropological Theory and Practice*, edited by Jeremy MacClancy and Agustín Fuentes, 242–255. New York: Berghahn Books, 2010.

Bentley, Eric. *The Life of the Drama*. London: Methuen & Co., 1965.

Bingham, Dennis. *Whose Lives Are They Anyway? The Biopic As Contemporary Film Genre*. New Brunswick: Rutgers University Press, 2010.

Birke, Lynda. *Feminism, Animals and Science: The Naming of the Shrew*. Buckingham and Philadelphia: Open University Press, 1994.

Boesch, Christophe. *Wild Cultures: A Comparison Between Chimpanzee and Human Cultures*. Cambridge: Cambridge University Press, 2012.

Boesch, Christophe and Michael Tomasello. "Chimpanzee and Human Cultures." *Current Anthropology* 39.5 (1988): 591–614.

Brooks, Peter. *The Melodramatic Imagination: Balzac, Henry James, Melodrama, and the Mode of Excess.* Yale and New Haven: Yale University Press, 1995.

Decker, Christof. *Hollywoods kritischer Blick: Das soziale Melodrama in der amerikanischen Kultur 1840–1950.* Frankfurt am Main and New York: Campus, 2003.

DeWalt, Kathleen M., Billie R. DeWalt, and Coral B. Wayland. "Participant Observation." In *Handbook of Methods in Cultural Anthropology*, edited by H. Russell Bernard, 259–299. Walnut Creek, CA: AltaMira Press, 1998.

Fossey, Dian. *Gorillas in the Mist.* London: Phoenix, 2001.

Galdikas, Biruté M. F. *Reflections of Eden: My Years With the Orangutans of Borneo.* Boston: Little, Brown, 1995.

Goodall, Jane. *Through A Window: 30 Years with the Chimpanzees of Gombe.* London: Weidenfeld and Nicolson, 1990.

Haraway, Donna. *Primate Visions: Gender, Race, and Nature in the World of Modern Science.* New York and London: Routledge, 1989.

———. "Morphing in the Order: Flexible Strategies, Feminist Science Studies, and Primate Revisions." In *Primate Encounters: Models of Science, Gender, and Society*, edited by Shirley C. Strum and Linda Marie Fedigan, 398–420. Chicago: University of Chicago Press, 2000.

Honneth, Axel. *The Struggle for Recognition: The Moral Grammar of Social Conflicts.* Cambridge, Massachusetts: The MIT Press, 1995.

———. "Reification: A Recognition-Theoretical View." The Tanner Lectures on Human Values, delivered at the University of California, Berkeley, March 14–16, 2005.

van Lawick-Goodall, Jane. *In The Shadow of Man.* London: Collins, 1971.

McGrew, William C. *Chimpanzee Material Culture: Implications for Human Evolution.* Cambridge, UK and New York: Cambridge University Press, 1992.

McHugh, Susan. *Animal Stories: Narrating Across Species Lines.* Minneapolis and London: University of Minnesota Press, 2011.

Payne, Mark. *The Animal Part: Human and Other Animals in the Poetic Imagination.* Chicago and London: The University of Chicago Press, 2010.

Pollock, Mary Sanders. *Storytelling Apes: Primatology Narratives Past and Future.* University Park, Pennsylvania: The Pennsylvania State University Press, 2015.

Sapolsky, Robert M. *A Primate's Memoir.* London: J. Cape, 2001.

Sommer, Marianne. *Foremost in Creation: Anthropomorphism and Anthropocentrism in National Geographic Articles on Non-Human-Primates.* Bern: Peter Lang, 2000.

Sommer, Volker. "The Anthropologist as a Primatologist: Mental Journeys of a Fieldworker." In *Centralizing Fieldwork: Critical Perspectives from Primatology and Biological Anthropology in the Lens of Social Anthropological Theory and*

Practice, edited by Jeremy MacClancy and Agustín Fuentes, 32–48. New York: Berghahn Books, 2010.

Strum, Shirley C. *Almost Human: A Journey into the World of Baboons*. New York: Random House, 1987.

Strum, Shirley C., and Linda Marie Fedigan. "Changing Views of Primate Society: A Situated North American View." In *Primate Encounters: Models of Science, Gender, and Society*, 3–49. Chicago: University of Chicago Press, 2002.

Takasaki, Hiroyuki. "Traditions of the Kyoto School of Field Primatology in Japan." In *Primate Encounters: Models of Science, Gender, and Society*, edited by Shirley C. Strum and Linda Marie Fedigan, 151–164. Chicago: The University of Chicago Press, 2000.

Tompkins, Jane. *Sensational Designs: The Cultural Work of American Fiction 1790–1860*. New York and Oxford: Oxford University Press, 1985.

Whiten, A., J. Goodall, W. C. McGrew, T. Nishida, V. Reynolds, Y. Sugiyama, C. E. G. Tutin, R. W. Wrangham, and C. Boesch. "Cultures in Chimpanzees." *Nature* 399.6737 (1999): 682–685.

Whitlock, Gillian. "Remediating Gorilla Girl: Rape Warfare and the Limits of Humanitarian Storytelling." *Biography* 33.3 (2010): 471–497.

Williams, Linda. "Melodrama Revisited." In *Refiguring American Film Genres: Theory and History*, edited by Nick Browne, 42–88. Berkeley and Los Angeles: University of California Press, 1998.

Zurn, Christopher F. *Axel Honneth: A Critical Theory of the Social*. Cambdrige and Malden: Polity Press, 2015.

PART III

Constructions

CHAPTER 8

Taxidermy's Literary Biographies

Susan McHugh

INTRODUCTION

Stolen from his grave and mounted by French taxidermist Jules Verreaux in the early 1830s, the Tswana man labeled erroneously as "the Bushman" and known popularly as "el Negro de Banyoles" remained on public view for over 80 years in Spain's Darder Museum, well into the 1990s, until an international effort concluded with his being reinterred in Botswana in 2000. Along the way, social justice began to seem a less likely outcome when his remains became a rallying point for an unapologetically racist and colonialist local argument against plans for his return, voiced by Spaniards who supported the museum directors' unsuccessful but nonetheless popular campaign to keep him. Taxidermy historian Pat Morris notes that, when he examined the specimen after its removal from public display in 1997 and well after the international repatriation effort was underway, the people closest to the institution still embraced its story that the skin and some bones of a dead African man presented a suitable object for aesthetic display. In the "tee shirts and lapel badges [that] also went on

S. McHugh (✉)
University of New England, Biddeford, ME, USA

© The Author(s) 2018   141
A. Krebber, M. Roscher (eds.), *Animal Biography*,
Palgrave Studies in Animals and Literature,
https://doi.org/10.1007/978-3-319-98288-5_8

sale locally in support of the museum and its 'bushman,'"[1] Morris locates a reactionary narrative that prompts questions about how human lives enter into the limits of animal biographies.

While I intend no disrespect to the dead in making the comparison, the struggle over seeing the Tswana man's remains as human illuminates the difficulty of being an "autobiographical animal." A key problem with animal biographies—their inability to represent a single historical subject—emerges as a challenge for some people's stories as well through taxidermy and its representation in literary history. Part of the challenge to writing even a straightforward biographical account of a piece of taxidermy is its social function as a site that both displays the collective narrative that a specimen represents as well as enfolds the narratives that accrue in the provenance of the object's creation and preservation. Never simply a container of biographies, taxidermy mediates human and animal stories.

Accounting for the recently rising popularity of recycled or reclaimed taxidermy, self-styled curator, collector, and artist Morgan Mavis asserts, "Taxidermy is the embodiment of a story."[2] But whose story? That of the creature on display, the group or species it represents, those responsible for its death, the artisan who assembles one or several creatures to make the object? And, over time, the vermin who inevitably degrade taxidermies, the conservators who try to maintain them, plus many more casual observers who join in the struggle to make sense of who or what taxidermy represents?

A few historians have addressed these questions in far greater detail than literary scholars, often through attempts to document humans as well as animals who become historical figures through association with particular examples of taxidermy. In the process, they reveal how the "bio" of taxidermy often confuses biology and biography, as it concerns relations among people and between species plus relations with other representational objects as well.[3] When "writing the biography of a natural history specimen," historians say they must "recontextualize the process [of creating the taxidermic display] historically, socially, and culturally, both within the scope of the 'afterlives' of the animals in the museum, and within the limitations inherent in the source situation, in order to give [back to] the animals a life before death."[4] Underscoring that the vast majority of

[1] Morris, *History*, 93.
[2] Quoted in Poliquin, *Breathless*, 169.
[3] Alberti, "Introduction," 2–3.
[4] Thorsen, *Elephants*, 10.

taxidermies take animal and not human form, the choice of phrasing here also indicates how taxonomic hierarchies haunt the history of taxidermy. The natural history aesthetics through which taxidermy emerged can only idealize a past material presence brought through preservation into a sort of life after death through careful choreographies of proximities that in the past all too often mapped human/animal differences onto those of colonial centers/margins. Narrative proves indispensable to the process, for it is "through the stories that we tell about them [... that taxidermies] spring into an afterlife."[5] Mapping how fictional taxidermy stories illustrate different notions of who gets to tell them, for whom, and at whose expense, I want to suggest that a genealogical analysis of literary representations can add to historical accounts a greater sense of how a creature made into a realistically lifelike form by people preserving and assembling parts of the dead is made to conceal its own function as a site of contested narratives, and with what related consequences for vulnerable living bodies.

While the earliest taxidermy collections date back to the 1500s, the practice of mounting skins in pursuit of a lifelike aesthetic gained momentum much later in the 1700s, coinciding with the intensification of European colonization around the world. Although by the 1900s collecting mania gave way to desires to protect, save, or conserve increasingly rare critters, along the way taxidermy became deeply entrenched in the colonial histories of extermination and thus an apt figure for stories of where extinction meets genocide. In some cases sharing the histories of coercion of live indigenous people put on public display for exhibitions, fairs, museums, and zoos, the heroic narratives of specimen procurements that are commonly the focus of taxidermy histories direct uneven consideration toward the different human populations who people the taxidermied animal's biography. But literary writers increasingly tell different stories that enlist some taxidermic forms instead in resistance to racism and colonialism.

Reduced to skin and mounted for display alongside similarly prepared animals, humans turned into such specimens are not just brutal reminders of colonialism's skin fetish.[6] Gutted of life stories, humans treated like the Tswana man witness a deadly discursive conflation of animality and aboriginality through which some bodies are rendered to be revered as primitive, wild, and above all lost objects. In this context, the

---

[5] Swinney, "Afterword on Afterlife," 230.
[6] Wakeham, *Taxidermic*, 5.

disproportionately large spectacle of taxidermized humans in fiction as opposed to fact gains interest, as do their many parallels to the story of the Tswana man.[7]

That said, at face value, it might seem counterintuitive to look to literary writing to reveal the operations of visual display in the many lives of taxidermy, for it could easily be argued that literature only ever shows people's perceptions of taxidermy. Vibrant materials—the real fur, the actual feathers, the true scales—are said to be the defining quality of a taxidermic mount,[8] perhaps because the European history of taxidermy as a strictly secular form requires that its enchantments remain reducible to mere matter.[9] However, as many contemporary artists have shown, taxidermy's command of the visual story of the life that it is meant to resemble is never absolute, for the spell it casts of pure nature or scientific objectivity is readily broken by representing taxidermy through other visual forms like installation art and photography.[10] Akin to photography's spectral remediation of what presents itself in taxidermy as the material fact of death,[11] literary representations separate the matter at hand from the stories that guide perceptions of it, opening up a critical distance in which other perspectives can take shape.

Part of the difficulty of mapping such potentials is that, unlike the photos and artworks along with the mounted animals themselves, fictional taxidermies are hard to find. In sharp contrast to the millions and more taxidermized bodies stored and displayed worldwide, scarcity has been the rule for their literary counterparts, that is, until recent decades, when writers began to explore how taxidermy operates as exceptionally storied stuff. Turning away from villainizing stories of taxidermists—commonly known as "stuffers"—and toward tales of the taxidermized object, contemporary fiction writers are realizing this potential most clearly when they treat taxidermy mounts as central subjects.

---

[7] Morris avers that seven full taxidermy mounts of people presently exist, amid stories of several others that cannot be confirmed because "museum curators are somewhat secretive on this issue," see Morris, *History*, 90.

[8] Desmond, "Postmortem," 161.

[9] Poliquin distinguishes taxidermy from "most other processes of bodily preparation" precisely through this "distinction between the palpable world of materials and the spiritual otherworld of material forces," see Poliquin, *Breathless*, 23. I would add that she also identifies an aesthetic wherein taxidermized humans became enframed in animal worlds by identifying taxidermy as a "secular art for portraying the physical sizes and shapes of animals" (Ibid., 25).

[10] Aloi, *Natural History*.

[11] Turner, "'Stuffed' Animals," 8.

STUFFERS

Like the thing itself, a taxidermy's biography involves multiple subjects. A well done taxidermy mount may appear full of life, but its history reveals it to be full of lives as well as deaths that are not so easily seen. Created by cobbling together assortments of materials like skins and skulls, fur and feathers, wood and wax from different individuals and species, taxidermy can be full of more creatures than meet the eye. Behind it all lurks a peculiar specter, the taxidermist, who is not so much a creator as a choreographer of these diverse entities, and who conventionally fashions them into individuated and coherently speciated forms.

From skins that have been cleaned and chilled properly, taxidermists can mount critters who have died of any number of causes, including accidents and old age. Reserving the term "trophies" for animals killed in a hunt, in such cases, hunters, makers, and owners of taxidermied animals can contribute in different roles at different stages of a process that will include multiple taxidermists, if the specimen is large, as well as owners if maintained over many years. In public or private display, taxidermy also has an audience, and other kinds of consumers as well. Damage from insects and microorganisms remains a perennial concern for conservators, fast becoming a dire one for the last remaining specimens of rare or extinct species. Yet taxidermists have become increasingly narrated as in command of the story, most extremely when cast as villains.

"He indulged the occupation he was known for so that he could earn the occupation that gave him pleasure" begins ordinarily enough in Téa Obreht's 2011 bestseller *The Tiger's Wife* to describe the character Dariša, who becomes a successful itinerant hunter and pelt-peddler only by following his initial passion for taxidermy.[12] Hearkening back to a fragile peacetime in the Balkans before the Second World War and recounted within a frame story set during the Bosnian genocide, Dariša's story voices a sense of nostalgia for a time when taxidermists were not damned for what they do. "Generally not highly esteemed" in real life as the practice fell from scientific craft to rustic hobby by the mid-twentieth century,[13] the fictional makers of taxidermy devolve in the same period from seedy to downright criminal, eventually becoming appropriate targets of backlash for horrors inflicted on humanity.

---

[12] Obreht, *Tiger's Wife*, 242.
[13] Morris, *History*, 359; Star, "Craft vs. Commodity."

Written within the period in which Dariša comes of age, Ernest Hemingway's 1926 novel *The Sun Also Rises* indicates where and how the slippage began. Main character Jake and his pal Bill pause in front of a taxidermy shop window, ponder a purchase, and "pie-eyed" Bill famously slurs, "Road to hell paved with unbought stuffed dogs. Not my fault." Hemingway scholars have long debated the various possible meanings of the taxidermized dog, following the manuscript trail through which the object was added to the story quite late in the production process. Is it a typical Hemingway "trifle" that calls attention to a shift in philosophical focus?[14] A metaphor for "out-of-place, nonstandard" human bodies that enables indirect expression of anti-ableist sympathy with the war-wounded Jake?[15] A historical allusion to the fate of Sergeant Stubby, a real-life canine hero of the Great War, who after his death was mounted and displayed in the American Red Cross Museum shortly before Hemingway finished the novel?[16] Another option arises later in the novel with Jake's facetious introduction of Bill to his beloved Brett as a taxidermist—followed by Bill's demurral, "That was in another country. And besides all the animals were dead"—suggesting a still more obvious possibility that, even among these misogynistic, US-expat, bullfighting-aficionado wastoids, a far more despicable character becomes imagined through the taxidermized animal.

Decades earlier, more detailed examples like Mr. Venus in Charles Dickens's 1865 novel *Our Mutual Friend* and H.G. Wells's title character in the 1894 story "The Triumphs of a Taxidermist" sow a seediness into perceptions of a profession that at the time was burgeoning to include all kinds. Although these same authors who created super-creeps like Bill Sikes and Dr. Moreau do not portray taxidermists as decided villains, there is a distinctly unsympathetic thread woven into their taxidermizing characters's affinities with crime. Confessing to his would-be victim, Dickens's Mr. Venus admits complicity in an elaborate but aborted blackmail scheme, while Wells's taxidermist, when well into his cups, brags about having deceived customers with fake specimens, exposing an ugly side of the profession. But the latter's self-professed triumph in having taxidermized a human being— claiming, "I stuffed a nigger once. No, there is no law against it"—more directly anticipates imaginings of his type as bigoted and potentially murderous, a sensibility that gathers force by the mid-twentieth century.

---

[14] Cheatham, "Sign the Wire," 27.
[15] Fore, "Life Unworthy," 82.
[16] Adair, "Hemingway's *The Sun Also Rises*."

Titular *Psycho* Norman Bates famously claims "just taxidermy" as his only pastime in Robert Bloch's 1959 novel, a detail given far more prominence in the form of large, whole-bird specimens that visually presage where his passion will lead in Alfred Hitchcock's 1960 film adaptation. The many parallels to the contemporaneous, true-crime story of Ed Gein bolster the sense that *Psycho* marks the arrival of a modern horror subgenre that features a homespun killer whose obsessions, including taxidermy, revolve around everyday life.[17] And correlation invites speculation about causation: in the stories of both Bates and Gein they first preserve the corpses of animals, then those of their mothers, and afterward become murderers, outlining a developmental narrative formula through which taxidermy is understood as conflated with deviance not as a corrective to but rather as the outcome of the history of colonial trophy hunting. The historical connection becomes the focus of inquiry in far more recent fictions, and largely through feminist critique.

Published in the same year as the novel *Psycho*, Roald Dahl's short story "The Landlady" more clearly sets taxidermy on a developmental spectrum as a stepping-stone to killing and stuffing people. An early representation of a female taxidermist, the title character moves from stuffing her pet parrot and dog to murdering and mounting her lodgers, a point made more explicit in Dahl's adaptation of the story to a television screenplay, which realizes the dying narrator's horror of being added to the landlady's taxidermy collection. With nods to earlier literary animal taxidermies like Hemingway's dog and Gustav Flaubert's parrot (to be discussed below), the story's stuffed pets offer a foretaste of violently violated human intimacies, intensifying the horror of taxidermists as honing grisly techniques on animals whose mounted forms in turn presage violence against other humans, who curiously are all caucasians, like themselves. Dahl's story thus indicates how gender and sex come to overtake racial politics in taxidermist-centered fictions.

The postwar emergence of the taxidermist-murderer trope also suggests how facts grotesquely blend into horror fictions of taxidermy. Gein's inspiration for making home furnishings out of human skin was the rare but widely reported desecration of corpses of Nazi concentration camp victims, only not, as the war-propaganda stories usually go, to make human-skin lampshades but more restrictively (as Gein likely did not know) to archive tattoos.[18] Inspired by made-up stories, his horrific actions—including the murder and dismemberment of two women and

[17] Humphries, *American Horror*, 85.
[18] Alban, "Human Skin."

fashioning home furnishings with human skin, including that of already-dead women that he disinterred—are widely credited with inspiring a pattern in horror fiction and film in which taxidermizing men victimize women and girls.

Stories representing taxidermists as male and their victims as female leverage a shift in representational history, in which taxidermy once served as a powerful metaphor connecting violence, capitalism, and heteronormativity—the "teddy bear patriarchy" that Donna Haraway identifies as reflected in and encouraged by the shifting aesthetics of museum taxidermy dioramas toward modeling what would later be termed nuclear families as early as the turn of the last century[19]—and also explains why taxidermists eventually become targets of feminist backlash in novels and film. So powerful have these associations become that female characters who fight off "taxidermist-murderers" in popular films, including Stretch in *The Texas Chainsaw Massacre, Part 2* (1989) and Clarice in *The Silence of the Lambs* (1991), are seen as heroes rather than victims, momentarily slipping the patriarchal ordering of taxidermy if not quite taking out the sexist, racist, and colonialist systems that lend it such significance.[20]

Literary fictions by women writers such as Alice Munro's 1993 short story "Vandals" and Alissa York's *Effigy* (2007) more effectively problematize the patriarchal stranglehold on taxidermy by expanding the trope of taxidermist to include sex criminals as well as their taxidermizing avengers. Pursuing a more limited feminist critique, Kate Mosse's 2014 novel *The Taxidermist's Daughter* likewise features a sexually abused female taxidermist, who eventually uses taxidermied humans as a means of expressing as well as avenging otherwise unspeakable crimes. Set at the turn of the twentieth century, when "taxidermy was not considered a suitable job for a woman" but when women and girls also often contributed in significant ways to family-run shops,[21] Mosse's novel clarifies how title character Constantia "Connie" Gifford secretly gains both the skills of and passion for avian taxidermy from her father Crowley, who is imagined as a contemporary rival of real-life Victorian taxidermy-tableau-superstar Walter Potter, and who inadvertently also inspires another woman, Cassandra or Cassie, to apply the same skills in revenge against the men who gang-raped then attempted to murder her. As the characters' names suggest, the novel

[19] Haraway, *Primate Visions.*
[20] Niesel, "Horror."
[21] Mosse, *Taxidermist's,* 14; Morris, *History,* 210.

is not big on subtlety, but it does follow Munro's and York's shift away from the biography of the taxidermist in favor of the many human, animal, and object stories that converge in the practice of taxidermy itself. In Mosse's story, complex ethical considerations follow from this shift, in part because unlike the other two it depicts taxidermized humans as animalized.

Competing definitions of what constitutes best practice within *The Taxidermist's Daughter* undermine certainties about whether the display of dead and mutilated rapists is terrible or justified. For Connie, who like York's fictional taxidermizing girl does not appear to kill any of her own mounts, taxidermy achieves not exercises of power but idealized achievements of parity: "Each creature had left its imprint on her as much as she had left her mark on it."[22] Cassie's final tableau, in which she reveals the mounted specimens of all but one of her violators in order to terrorize that remaining one, certainly violates Connie's guiding esthetics for her craft that "more than anything [...] is about beauty."[23] But, by the definition attributed to her father Crowley—who rejects the term taxidermist as "too fancy" because "it took away from what he was doing," which was "telling stories"[24]—Cassie's tableau succeeds in doing what the law will not and "polite" society cannot do, namely, tell the story of how these monstrous men brutally violated then left her for dead, only to get their comeuppance when she takes justice into her own hands. As taxidermy, they are made to tell her story while simultaneously rewriting their own biographies as animals through her careful choreographies of bird elements with their bodies in her displays. Adding to each corpse some distinctive attributes of the different bird species with which each man code-named himself in life, Cassie's attempt to render or reveal them as animals forges a fragile link to taxidermy's colonialist histories that remains otherwise unacknowledged in the novel, except as an entrée for teddy bear patriarchy to restore order.

Bringing the taxidermist-murderer story to a real-world context in which stuffers do not appear to be more likely than others to become violent criminals, Mosse's mystery nonetheless relies on the male taxidermist Crowley to be a drunken failure as a father figure, thereby making himself a prominent suspect in the murders. His redemption at the end coincides with Cassie's narratively convenient death, and his subsequent and sober wedding to his daughter's nurse confirms the restoration of patriarchal

---

[22] Mosse, *Taxidermist's*, 15.
[23] Ibid., 213.
[24] Ibid., 216.

order. As the instruments of feminist backlash devolve to killjoys, all the while remaining white inheritors of the imperial order signaled by their predecessors, a profound sense of uncertainty regarding the taxidermized object as a container of its maker's or an animal's story signals the more disruptive potentials growing in taxidermy's literary biographies.

OBJECTS

"When you write the biography of a friend," wrote novelist Gustav Flaubert, "you must do it as if you were taking *revenge* for him," a line that much later resurfaces as the epigraph of Julian Barnes's 1984 novel *Flaubert's Parrot*. Wavering between ironic appropriation and postmodern blank parody, the epigraph speaks to the basic conundrum of the novel: can writing an author's life be a friendly avengement, or does literary biography invariably devolve to exercises in "mindless parroting" of the author?[25] Complicating the problem further is the book's titular subject: the taxidermized parrot who once stood on Flaubert's writing desk and served as a model for a character in one of his fictions. The pursuit of the bird—that is, of the fate of the particular specimen that inspired Flaubert to create what may well be the first stuffed parrot in fiction—provides a frame story aligning biography and taxidermy as particular kinds of objects that are crafted in tension with their affective values.

Absurd though it sounds today, taxidermy's role as creative muse has a colorful provenance, including the mount now on display at the Free Library in Philadelphia of Dickens's pet raven Grip, who was taxidermized after the bird's death and hung over the writer's desk in order to continue to inspire him. During the time of Grip's life and death with him, Dickens was developing a raven character of the same name in *Barnaby Rudge* (1841) that would forge a chain of influence over other artists' renderings of black birds, including Edgar Allen Poe's 1845 poem "The Raven" and, in turn, Paul Gaugin's 1897 painting *Nevermore*. As an animal mount, Grip proves a rare inspiration for literary engagements with animal biography, and Barnes's novel helps to explain why.

Flaubert's Parrot begins with amateur literary scholar Geoffrey Braithwaite setting out to find the real taxidermized parrot that served as an inspiration for the character Loulou in Flaubert's 1877 story "A Simple Heart." Upon seeing the first of what are revealed to be a series of candi-

---

[25] Baker, *Postmodern Animal*, 29.

dates for Flaubert's one true parrot, Braithwaite instantly feels "ardently in touch with this writer who disdainfully forbade posterity to take any personal interest in him," which is why he goes to great lengths to determine if it is indeed *The One*.[26] Barnes's phrasing here emphasizes the contrast between Braithwaite's vision of the taxidermized parrot as an object of transference for human affect and Flaubert's concern for how objects prestructure such extensions of human feeling.

In Flaubert's story, Loulou proves the only wonderful thing in the life of Félicité, who is illiterate, impoverished, and cruelly used by family, friends, and employers. When Loulou dies, she is easily persuaded to have him taxidermized, and despite growing signs of decomposition over the years the mount of him remains her most beloved possession. Clutching at Loulou's tattered remains on her own deathbed, Félicité's final vision of the Holy Ghost as a parrot steers the story toward sacrilege, if not outright contempt for its protagonist. If Flaubert's emphasis on the unpleasantnesss of cohabiting with parrots thwarts sympathetic identification,[27] then the absence of Flaubert's vividly live parrot throughout Barnes's story all the more clearly undercuts the reasoning behind her passion for it.[28] Read through Braithwaite's final revelation that the stuffed parrot that once sat on Flaubert's writing desk is indeterminable—the trail of the original turns out to have been long lost upon the author's having returned it to a collection that once included at least 50 others just like it—the stuffed parrot appears all the more reduced in Barnes's vision to an emblem of postmodern irony. Or, more precisely, *Flaubert's Parrot* aligns with what Fredric Jameson identifies as the emergence of postmodern pastiche, a style that, like speaking in a dead language, has no normative standard from which to devolve into satire.[29] Yet, with the potential for the bird's material presence remaining hedged by anonymity, the eponymous bird as a taxidermic object also gains new meaning as a site of converging stories.

Musing that a parrot is a more logical choice of animal figure than the iconic Christian dove for the Holy Ghost in part because it is capable of speech, Barnes's Braithwaite affirms Flaubert's own diagnosis that Loulou and Félicité's story "is not at all ironical as you may suppose but very seri-

[26] Barnes, *Flaubert's Parrot*, 7.
[27] Scholtmeijer, "What is Human?," 132.
[28] Baker, *Postmodern Animal*, 32.
[29] Jameson, *Postmodernism*, 195.

ous and sad."[30] In the novel as in the story that inspired it, the principal
character becomes increasingly isolated in a life marked by loss of all personal ties, shadowed all the while by parrot lives diminished to taxidermies.
In Barnes's final lines a connection between taxidermized animals and a
wider sense of damage is entertained, if only to be summarily dismissed.

From Flaubert's description of Loulou in his glory, the bird appears to
be a blue- or turquoise-fronted Amazon parrot (*Amazona aestiva*), a gre-
garious and once widespread species who like so many others became the
victim of people's greed for pets, feathers, skins, and taxidermies. Standing
in a natural history archive, Braithwaite remarks:

> Everywhere I looked there were birds. Shelf after shelf of birds, each one
> covered in a sprinkling of white pesticide. [...] There, standing in a line,
> were the Amazonian parrots. Of the original fifty only three remained. They
> gazed at me like three quizzical, sharp-eyed, dandruff-ridden, dishonorable
> old men. [...] I stared at them for a minute or two and then dodged away.
> Perhaps it was one of them.[31]

Moving from a singular writing-desk ornament to an archive of museum-
display extras, the "animal-thing"[32] appears to Braithwaite as indistin-
guishable among so many others, but along the way the taxidermies
themselves signal the dismantling of what should be ordinary life to these
exceptionally social creatures. Written and published in the 1980s, when
the annual destruction rates of Amazonian forests ramped up to the
previously unprecedented percentages that continue today, the scene
opens connections between decimations of parrot populations along with
the indigenous cultures that the forests once supported, except that
Braithwaite (and by extension Barnes) chooses not to connect the dots.
While the initial encounter with a beautifully displayed specimen made
Braithwaite feel immediately connected to the long-dead Flaubert, his
final encounter with an insecticide-dusted Amazon parrot group in a
French museum's taxidermied-bird storage room proves intimidating,
overwhelming, something to "dodge" rather than explore.

The dodging aligns all the more precisely with colonialism if indeed one
of them is Flaubert's Loulou, who cannot help but share in human suffering from his very first appearance. "A Simple Heart" introduces Loulou

---

[30] Quoted in Scholtmeijer, "What is Human?," 130.
[31] Barnes, *Flaubert's Parrot*, 216.
[32] Poliquin, *Breathless*, 34.

alongside "a negro," and both together as possessions of a white family who have recently returned to France from America. In these spare details, the story rehearses without comment a discursive flattening together of exotic animal and black human, presumably a slave, that accompanies the movement of their bodies from colonial margins to centers here, and that informs how the legacies of imperial rule inform the human and animal afterlives of taxidermy in literary history.

Writing decades after Flaubert, Wells's menacingly racist taxidermist introduces at the turn of the twentieth century what by today has become a singularly inspirational kind of object for fiction, if not for many actual taxidermists. Along with his boasts about conning customers by faking specimens that in turn ratchet up desires for the deaths of rare and fragile animal species, the claim of the title character of "The Triumphs of a Taxidermist" to having "stuffed a nigger" and "used him as a hat-rack," swearing he would do it again if only it were not so difficult to "get skins," outlines the linkages whereby exotic animals are aligned with nonwhite people through the eyes of those who stand to profit from their sufferings and deaths. And, while miniscule in terms of numbers, the mounting of the skins of largely black African people by and for white Europeans appears to have found a flash point in taxidermy's literary biographies with the telling and retelling of one particular person's story that intensifies in the decades leading up to the repatriation of the Tswanan man from the Spanish museum.

Well into the twentieth century, with the publication of modern Austrian literary lion Robert Musil's final and unfinished novel *Der Mann ohne Eigenschaften* [*The Man without Qualities*] (1940), the biographical subjects of actual human taxidermy come to weigh heavily on the literary imagination. Musil's character Soliman, an African boy raised to be a servant in a white family, appears partly inspired by the story of Angelo Soliman, who over a century earlier was born into the Kanuri people of western Africa, then stolen as a child and sold to Europeans. A slave who later became a freeman, Soliman was a "court Moor," a kind of rich person's plaything akin to an exotic pet, whose career eventually flourished in the eighteenth-century Vienna of Emperors Joseph II, Leopold, and Franz, where he became a pioneering freemason, expert chess player, Christian, tutor, and scholar. Yet, upon Soliman's death and against his daughter's repeated and insistent protests, Emperor Franz ordered his corpse skinned, mounted, and exhibited "in a fine glass case," placed on view in the imperial cabinet as part of a collection that included several animal and a couple of other human taxidermies until all was destroyed in a fire decades later.[33]

Musil's story offers some clues as to how the human as taxidermized object inspires a different narrative trajectory from that of the murderous stuffer. The obvious differences between the historical figure, treated so disgracefully after his death, and the fictional character who disgraces himself in life, draw attention away from their greater significance to the author's purported "failure" to reconcile metaphor and reality.[34] The current critical trend toward reading Musil's poetics as political emphasizes how, rather like *Flaubert's Parrot* in its very gone-wrongedness, his fictional Soliman proves pivotal to reimaginings that eventually break away from the cycle of exoticization and exploitation, and that require more explicit reckonings with animal biographies.

Like Dickens's Grip, a literary-historical figure hovering between taxidermic fact and lively imaginings, Musil's Soliman and the man before him are linked to a wide range of creative responses. In recent years, the bulk of the retellings of Soliman's story have been on stage and in German, beginning with Conny Hannes Meyer's *Die schwarze Bekanntschaft oder Angelo Soliman* [*The Black Acquaintance or Angelo Soliman*] (1983). Other examples include Ludwig Fels's tragic play *Soliman* (1991)—which in turn inspired a ballet choreographed by Bert Gstettner titled *Angelo Soliman, ballet d'action*[35] (1996)—and Andreas Pflüger and Lukas Holliger's comic opera *Der schwarze Mozart* [*The Black Mozart*] (2005). Following Musil's example, these texts struggle to make sense of the racist and colonialist ideologies that inform the horrific afterlife of Soliman as a taxidermic display. Fels, for instance, spins out a murder plot driven by sexual jealousy, whereas Pflüger and Holliger sketch a continuum of objectification in life and death through Soliman's ghost and wax-figure displays (in lieu of attempting to portray the taxidermized human with a live actor). Despite taking very different approaches regarding the facts of Soliman's life and death, these texts together work to reinforce an older biographical vision of Soliman as primarily a victim,[36] and thereby run the risk of extending his exploitation through racist and colonialist discourses.[37]

---

[33] Morris, *History.*
[34] Grill, *The World*, 181.
[35] "Ballet d'action" is the technical term for a ballet with a plot.
[36] Firla, "In Search of."
[37] Read, *Angelo Soliman*, 47.

More recent texts indicate how his afterlife as taxidermy proves more significant to the recovery of Soliman's story.

With a growing sense of the biographical Soliman's agency and accomplishments,[38] twenty-first-century artistic and literary renderings become more explicitly critical of why he was taxidermized. Gergely Péterfy's award-winning 2014 historical novel *Kitömött barbár* [*The Stuffed Barbarian*] imagines Soliman's story through the eyes of his friend and fellow "barbarian" in Vienna, the Hungarian literary tour-de-force Ferenc Kazinczy, and the story of their friendship in turn through the eyes of Kazinczy's wife Sophie Török, confronted with Soliman as specimen in the Viennese Imperial Natural History Collection. Dramatizing the taxidermized mount as produced from the historical man through a diffracted storytelling technique, the novel clarifies how taxidermy serves as "a multivalent sign: a specimen of the 'African race' for contemporary scientists, an object of fright or amusement for visitors of the museum, a sign of Western racism for today's reader, an object of meditation for Sophie— and we could continue the list."[39] By contrast, the living man at the heart of the novel asserts a sense of intention if not control over how he will be read. In a pivotal scene, the living Soliman chooses to wear Orientalist or Moorish clothes in public alongside Kazinczy in his Hungarian national dress, together asserting themselves as "barbarians" in a strange land. The choices of the living man pointedly contrast his representation as a taxidermy on imperial display, clad only in the beads and feathers that worked to equivocate him with the taxidermized animals alongside which he was installed in his own museological afterlife.

Long after the object itself was destroyed, what might be called the human-animal-thing made of Angelo Soliman's skin continues to elicit powerful affective responses. *Exhibit B*—an ongoing and controversial installation artwork by South African artist and playwright Brett Bailey that has been staged in several European cities, beginning in 2010—imagines a different display for Soliman's corpse. As a whole, "*Exhibit B* takes the form of live actors playing the roles of objectified historical (and contemporary) people,"[40] all of whom are black Africans. Settings are crafted to

---

[38] Read charts this changing perception of Soliman's agency through the sequence of biographies published by Monika Firla in 1993, 1996, 2001, and 2003 (see Firla, "Viennese African," 19–20).

[39] Orzóy, "Stuffed Barbarian."

[40] Bailey, "Personal."

reference "people shows" and other ethnographic displays of indigenous Africans once popular in Europe and the United States alongside re-creations of more recent crime scenes, all in order to call attention to "current dehumanizing policies toward immigrants in various parts of the world."[41] Perceptions of Bailey as a white man extending those practices inspired protests and even riots empowered by the large role given to audiences in the artwork itself.

Listed as one of the artwork's materials alongside historical details on the signage for each tableau, spectators are conceived as an integral part of *Exhibit B*. Actors, all locally recruited and self-identified as black, are practiced to remain silent and motionless except to make uncomfortable eye contact with viewers, who are made to feel their own discomforting power to look at others. Immobile human bodies illustrate the power of the colonial gaze that the living actors' eyes alone powerfully unsettle from within these tableaux, according to the actors and viewers, who attest to experiencing profound revelations regarding visceral feelings of racism and colonialism as part of the aesthetic experience.[42] Berthe Njole is an actor who in three different iterations of the installation portrayed the Khoikoi slave known as Saartje or Sarah Baartman, who was exhibited alive in nineteenth-century Europe as the freak "Hottentot Venus" and in death as body parts in museums in France for a century and a half afterward, before being repatriated in South Africa in 2002, two years after the Tswana man's remains were returned to Botswana. Njole tells a powerful story about her performance as Baartman in *Exhibit B*: "A group of guys came in. They were laughing and making comments about my boobs and body. They didn't realize I was a human being, they thought I was a statue. Later they returned and each one apologized to me in turn."[43] The anecdote becomes all the more intriguing as a microcosm of the European affective trajectory regarding Baartman's actual remains, as well as in the absence of similar stories focused on the installation's representation of Angelo Soliman.

Several of the tableaux include nonhuman taxidermy, whether as the furnishings of a room in which a woman is shackled to a colonial officer's bed, or as the décor of museum-like spaces. In the scene titled "The Age of Enlightenment," a figure arranged to resemble an embalmed corpse on display is dressed in tailored clothes and a turban nearly identical to those

[41] Bailey, "Third World."
[42] Ibid.
[43] O'Mahony, "Edinburgh's."

worn by Soliman in portraits taken from life. In Bailey's words, the staging creates "a way of honoring [him] with the tomb he never had."[44] Only a mounted bird overlooks the figure, who like the body of Soliman also has a museum-catalog-like numbered tag prominently attached. Proximity to the animal's prominently displayed skin in this tableau offers a creative solution to the difficulties of re-creating human taxidermy with live actors not because the one is a stand-in for the other but rather because together they instantiate the lesson of taxidermy's literary biographies: never simply a record of one life, a taxidermied body represents how proximities of different bodies serve relations of power. Embodied skin and taxidermy can never be viewed the same—one is affected, the other only elicits affect— yet the depiction of Soliman in *Exhibit B* indicates how creative integrations of their representation loft a powerful counter-narrative to conceiving race and species as merely matters of discursive power-play.

The same decade in which the novel and film *Psycho* were released also witnessed the publication of *Black Skin, White Masks*, Franz Fanon's 1952 psychological deconstruction of racism. A pioneering book in the black-consciousness movement, it identifies racial inequality as leveraged in colonial contexts through the regulation of visible-surface encounters of skin colors as contrasting through what Fanon terms a "racial epidermal schema." In other words, racism involves not simply the internalization of inferiority by individuals but a doubled process that includes what Fanon terms "epidermalization" or extension of racial difference from embodied qualities to socioeconomic processes like language acquisition that leave material traces.

The point in reading taxidermy through Fanon's theory is not simply to say that reducing people to just their skins is monstrous, whether as imaginary Nazi lamp shades or historical taxidermies like those of Soliman and the Tswana man, but rather to account for how skins are stretched far beyond their biological function of encasing bodies. In a rare study of the metaphoric affinities of taxidermy and racialization in the representational histories of indigenous peoples, Pauline Wakeham clarifies that, "as both biological tissue and discursive schema overdetermined by colonialism's obsession with racial and species categorization,"[45] skin at once is seen to

---

[44] Bailey, "Third World."

[45] Wakeham, *Taxidermic*, 25. Fanon's description of a "corporeal" that gives way to "racial epidermal schemas" informs how more recent theoretical projects like those of Wakeham along with Alexander Weheliye work, according to the latter, to "tackle notions of the human

envelop and separate nonhuman bodies, and its mounting provides an opportunity for the visible display and extension of racist-imperial power. Such an approach begins to explain the important difference enacted by shifting attention away from taxidermizers' intentions and toward the taxidermized object that is provisionally staged through the literary fictions that pinpoint affective affinities of humans and animals by reanimating specimens from the past as vital players in the present political struggles of populations that continue to be endangered by the legacies of racism and colonialism.

Like a city or a species, taxidermy is a cultural phenomenon through which the stories of individuals become inextricable from those of many more agents. Among the cultural lives of things, a piece of taxidermy—an "animal-thing" that is "no longer quite an animal" yet hardly "mistaken for anything other than an animal"—has specially "strange, unsettling power[s]"[46] that are specific to times, places, ideas, and interactions and inextricable from the conundrums as well as opportunities of animal biographies. Taxidermy's stories are constantly multiplying,[47] if also increasingly linked to histories of exploitation, through literary representations. If a basic instability makes taxidermic form attractive for aesthetic explorations of how biographies become human, then its flickering status as cultural along with biological "stuff" is what explains taxidermy's appeal for creative interventions into what counts as actual animals' stories, broadly writ, at the turn of the twenty-first century.

WORKS CITED

Adair, W. "Hemingway's *The Sun Also Rises*: The Dog in the Window and Other War Allusions." *Hemingway Review* 34.1 (2014): 76–81.
Alban, D. "Books Bound in Human Skin: Lampshade Myth?" *Harvard Law Record* (2005). http://hlrecord.org/2005/11/books-bound-in-human-skin-lampshade-myth/. Accessed November 11, 2005.

as it interfaces with gender, coloniality, slavery, racialization, and political violence without mapping these questions onto a mutually exclusive struggle between either the free-flowing terra nullis of the universally applicable or the terra cognitus of the ethnographically detained" in Weheliye, *Habeas Viscous*, 24.

[46] Poliquin, *Breathless*, 34.

[47] The meanings of taxidermic trophies are elaborated as "always specific to a time, a place, an animal, a hunter, a collector, a gallery visitor" in Rothfels, "Trophies," 136.

Alberti, Samuel J.M.M. "Introduction: The Dead Ark." In *The Afterlives of Animals: A Museum Menagerie*, edited by Samuel J.M.M. Alberti, 1–16. Charlottesville: University of Virginia Press, 2011.

Aloi, G. *Speculative Taxidermy: Natural History, Animal Surfaces, and Art in the Anthropocene*. New York: Columbia University Press, 2018.

Bailey, B. "Personal Communication." 20 February 2016.

———. "Third World Bun Fight: *Exhibit B*." http://thirdworldbunfight.co.za/exhibit-b/. Accessed September 15, 2017.

Baker, S. *The Postmodern Animal*. London: Reaktion Books, 2000.

Barnes, J. *Flaubert's Parrot*. New York: McGraw-Hill, 1984.

Cheatham, G. "'Sign the Wire with Love': The Morality of Surplus in *The Sun Also Rises*." *Hemingway Review* 11.2 (1992): 25–30.

Desmond, J. "Postmortem Exhibitions: Taxidermied Animals and Plastinated Corpses in the Theaters of the Dead." *Configurations* 16.3 (2008): 347–377.

Fanon, F. *Black Skin, White Masks*. New York: Grove Press, 2008.

Firla, M. "In Search of the Viennese African, Angelo Soliman (ca. 1721–96): From Educator of a Hereditary Prince to Stuffed Exhibit." *Tinabantu* 2.1 (2004): 72–90. http://m.delphiforums.com/cltalk/messages/811/26. Accessed September 15, 2017.

Fore, D. "Life Unworthy of Life? Masculinity, Disability, and Guilt in The Sun Also Rises." *Hemingway Review* 26.2 (2007): 74–88.

Grill, G. *The World as Reality in Robert Musil's* The Man Without Qualities. Rochester: Camden House, 2012.

Haraway, D. *Primate Visions: Gender, Race, and Nature in the World of Modern Science*. New York: Routledge, 1990.

Humphries, R. *The American Horror Film: An Introduction*. Edinburgh: Edinburgh University Press, 2002.

Jameson, F. *Postmodernism, or The Cultural Logic of Late Capitalism*. Durham: Duke University Press, 1991.

Morris, P. *A History of Taxidermy: Art, Science, and Bad Taste*. Ascot: MPM, 2012.

Mosse, K. *The Taxidermist's Daughter*. London: Orion, 2014.

Niesel, J. "The Horror of Everyday Life: Taxidermy, Aesthetics and Consumption in Horror Films." *Journal of Criminal Justice and Popular Culture* 2.4 (1994): 61–80.

Obreht, T. *The Tiger's Wife*. New York: Random House, 2011.

O'Mahony, J. "Edinburgh's Most Controversial Show: Exhibit B, a Human Zoo." *The Guardian*, August 11, 2014. https://www.theguardian.com/stage/2014/aug/11/-sp-exhibit-b-human-zoo-edinburgh-festivals-most-controversial. Accessed September 15, 2017.

Orzóy, A. "The Stuffed Barbarian/Kitömött Barbár." *Literaturhaus Europa*, 2015. http://www.literaturhauseuropa.eu/en/observatory/blog/thestuffed-barbarian-kitomott-barbar. Accessed September 15, 2017.

Poliquin, R. *The Breathless Zoo*. University Park, PA: Pennsylvania State University Press, 2012.

———. "The Matter and Meaning of Museum Taxidermy." *Museum and Society* 6.2 (2008): 123–134.

Read, E.E. *Angelo Soliman Then and Now: A Historical and Psychoanalytical Interpretation of Soliman Depictions in Modern German Literature*. Master's thesis, University of Tennessee, 2006.

Rothfels, N. "Trophies and Taxidermy." In *Gorgeous Beasts: Animal Bodies in Historical Perspective*, edited by Joan Landes, Paula Young Lee, and Paul Youngquist, 117–136. University Park, PA: Pennsylvania State University Press, 2012.

Scholtmeijer, M. "What Is 'Human'? Metaphysics and Zoontology in Flaubert and Kafka." In *Animal Acts: Configuring the Human in Western History*, edited by Jennifer Ham and Matthew Senior, 127–143. New York: Routledge, 1997.

Star, S.L. "Craft vs. Commodity, Mess vs. Transcendence: How the Right Tool Became the Wrong One in the Case of Taxidermy and Natural History." In *The Right Tools for the Job*, edited by Adele E. Clarke and Joan H. Fujimura, 257–286. Princeton, NJ: Princeton University Press, 1992.

Swinney, G. "An Afterword on Afterlife." In *The Afterlives of Animals: A Museum Menagerie*, edited by Samuel J.M.M. Alberti, 219–233. Charlottesville: University of Virginia Press, 2011.

Thorsen, L.E. *Elephants Are Not Picked from Trees: Animal Biographies in Gothenberg Natural History Museum*. Aarhaus: Aarhaus University Press, 2014.

Turner, S. "Relocating 'Stuffed' Animals: Photographic Remediation of Natural History Taxidermy." *Humanimalia* 4.2 (2013): 1–32.

Wakeham, P. *Taxidermic Signs: Reconstructing Aboriginality*. Minneapolis: University of Minnesota Press, 2008.

Weheliye, A. *Habeas Viscous: Racializing Assemblages, Biopolitics, and Black Feminist Theory*. Durham: Duke University Press, 2014.

CHAPTER 9

Caesar: The Rise and Dawn of a Humanimalistic Identity

Daniel Wolf

It is a common approach to use animals to tell stories about humans. From Pliny's natural history to George Orwell's *Animal Farm* animals have been used to symbolize specific human characteristics. At the same time, stories about animals themselves are still rare in the genre of film, other than in documentaries. However, if they appear as characters, they will usually be anthropomorphized. And even though anthropomorphism is not necessarily bad or unscientific,[1] the animals might disappear behind the veil it creates, since they are only representatives of human features. As Lorraine Daston and Gregg Mitman argue: "Considered from a moral standpoint, anthropomorphism sometimes seems dangerously allied to anthropocentrism: humans project their own thoughts and feelings onto other animal species because they egotistically believe themselves to be the centre of the universe."[2] Nevertheless, even though anthropomorphism has the potential to conceal certain aspects of animals, it can be argued, as

---

[1] Mitchell, "Anthropomorphism," 100; Mitchell et al., *Anthropomorphism*, 3–5.
[2] Daston and Mittman, *Thinking*, 4.

D. Wolf (✉)
University of Kassel, Kassel, Germany

© The Author(s) 2018   161
A. Krebber, M. Roscher (eds.), *Animal Biography*,
Palgrave Studies in Animals and Literature,
https://doi.org/10.1007/978-3-319-98288-5_9

Fig. 9.1   The Road to the Planet of the Apes. © swolf, schwarzerwolfweisserwolf. com 2016

does Emanuela Cenami Spada, that it cannot be completely avoided when studying animals: "Anthropomorphism [...] is the name that describes a prejudice detectable only a posteriori [...]. [W]e must refer to our human experience in order to formulate questions about animal experience."[3] This means that the first access path to a nonhuman is necessarily anthropocentric and thus anthropomorphic. In addition, Spada considers it a fallacy to turn to mechanomorphic descriptions, as they would produce similar errors while seeming to be more objective.[4] Similarly, while assuming the possibility of avoiding an anthropocentric perspective, H. Lyn Miles argues for a "pragmatic anthropomorphism"[5] as a necessity in comparative studies with apes, especially in ape language research.

Accepting the claim of anthropomorphism as a necessary risk in scientific research, it is not surprising that a nonhuman character in a movie is dependent on anthropomorphism to make the challenges he has to overcome relatable to the viewers' experiences. The strong presence of a topic in popular culture shows that people identify themselves with the ideas presented and establish these perceptions through visual confirmation. In addition, popular media influences the perception of scientific results: "Screened representations translate concepts into moving images, living pictures, and thus make them immediate in a way that an abstract and thus dead (or more precisely not-yet-living) concept could never be. [...] As a result, we learn to see ourselves differently."[6] This potential impact is why

---

[3] Spada, "Amorphism," 49.
[4] Ibid., 40–42.
[5] Miles, "Anthropomorphism," 385.
[6] Hauskeller et al., *Palgrave Handbook*, 4.

Fig. 9.2   Caesar, *Rise of the Planet of the Apes*, 00:62:19. © swolf, schwarzerwolf-weisserwolf.com 2016

the following pages are dedicated to a fictional character: a very unique person named Caesar (Fig. 9.2), one of the protagonists in *The Planet of the Apes*.

JUST ANIMALS? THE APES IN *THE PLANET OF THE APES*

The main questions for the following considerations are what impact the anthropomorphization of the apes in the movies *Rise of the Planet of the Apes* (2011) and its prequel *Dawn of the Planet of the Apes* (2014) has on the perception of those animals in relation to humans and whether it is resolved a posteriori to create a posthuman character. *The Planet of the Apes*—the original novel by Pierre Boulle (1963) as well as the original movie saga (1968–1973)—creates a fictional world in which, in contrast to our own, apes are the dominant species, while humans, creatures without speech or the ability to use tools, have taken their place in the wild. The most recent screen adaptions in 2011 and 2014—on which the following pages will focus—tell the story of the genesis of this world, tightly bound to the biography of Caesar, an ape who not only gains the ability to talk but establishes a humanlike society of apes, which in many ways seems at first to work better than its human counterpart, but finally only manages to recreate humanity's failures. The movies seem to focus on the animal's perspective, which is why they might be interpreted as an approach to a posthuman cinema.[7] There are many aspects which validate this perspective. To name just a few examples, the movie posters exclusively presented the primates as characters. In relation to the animals, the human actions become more and more inconsequential over the course of the movies. And furthermore, the director Rupert Wyatt even called it a story about equal rights for apes.[8]

With an animal as the main protagonist there seems to be a nonhuman focus, but as his biography will show, Caesar cannot be categorized as an animal at all. He cannot be defined as a "natural" being in the sense of a biological affiliation to a singular species, even if we ignore the facts that he is a completely hypothetical ape whose personality is created by humans, based on the imagination of the effects of artificial evolution,[9] and represented by a human actor through motion-capture-technology (Fig. 9.3). Even if the narrative of the movie alone is taken into account, it is questionable to attribute an animal status to him, since the human interference through genetic engineering as well as his social education cast doubt on his ontological status. Regardless of whether the fictionality of the film is ignored, Caesar is still an artificial being, since he only came into existence through genetic engineering that gave him humanlike cognitive skills.

Irrespective of the question of whether these changes are considered improvements, he is definitively anthropomorphized. And while these genetic changes might not make him human, he is also not an ape anymore. Consequently, the main concern of the *Rise of the Planet of the Apes* is the question of Caesar's identity, as a look at his biography will show. Before meeting Caesar, the viewer is introduced to his mother, a genetically modified ape in a laboratory, where the scientist Will Rodman (James Franco) is looking for a cure for Alzheimer's disease. At the beginning of *Rise of the Planet of the Apes* men are hunting apes. The camera follows one

---

[7] An example for this ascription can be found in the *Palgrave Handbook of Posthumanism in Film and Television*: "[T]he Apes films' most political message is their performance of a posthuman narrative [...] haunted by humanist dispositions" (Henderson, "Haunts of Humanism," 321).

[8] Gosling et al., *Planet of the Apes*, 10.

[9] The development of Caesar's supreme cognitive skills is induced by medication given to his mother, as well as himself, changing his DNA.

Fig. 9.3 Motion-capture—Andy Serkis/Caesar at the veterinarian, *Rise of the Planet of the Apes*, 00:19:42. © swolf, schwarzerwolfweisserwolf.com 2016

specific ape who is caught and put in a crate. While she tries to get out of her prison through a small window in the box, staring at the other apes, nostrils flaring, the camera closes in on her eye and—zooming out—shows her sitting chained in a cell with grey concrete walls in a laboratory. She is solving a Lucas Tower, a mathematical brain teaser, without hesitation in only 20 steps, where 15 steps would be a perfect score.[10] With this visualization of her memory, the jungle is introduced as the natural habitat for an ape as well as the longing for freedom as a natural desire. In addition, it is made clear that she would not have been able to solve this task without the human influence in form of genetic changes, since the first reaction to the speed with which she completes her task is Rodman's question: "What are we giving her?"[11] It is also stated explicitly that she was unable to complete the task by any means before she got the treatment with the so-called ALZ-112, a gene therapy that allows the brain to create its own cells.[12]

---

[10] Wyatt, *Rise*, min. 1–3.

[11] Ibid., min. 4. (All transcriptions in the following are my own.)

[12] Ibid., min. 5.

She is called "Number 9," which shows that she is treated as an object. Only one human character at the Gensys Lab (where the beginning of Caesar's story takes place), the chimp handler Robert Franklin (Tyler Labine), calls her "Bright Eyes," granting her some individuality (even though it is merely a descriptive name,[13] as it refers to the human influence since her eye-colour turned from brown to a bright gold-green when the drug was administered).[14] Although he is the only one who sees the apes as "personalities, with attachments,"[15] not just as material for the tests, he has to put her down after the experiments fail. Yet he refuses to kill the newborn Caesar,[16] rather giving him to Rodman, who first declines responsibility for "company property,"[17] but then takes the newborn chimp with him, because he cannot put him down himself either.[18] After recognizing his increased intelligence, he decides to proceed with the experiments on him at home, and they finally develop some kind of father-son relationship.[19] Consequently, Caesar spends his childhood in a human family, where he feels accepted as one of them, but all other interactions refer to his difference and lead him to question his identity.

BECOMING CAESAR

Caesar starts his life as an object, the property of a company, which has to be disposed off because it has lost its financial value. But he is also an individual living being, thus invoking pity in the humans responsible for this

[13] The name of Caesar's first son who appears in the first scene of *Dawn of the Planet of the Apes*, "Blue Eyes," refers back to her and—even though originating in an objectifying treatment—might be interpreted as reference to the intimate relation between Caesar and his human family, his longing for his own origin (or identity) as well as his acceptance of his life starting as a human possession, which means an acceptance of his animality. He mostly overcame these questions of identity in the course of the first movie.

[14] Interestingly, Franklin is also the first human who contracts and dies of the so-called *simian flu*, an unexpected side effect of the drug. His empathy towards the apes comes into conflict with his inability to actually do something to stop their suffering that is a result of self-interest, as he is afraid of losing his job if he were to interfere (ibid., min. 10), which ultimately proves to be his death sentence. Because he follows his orders against his better knowledge, he is guilty through action as well as omission. It also makes the apes not active perpetrators but a passive medium of the humans' own creation.

[15] Wyatt, *Rise*, min. 8.

[16] Ibid., min. 11.

[17] Ibid., min. 10.

[18] Ibid., min. 9–11.

[19] Ibid., min. 14–15.

disposal. He is a chimpanzee, a wild animal, yet living like a domestic animal, regarded as a human family member by his foster father and grand-father, even though he is still part of his foster father's research with an experimental drug. He even has his own room and wears human clothing, illustrating his adaptation to a childlike status. But he is still treated as a dangerous beast by almost every other human he meets. He is part of a family, but also a test subject. He is the son of a lab-animal, but—with the exception of his birth—has never been in a laboratory himself. He is taught to understand human language and to use sign language, but he is not able to communicate with people or apes outside his home. He is not locked up, but cannot go out on his own either. Therefore, he does not know what it is like to be caged, nor does he know what it is like to be free. His cognitive skills are equal to those of humans, he lives and behaves mostly like a human being, but he is treated differently because of his appearance. He is at the threshold of being human as well as being an ape, but always remains almost human as well as almost ape. This liminality makes it impossible to define his status consistently. This position corre-sponds with Deleuze and Guattari's concept of becoming. As they say: "[…] becoming is not to imitate or identify with something or someone."[20] Instead, it is a form of worlding that enables species to become attuned to each other's perspectives: "What is real is the becoming itself, the block of becoming, not the supposedly fixed terms through which that which becomes passes."[21] Caesar is unable to decline one of the sides of his iden-tity, and instead remains in a constant state of becoming, unable to iden-tify completely with either humans or with apes.

   In accordance with this concept of becoming, the filmmakers portrayed Caesar as more than an ape, as an almost-human being, able to take the perspective of humans or apes alike. Andy Serkis—the actor playing Caesar—pointed out when he was asked whether becoming Caesar was the same process as becoming "a real person"[22] that while for acting King Kong he had studied mountain gorillas in Rwanda to capture authentic apelike behaviour, he did not think this necessary in order to play Caesar since "[…] he's really an ape-plus—he's brought up among humans, he's evolving very rapidly. So I approached him almost as a human in ape skin,

---

[20] Deleuze and Guattari, *Plateaus*, 272.
[21] Ibid., 238.
[22] Forrest, "Andy Serkis Interview."

having human feelings while being trapped inside an ape's body."[23] As a consequence Serkis did not study apes for his role, but individuals. Following his research, he did not create an ape with character, but a character who is also an ape. Serkis' approach is in line with the series' director Rupert Wyatt, who wanted the actors to not just imitate ape behaviour, but play specific characters which are also apes. He wanted an actor who would play Caesar like a human, instead of just imitating a chimpanzee.[24] Hence Caesar is portrayed not really as an ape, but just as obviously he is not a human being either.

In consequence, the main concern of *The Rise of the Planet of the Apes* becomes defining his identity for himself as well as for the viewer. This problem is pointed out by Caesar himself, who asks "What is Caesar?"[25] following a confrontation between him and another animal—a German Shepherd on a leash—which makes him aware of his own leash and in extension his ambivalent ontological status in comparison to the human members of his "family." The leash, which he has to wear outside the house, is a specific symbol of his difference and especially of his awareness of this difference. He does not question its necessity until he and his foster father pass the family with the German Shepherd. Caesar recognizes the dog's leash and touches his own,[26] a gesture which is identifiable as moment of recognition of his animal nature, as well as the related restraint of his freedom (Fig. 9.4).

Such realization raises the question of his oscillating identity between animal and human, as even the people closest to him do not treat him like one of their own. At this point he starts to question his place in the world, but still longs for human acceptance. Nevertheless, it becomes clearer that Caesar can never be a real member of the family (let alone human society), because his visible animality cannot be ignored. Thus, the inconsistency between Caesar and his surroundings, and therefore the need for an essential change of either himself or his environment, is established. This contradiction inevitably erupts in a following conflict, in which Caesar attacks a neighbour in an attempt to protect his family. As a result, Animal Control takes him to a Primate Shelter, where he is caged and abused.[27] Even

---

[23] Ibid.
[24] Gosling et al., *Planet of the Apes*, 11.
[25] Wyatt, *Rise*, min. 27.
[26] Ibid., min. 26.
[27] Ibid., min. 33–34.

Fig. 9.4 Caesar recognizing his leash, *Rise of the Planet of the Apes*, 00:24:58. © swolf, schwarzerwolfweisserwolf.com 2016

though he was only trying to protect his family, as the neighbour approached his foster grandfather in an aggressive manner,[28] his animality and therefore his difference becomes obvious. For one instant, Caesar's own reaction is inhuman, as he bites off one of the man's fingers. He withdraws instantly, and his expression shows his own surprise and shame at having given in to this animalistic impulse, while his punishment reinforces his awareness of this difference.

The incident compromises Caesar's identity even further and leads to the final turning point in his relationship to humans, not least as a result of his experiences at the Primate Shelter, where his first contact with other apes since his birth takes place. It is obvious that he does not fit in with them either, illustrated, once more, by his human clothing. The guards point out straightaway that "[i]t might cause problems with the other apes"[29] but either do not care or even favour a conflict. Yet even without his clothes, his difference is undeniable, but guards' comments visualize the necessity to take a side—he will not be able to fit in with the other apes unless he leaves his contact to humans behind and finds his "inner ape."[30] Thus it is established that he cannot be both, or he will not be anything. Consequently, at Caesar's first direct encounter with the other apes, they punish him for being humanlike, when their current leader Rocket rips off

[28] Ibid., min. 32.
[29] Ibid., min. 41.
[30] Cf. Gosling et al., *Planet of the Apes*, 53.

his sweater and attacks him.[31] Even though he appears to have joined a community of natural companions, his mind and body remain inconsistent. While he feels at home among human beings, his appearance separates him from them and leads to conflict. He still fits neither to the world of animals nor to that of humans. Additionally, he experiences human violence by the guards and feels betrayed by his former family members, who are not able to help him. The contact with humans is now primarily shaped by disappointment, and the change of loyalty is unavoidable. Seeing the suffering of the other apes leads to his choice of identity: He starts to see them as his "own kind" and turns his back on humanity.[32]

Hereafter, Caesar chooses to change his environment to fit his own identity by using his humanlike abilities. He escapes the shelter by threatening a human visitor, stealing his pocket knife and using it to build a tool to pick the lock of his cage. He then releases the gorilla Buck, thereby securing his allegiance. With his help, he gains leadership by threatening the former dominant ape Rocket in front of the other apes.[33] Caesar disappears, steals the experimental drug which was given to him and his mother, returns and administers it to the other apes. Afterwards he leads them against their guards into the freedom of the forest, building their own society. Instead of just adapting to his new situation, Caesar chooses to alter the other apes and lead them into freedom. For this, he uses tools and anticipates the actions and anticipations of others—humans as well as apes. He follows a complex, long-term plan and relies on cooperation to carry it out. All these aspects, which are commonly used to prove an anthropological difference,[34] make it obvious that he would not have been able to accomplish anything without becoming more than "just an animal."[35]

---

[31] Wyatt, *Rise*, min. 43–45.

[32] Ibid., min. 61.

[33] Ibid., min. 53–55.

[34] "That we possess a basically primate 'hardware' hardly challenges our self-esteem. However, we become slightly uneasy when our 'software' is at stake: our mind." Most scientists hang on to claims of human uniqueness, assuming that "only humans create tools with foresight and for future utilisation; only humans keep utensils for re-use; only humans employ a variety of artefacts in a logical sequence" (Hof and Sommer, *Apes*, 158). On the discussion of the understanding of mental states and the ability of primates for anticipation, see, for example, Kaminski et al., "Chimpanzees."

[35] Reeves, *Dawn*, min. 106.

The other apes confirm such need to change, as they also have to improve their cognitive abilities in order to overcome their position as caged animals. These apes are not able to do this by staying as they are, for without the ability to think like a human cooperation seems impossible. To gain freedom they need to evolve, because "Apes stupid"[36] as the orangutan Maurice puts it, referring to their inability to work together.[37] Caesar, in contrast, is an exceptional individual, able to create a threat, while the other apes merely "ape" his actions. Through his liminality he questions human supremacy. It is no longer secure that "The animal is forever positioned on the other side of an unbridgeable gap, a gap that reassures the Human of his excellence by the very ontological impoverishment of a lifeworld that cannot be its own end or know its own condition."[38] While the necessity to gain the cognitive skills associated with human exceptionalism in order to change the established hierarchy confirms human supremacy in principle, the potential of the apes to assimilate these abilities challenges this gap. Combined with abilities supposedly unique to humans, such as reason, culture, and language, Caesar's simultaneous remaining apish characteristics represent a gradual rather than an essential difference of the species.

"Becoming With"

Accepting such equality between humans and apes would make *becoming with* a necessity, ultimately requiring humans to share their world: "If we appreciate the foolishness of human exceptionalism, then we know that becoming is always becoming *with*—In a contact zone where the outcome, where who is in the world, is at stake."[39] Since such becoming with is of course the topic of *The Planet of the Apes*, the question of how apes and humans interact and how the "becoming with" changes them is to be contemplated. According to Haraway, a successful process of "becoming with" depends on mutual respect: "To knot companion and species together in encounter, in regard and respect, is to enter the world of

---

[36] Wyatt, *Rise*, min. 64.

[37] Maurice is the only other ape Caesar is able to communicate with, since he learned to use sign language in a circus (ibid., min. 48). Obviously, it is not considered a problem for an ape to use language if he has been taught. They just usually lack the tools to express themselves.

[38] Haraway, *Species Meet*, 77.

[39] Ibid., 244.

becoming with, where *who and what are* is precisely what is at stake. [...] Species interdependence is the name of the worlding game on earth, and that game must be one of response and respect."[40] In the dystopian future presented in *The Planet of the Apes* humanity fails to do just that, and its punishment is severe and immediate. Through its refusal to respond to the apes and their changed behaviour in a reasonable, respectful way, humanity loses its world.

Nonetheless, Caesar and the main human protagonist of the prequel *The Dawn of the Planet of the Apes* Malcolm (Jason Clarke) respect each other and try to build a cooperative relationship in which the productive process of "becoming with" seems possible. At the end of the movie, they even emphasize that they had believed in the possibility of "becoming with," but were ultimately disappointed, as Caesar replies "I did too" to Malcom's claim "I thought we had a chance."[41] But they cannot ward off the final conflict as a result of mistrust and fear of their otherness. So they are at a point of no return. Apes and humans cannot live in peace, even though they are pretty much the same; or maybe they cannot precisely because of such similarity, at least according to Eduardo Viveiros de Castro: "The difference between species is not a principle of segregation but of alternation: for what defines the specific difference is that two species (unlike two given individuals) cannot both 'be' human at the same time, which means that both species cannot perceive themselves as human one for the other, or else they would cease to be two different species."[42]

Consequently, the apes are not "becoming" in the processual meaning of either Haraway or Deleuze and Guattari, but in the sense of transforming into a new if humanlike form. As the story proceeds in the second movie, the humanization of the apes intensifies, concerning their behaviour as well as their bodily appearance. Sometimes the apes still act as could be expected from animals, when a gorilla beats his chest,[43] or the use of submissive gestures of apes several times in the movies,[44] which are

---

[40] Ibid., 19.
[41] Reeves, *Dawn*, min. 114.
[42] De Castro, "Notion of Species," 18.
[43] Wyatt, Rise, min. 80.
[44] Ibid., min. 23.

based on the behaviour of actual chimps.[45] Yet ultimately the apes prove [...] humanised. In *Dawn of the Planet of the Apes* (2014), the intelligent ape-protagonist Caesar demonstrates within the first five minutes heroic human capacity for bravery in the face of a grizzly and for concern over the injury to his son. These anthropocentric qualities are foregrounded, as a primitive form of humanlike ape society is valorized."[46] Through their humanlike features, gestures, and behaviour and especially their developed social structure, they are characterized as almost humans. They hunt like humans, use tools—especially weapons—ride horses and wear war paint.[47] In one scene Caesar closes the eyes of a dead gorilla, copying human funeral rites.[48] Their family structures are more human than apelike, and they even have schools.[49]

Thus, the apes do not develop their own culture but assimilate that of the humans. This becomes especially obvious in their language. In *Rise* and *Dawn of the Planet of the Apes* the apes communicate through sign language at first, later they start speaking English, if with improper syntax. They use human gestures and human language. They use icons, of which the (symbolic) representation of the window in Caesar's room is the most prominent in both movies (Fig. 9.5). It stands for "home" as well as "freedom," depending on the context. Implicating an advanced, multidimensional use of symbols, it combines both perspectives and the contradicting longings connected with them: looking through the window from the outside and from the inside. Moreover, the apes also use icons as a kind of written history, with an obvious resemblance to cave paintings (Fig. 9.6). This indicates a comparability of the nature of apes and humans and implicates that the apes are just on a lower step on the evolutionary ladder, presenting them as incomplete beings: an impression that is also supported by the missing structure in their spoken language. They are presented as an image of human evolution, as is commonly used in primatology, thus telling a story of where humanity is coming from, as well as indicating what the apes will become.

---

[45] Cf. Gosling et al., *Planet of the Apes*, 56, 110–112.
[46] Carbonell, "Contest of Tropes," 158.
[47] Reeves, *Dawn*, min. 4–6.
[48] Wyatt, *Rise*, min. 88.
[49] Reeves, *Dawn*, min. 9–10.

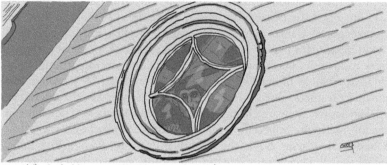

Rise of the planet of the apes 00:30:30h : Caesar's window

Rise of the planet of the apes 00:41:12h : window sign

Fig. 9.5 Window and Caesar creating the symbol for home/freedom, *Rise of the Planet of the Apes*, 00:30:30 and 00:41:12. © swolf, schwarzerwolfweisserwolf. com 2016

HUMANIMALS: MAKING APES—BODY AND MIND

The appearance of the apes supports this evolutionary process, as their bodies are similarly taken over by human features as their behaviour. Their evolution is shown as a process of becoming significant beings. What they are is accordingly not important, but only what they might transform into. The central image to purport this idea is Robert Zallinger's visualization of evolution in *The Road to Homo Sapiens*[50] (1965), which implicates that apes are

---

[50] Also known as *March of Progress*.

Fig. 9.6   Ape history, *Dawn of the Planet of the Apes*, 00:08:41. © swolf, schwarzerwolfweisserwolf.com 2016

just an earlier, *incomplete* version of humans. The creatures in *The Planet of the Apes* movies reflect Zallinger's image, since not only their behaviour but also their bodily appearance adopts human features; their specific vocabulary of movement combines ape and man (Fig. 9.1). This chimerical appearance is also supported by a couple of changes in their faces, of which the eyes are the most anthropomorphized attributes (Fig. 9.2). This is an important visual decision, since cross-species communication is a complicated matter.[51] For example, according to the cooperative-eye-hypothesis[52] the distinctive features of the eyes are important for the mimic communication of humans, enabling them to "[...] engage in frequent, large-scale, complex, even institutionalized cooperation with non-kin to a degree unprecedented among

---

[51] "Language is often viewed as a bugbear for any cross-species comparisons, in that language is believed to be a species-specific behavioural propensity which bears no comparison with the communication systems of other species. Programs orchestrated to teach nonhumans language are objected to as fraught with unverified anthropomorphic inference and description" (Mitchell et al., *Anthropomorphism*, 11). Lacking a common language, human-animal communication has to rely on behaviour, on gestures and actions that can be interpreted in a much more varied way and thus might lead to misunderstandings. Even the basics are still questioned as there is no common ground if anthropomorphism is to be allowed or if it is unscientific.

[52] Kobayashi and Kohshima, "Unique Morphology."

the primates [...]."[53] In addition, through their symbolic conception as *windows to the soul*, the humanized eyes implicate the nullification of a different state of human and animal in this regard. The reasoning for these changes is especially important: according to the creators of the movies they needed to look "more intelligent,"[54] implicating that the viewers are predisposed to perceive real apes as stupid. The changes make it easier for the viewer to understand the apes' facial expressions and to identify with the characters, but also affect the perception of the (re-)presented animals—the other being cannot be perceived as other anymore, if its otherness is taken from it. This seems to be the case when humans are playing animals which evolve into humans and therefore also behave like humans.

In addition to the general changes in the appearance of the apes, the main characters are marked. Their marks and attributes are of course designed to help the human viewers recognize them and are not important for the communication between the apes themselves. The viewer needs—or is thought to need—hints to recognize them as individuals: Caesar has a birthmark, which Charles Rodman (his foster grandfather) points out even before he names him,[55] thus indicating that such attributes are necessary to identify individuals within another species; Koba (Toby Kebbell), another ape from the Gensys Lab and Caesar's main antagonist, is missing an eye and has several scars (Fig. 9.7); Rocket has pale skin; and Caesar's son Blue Eyes has three big scars on his chest from a fight against a bear. These body-marks also represent the apes' personalities. The scarred body of Caesar's son is a lesson learned about recklessness, as well as a constant reminder of Caesar's heroism and the love for his family. Caesar's features are symmetrical, associated with inner balance, while the asymmetrical features of Koba (Fig. 9.7) are instinctively perceived as unsettling. In addition, their bodies keep the characters' backgrounds visible. Irrespective of his current actions, Koba is a permanent reference to human cruelty. His appearance always shows the kind of relation which connects him with humanity. This way, the negative aspects of human-animal relations are always visually present through Koba. His body reflects his experiences. Pointing at his scars and referring to them as "human work"[56] in one scene, he even points as much out himself. His scars, then, are the embodied representations of humanity's failures. They signify visu-

---

[53] Tomasello et al., "Reliance on Head," 314.

[54] Gosling et al., *Planet of the Apes*, 11.

[55] Wyatt, *Rise*, min. 12.

[56] Reeves, *Dawn*, min. 38.

Fig. 9.7   Koba, *Rise of the Planet of the Apes*, 00:46:15. © swolf, schwarzerwolf-weisserwolf.com 2016

ally that he was exposed to human influences long enough to adopt their behaviour, while having internalized what he has suffered: deception, betrayal, and aggression. Even though he attributes these to humans in general and considers apes to be better than that, he uses all the abilities he despises, even in interaction with the other apes.

BECOMING KOBA

A crucial scene in Koba's becoming is his attempt to infiltrate the arsenal in the human base during *The Dawn of the Planet of the Apes*.[57] Similar to Caesar's escape from the Primate Shelter in the first movie, he shows supreme cognitive abilities and empathic skills. He lies to the other apes, telling them he is going hunting. When he discovers a stack of weapons,[58]

[57] Ibid., min. 44–46.
[58] Ibid., min. 45.

he instantly recognizes the threat they represent to the apes, implicating an understanding of foresight concerning the production or hoarding of such devices by humans. He also shows a keen insight into the future utilization of those tools for himself. Furthermore, he is well aware of the human concept of an ape as well as the inability of humans to accept the abilities of the apes as a reality. He uses their denial, first to escape by imitating a stupid animal[59] and then repeating this trick later to get close to a gun and kill his human opponents.[60] In addition to his cognitive skills, his body enables him to choose tactics the humans are not aware of. This is shown early in the movie, when he climbs over the Golden Gate bridge— introduced in *The Rise of the Planet of the Apes* as the symbolic barrier between human civilization and the presumably more natural habitat of the apes—moving hand over hand along the top to escape the view of their sentries.[61]

As such, Koba is in a similar position as Caesar but embraces his dual identity to gain dominance over humans and apes alike. Instead of trying to fit in, he uses the inconsistency of his appearance and his abilities to defeat his enemies. In his selfishness and brutality, he thus proves the antithesis to Caesar's moral superiority. Ironically then, not Caesar seems human but Koba, who also becomes the final antagonist in *The Dawn of the Planet of the Apes* while the actual humans seem to be reduced to no more than a mere footnote of the main storyline. Koba's experiences with humans have been extremely painful, to which the many scars on his body are a testimony. As a consequence, he is willing to do anything to get his revenge on humanity, even killing another ape,[62] thereby breaking the central law of the newly developed society of apes, "Ape not kill Ape."[63] Thus, Koba represents the possibility of adoption of human flaws and, accordingly, the human-animal equality in regard to the potential of the apes to repeat the mistakes of humanity and eventually follow them into extinction.

Unable to believe that the humans will not attack one day, he thinks he has to confront Caesar and his predominantly peaceful handling of the humans who intrude the apes' habitat. The mistrust leads to open con-

---

[59] Ibid., min. 46.
[60] Ibid., min. 63–64.
[61] Ibid., min. 44–45.
[62] Ibid., min. 95.
[63] Ibid., min. 9.

frontation among apes as well as between apes and humans. After he has seen the arsenal of weapons, he argues that Caesar is putting the apes in danger and challenges his leadership.[64] When his attempt fails,[65] he plots against Caesar and tries to kill him, while laying the blame on the humans by using one of their guns.[66] With Caesar left for dead, Koba leads an attack on the human battlement, resulting in the death of many of the apes[67] and the imprisonment of humans and apes alike who get in his way.[68] With Koba's abilities to plan ahead, use tools and anticipate the behaviour of other beings, he seems to be as smart as Caesar, but he proves much more aggressive. If Caesar combines the best ape and human characteristics, Koba combines the worst. The way he wants to lead the apes is very much the way that destroyed human society in the first place. Koba's actions lead to Caesar's final realization that good or bad is not a question of nature—or species to be more precise—but arises out of experiences: "I am to blame. I chose to trust him [Koba], because he is ape. I always think ape better than human. I see now how much like them we are."[69] For this reason the movies ultimately are not about the question of human survival in the face of an ape society, or at least not directly, but whether the apes might find a better way to live, or merely replicate humans in their self-destruction.

BECOMING HUMAN

The equalization of ape and human in theory seemingly dissolves the problem of Caesar's liminal identity, implying a utopia of a "becoming with" of humans and apes. Caesar perceives humans as morally equal, which means the conflict is no longer one between human and animal, but between good and bad characters. Nevertheless, the biological distinction remains relevant. This becomes obvious in the final confrontation between Koba and Caesar. Even though they fight as apes, using all their physical abilities, the final blow is not a physical, but an intellectual one which reflects the concept of anthropological difference. The violation of the apes' central law by Koba gives Caesar later a reason to deny him being an

---

[64] Ibid., min. 58.
[65] Ibid., min. 59.
[66] Ibid., min. 70–72.
[67] Ibid., min. 72.
[68] Ibid., min. 88.
[69] Ibid., min. 93–94.

ape, which is why he can finally kill him without himself breaking the rule "Ape not kill ape,"[70] to which Koba even refers to save his life.[71] The categorization as ape is what grants them their consideration. Caesar cannot just kill Koba, but first has to make him killable.[72] The categorization as "no ape"[73] is rendered necessary; Caesar could never use the death penalty on an ape, as it would invalidate his own law. But it is also an interesting decision, as it preserves the importance of species affiliation, and the status of other animals remains unquestioned.

Even though Caesar considers the species to be equals, making a distinction between ape or no ape—the other—remains relevant. He still cannot define them in other categories, thus re-instantiating the anthropological difference as simian difference. This matches de Castro's proclamation of anthropomorphism as a necessity: "There is only one point of view, the point of view of humanity. What changes is the point of view of this point of view: which species is seeing the world upon seeing itself as human?"[74] Therefore, when Caesar finally comes to terms with his identity and defines himself as ape, the human order is restored, if with apes at its centre instead of humans. Anthropocentrism is substituted by "simiocentrism." As stated by Phil Henderson, this is also where the movies fail:

Over the course of *Rise* and *Dawn of the Planet of the Apes* the old ontological animal/human binary is dissolved; not only is the human narratively decentred, but the very notion of a purely animal being becomes more and more untenable in light of all the boundary crashes and collapses. [...] Where the imaginative world begins to lose its lustre, however, is in the political subtext. Humanistic tropes are subtly re-instantiated in this text. [...] Here, the posthuman imagination clearly faltered, and fell back into the increasingly meaningless and unsustainable binaries that have for so long demarcated the political.[75]

---

[70] Ibid., min. 9.
[71] Ibid., min. 111.
[72] Haraway, *Species Meet*, 80.
[73] Reeves, *Dawn*, min. 112.
[74] De Castro, "Notion of Species," 17.
[75] Henderson, "Haunts of Humanism," 329.

The End...?

Even though the two movies focus on Caesar's biography and most of the story is shown from Caesar's point of view then, they still do not tell a posthuman story, due to the fact that they dissolve the other perspective by remaking it human. The apes are still only acknowledged inside "humanist frameworks"[76] and thus stay entwined in categories of human similarity and analogy whenever their worth as living beings is considered. In the end, the apes substitute humanity without any substantial changes. The supremacy of humanity is not challenged but confirmed, as the animals are not characters in their own right but only insofar as they appear as humans. The nonhuman characters, embodied by human actors, tell a story about humanity's place in the world, not a nonhuman world. Nevertheless, taking the point of view of a character who belongs to another species seems to be the best attempt to convey his perspective. The viewers are enabled to identify with Caesar and thus perceive him as a "real" person, as an equally considerable being. The change of perspective enables the viewer to transfer his anthropocentric view to the apes and consider the humans as "the other." Despite the general confirmation of the supremacy of human qualities, the exclusivity of these qualities is questioned. This, then, might be the posthuman quality of the *Planet of the Apes*-remakes at last.

Moreover, Caesar's becoming as perceived through the struggle with his identity "[...] replaces static modes of identification with the dynamic movement of life between and through congruent singularities. Because of their openness, becomings challenge the 'natural' order [...]."[77] Unfortunately, in pop-cultural movies there usually has to be an unambiguous ending. They need closure. Therefore, the character has to define his status and cannot remain in the transitional process of becoming. Thus, "[...] the need for separate categories of animal and human"[78] remains unscathed in the end. While mutual recognition as morally considerable beings whose perspectives have to be regarded in a respectful way is exactly what "becoming with" would afford, the transformation in the *Rise* and *Dawn of the Planet of the Apes* has to reach a conclusion, in which the binary, hierarchical structure of species' relations stay intact and the con-

---

[76] Haraway, *Species Meet*, 73.
[77] Powell, "Growing," 78.
[78] Haraway, *Simians*, 152.

flict is resolved. Instead of "becoming with," the apes just turn into humans, while the humans themselves become irrelevant. The movies fail to follow the "becoming with" apes to its necessary consequences of surrendering humanity's exclusive claim to the world. However, the sequential structure of the movies reopens the possibility of further developments. The end of Caesar's transformation at the close of *The Dawn of the Planet of the Apes* hence can be interpreted as temporary and the process remaining an ongoing becoming.

Works Cited

Carbonell, Curtis D. "A Contest of Tropes: Screened Posthuman Subjectivities." In *The Palgrave Handbook of Posthumanism in Film and Television*, edited by Michael Hauskeller, Thomas D. Philbeck, and Curtis D. Carbonell, 153–162. Hampshire, New York: Palgrave Macmillan, 2015.

De Castro, Eduardo Viveiros. "The Notion of Species in History and Anthropology." In *Anicka Yi Jungle Stripe*, edited by Susanne Pfeffer, 13–18. Kassel: documenta und Museum Fridericianum GmbH, 2016.

Daston, Lorraine and Gregg Mitman. *Thinking with Animals. New Perspectives on Anthropomorphism*. New York: Columbia University Press, 2005.

Forrest, Adam. "Andy Serkis Interview: 'I've just completed filming on Star Wars Episode VII'." http://www.bigissue.com/features/interviews/4619/andy-serkis-interview-ive-just-completed-filming-on-stars-wars-episode-vii. Accessed February 12, 2014.

Gosling, Sharon, Adam Newell, and Matt Hurwitz. *Planet of the Apes: The Art of the Films Dawn of the Planet of the Apes and Rise of the Planet of the Apes*. London: Titan Books, 2014.

Haraway, Donna. *Simians, Cyborgs and Women. The Reinvention of Nature*. London: Free Assoc. Books, 1991.

———. *When Species Meet*. Minneapolis, London: University of Minnesota Press, 2008.

Hauskeller, Michael, Thomas D. Philbeck, and Curtis D. Carbonell. *The Palgrave Handbook of Posthumanism in Film and Television*. Hampshire, New York: Palgrave Macmillan, 2015.

Hof, Jutta and Volker Sommer. *Apes Like Us. Portraits of a Kinship*. Mannheim: Edition Panorama, 2010.

Kaminski, Juliane, Josep Call, and Michael Tomasello. "Chimpanzees Know What Others Know, But Not What They Believe." *Cognition* 109 (2008): 224–234.

Kobayashi, Hiromi and Shiro Kohshima. "Unique Morphology of the Human Eye and Its Adaptive Meaning: Comparative Studies on External Morphology of the Primate Eye." *Journal of Human Evolution* 40 (2001): 419–435.

Miles, H. Lyn. "Anthropomorphism, Apes, and Ape Language." In *Anthropomorphism, Anecdotes, and Animals*, edited by Robert W. Mitchell, Nicholas S. Thompson, and H. Lyn Miles, 383–404. Albany: State University of New York Press, 1997.

Mitchell, Robert W., Nicholas S. Thompson, and H. Lyn Miles. *Anthropomorphism, Anecdotes, and Animals*. Albany: State University of New York Press, 1997.

Mitchell, Sandra D. "Anthropomorphism and Cross-Species Modeling." In *Thinking with Animals. New Perspectives on Anthropomorphism*, edited by Lorraine Daston and Gregg Mitman, 100–117. New York: Columbia University Press, 2005.

Powell, Anna. "Growing Your Own: Monsters from the Lab and Molecular Ethics in Posthumanist Film." In *The Palgrave Handbook of Posthumanism in Film and Television*, edited by Míchael Hauskeller, Thomas D. Philbeck, and Curtis D. Carbonell, 77–87. Hampshire, NY: Palgrave Macmillan, 2015.

Spada, Emanuela Cenami. "Amorphism, Mechanomorphism and Anthropomorphism." In *Anthropomorphism, Anecdotes, and Animals*, edited by Robert W. Mitchell, Nicholas S. Thompson, and H. Lyn Miles, 37–49. Albany: State University of New York Press, 1997.

Tomasello, Michael, Brian Hare, Hagen Lehmann, and Josep Call. "Reliance on Head Versus Eyes in the Gaze Following of Great Apes and Human Infants: The Cooperative Eye Hypothesis." *Journal of Human Evolution* 52 (2007): 314–320.

MEDIA

Rise of the Planet of the Apes, directed by Rupert Wyatt. © 20th Century Fox, 2011.

Dawn of the Planet of the Apes, directed by Matt Reeves. © 20th Century Fox, 2014.

CHAPTER 10

Postscript, Posthuman: Werner Herzog's "Crocodile" at the End of the World

Dominic O'Key

How do we imagine an animal biography in a posthuman world? How might it be possible to recover animal selfhood not from the archives of the past but from those of the future? Can we remember what is yet to happen? These are just some of the questions that are suggested by the postscript to Werner Herzog's 3D documentary *Cave of Forgotten Dreams* (2010), where the German director narrates a fabulated and speculative fiction in which supposedly mutated reptiles break free of their cages, make their way towards the Chauvet cave in southeast France, and gaze upon prehistoric cave paintings. Since the film's release, Herzog's postscript has largely been met with bafflement by film writers both academic and otherwise. These writers have taken the film's postscript to be little more than a characteristically "Herzogian" afterthought—that is, a throwaway moment of what Eric Ames calls the director's signature mix of "encounter and artifice"[1]—and subsequently describe the closing scene as at best "humor-

---

[1] Ames, *Ferocious Reality*, 2.

D. O'Key (✉)
University of Leeds, Leeds, UK

© The Author(s) 2018
A. Krebber, M. Roscher (eds.), *Animal Biography*,
Palgrave Studies in Animals and Literature,
https://doi.org/10.1007/978-3-319-98288-5_10

185

ous and capricious"[2] and at worst "irrelevant."[3] In this chapter, though, I will argue that *Cave of Forgotten Dreams*'s postscript is vitally important: important on its own terms, important for thinking about Herzog's documentary as a whole, important for reconsidering the director's much-debated documentary filmmaking style, and, most crucially, important for thinking about the central organizing theme of this volume, animal biographies. This is because the postscript, as I see it, constructs its own peculiar form of animal biography. Peculiar because Herzog seems not so much interested in recovering the real-life story of a particular reptilian which exists in the contemporary "now." Rather, Herzog uses his postscript to construct a "quasi-science-fictional scenario,"[4] a speculative biography of a fictional radioactive crocodile which exists in a future time after the human. One of my tasks in this chapter will be to explicate the significance of this fictionalized and future-derived animal biography.

In this chapter, I will outline an antinomous reading of Herzog's fabulated representation of nonhuman life: first, I will momentarily step "outside" of the film itself and argue that one way of reading Herzog's imagined animal biography would involve attending to its ironic inaccuracy. That is, the filmed animal's "true" biography, outside of the documentary's speculative world, is, on closer inspection, somewhat stranger than Herzog's fiction. Second, I will then return to the film itself, to the internal logic of Herzog's posthumanist fiction, and I will describe how Herzog's imagined "crocodile," although imagined as outliving the human species, is necessarily marked with the inscription of humanity's prior presence. As such, I will conclude that Herzog's "radioactive" reptilian bears witness to what I will call—following Georges Bataille, Jacques Derrida, and Bernard Stiegler—the catastrophic pharmacology of a technics that necessarily leaps ahead of itself. Although the nonhuman animal survives long into the future, its body—and even the posthuman world in which it exists—is irrevocably written or inscribed with the trace of humanity's technical activities. Herzog's animal biography therefore figures a single albino alligator as a metonym for humanity's ongoing inscription onto the world. My argument will thus centre on the claim that *Cave of Forgotten Dreams*'s postscript reveals how a posthuman future is not necessarily *post-script*.

---

[2] Lord, "Only Connect," 130.
[3] Rayns, "Cave of Forgotten Dreams," 52.
[4] Johnson, "Science," 930.

Humanity's script is written into the future, even onto the body of future albino alligators.

Before arriving at Herzog's speculations on crocodilian selfhood, though, I will first give a brief outline of *Cave of Forgotten Dreams* itself and argue for its preoccupation with the concept of the human. This will allow us to see how crucial it is that Herzog's postscript at once leaves humanity behind and then discovers its lingering presence within the imagined posthuman future.

IMPOSSIBLE ARCHAEOLOGIES: *CAVE OF FORGOTTEN DREAMS* AND THE HUMAN

Cave of Forgotten Dreams is a 3D documentary that focuses on the history and science research conducted at the Chauvet cave in southeast France. The cave, home to a veritable archive of over four hundred Upper Paleolithic paintings, was discovered in 1994 before being promptly sealed off from the public. Radio carbon dating approximates that the cave's collections of paintings, handprints, and nonhuman animal bones date back to around 30,000 BP. The Chauvet cave is therefore said to be unique in that it houses the oldest known volume of extant figurative art.[5] Afforded restricted but nevertheless unprecedented access to the cave and its team of multidisciplinary researchers, Werner Herzog casts his eye across the cave's topography and, in turn, rearticulates several of the wider thematics of his filmography. One such thematic preoccupation is the question of the human: from early films such as *Aguirre, the Wrath of God* (1972) to later documentaries like *Into the Abyss* (2011), Herzog's work unfolds contesting ontologies, forever probing humanity's conceptual limits within and against the natural world. This is one of the key reasons why Gilles Deleuze wrote in *Cinema 1* (1983) that Herzog "is a metaphysician. He is the most metaphysical of cinema directors."[6] What Deleuze points towards is the fact that Herzog's films dramatize humanity as having an uneasy and unstable foothold on the earth. As Herzog himself puts it in an early essay, echoing Martin Heidegger's fundamental question of metaphysics, "Why Being rather than Nothing?"[7] For Herzog, the human is always in question.

---

[5] Clottes, *Chauvet Cave*; cf. Pettitt and Bahn, "Alternative Chronology," 543.
[6] Deleuze and Guatarri, *Thousand Plateaus*, 186.
[7] Herzog, "Why Being Rather," 24.

With this ontological concentration in mind, *Cave of Forgotten Dreams*'s investigation of humanity's origins becomes apposite for contemplating and indeed grounding the human. Indeed, this is precisely what happens in the final interview of Herzog's film, with the Chauvet cave's director of research, Jean-Michel Geneste. The questions that Herzog puts to Geneste explicitly centre on the question of the human, especially anthropogenesis: "Do you think that the paintings in the Chauvet cave were somehow the beginning of the modern human soul? What constitutes humanness?"[8] Geneste's answers to these questions concretize the specific ways in which *Cave of Forgotten Dreams* conceives of the human:

> Humanness is a very good adaptation with the ... —in the world. [...] The human society needs to adaptate [*sic*] to the landscape, to the other beings, the animals, to other human groups and to communicate something, to communicate it and to inscribe the memory on very specific and hard things, like walls, like pieces of wood, like bones. This is invention of Cro-Magnon. [...] with the invention of the figuration—figuration of animals, of men, of things—it's a way of communication between humans and with the future to evocate [*sic*] the past, to transmit information that is very better than language, than oral communication. And this invention is still the same in our world today—with this camera, for example.[9]

Interviews are a vital component of Herzog's documentary practice. As Marcus P. Bullock argues, interviews form a "constellation of eccentric encounters"[10] that often unify the thematics of Herzog's films. Here, *Cave of Forgotten Dreams*'s vision is unified in that Geneste signals the film's development of a specific notion of "humanness." But what is this particular notion? Geneste's ontological delineation sees the human as perpetually adapting to the surrounding environment, a process of hominization in which communication is utilized as a tool for both present and future habituation. That is, language opens up the capacity for the transmission of memory from person to person, and from generation to generation. Humans "adapt" to their environment through their utilization of memory. This communication, Geneste tells us, is most significantly, effectively and even evocatively instrumentalized through the inscription of information onto the surface of the world itself: "to inscribe the memory on very

[8] *Cave of Forgotten Dreams.*
[9] Ibid.
[10] Bullock, "Lost Son," 237.

specific and hard things, like walls, like pieces of wood, like bones." Humans are thus envisioned as grounding themselves in their environment through haptics and technics—by which I mean the human's technical faculty and its uses of such a faculty—which discloses a performative physical adaptation or reshaping of the world that creates a shared imaginary to be passed on over time.

Cave of Forgotten Dreams can thus be read in the first instance as a film that pivots on the question of the human as a performer of inscription and speculation. Herzog's documentary engages with the Chauvet cave's parietal art as *inscriptions* that mark or carve out an ontology for humanity within the world. Concurrently, the film also suggests that humanity's perennial fascination with such artefacts, our very *speculations* on our origins, similarly constitute a distinctive mode of being. The fact that we paint, for example, and that we also ask *why* we paint, are both figured as immanent to the composition of humanness. Importantly, this concept of speculation is played out within the documentary's form itself. As an "essay film" that "renegotiates assumptions about documentary objectivity, narrative epistemology, and authorial expressivity,"[11] *Cave of Forgotten Dreams* foregrounds the unknowability of the Chauvet cave's paintings, emphasizing in turn the open-ended process of speculation as a defining feature of the human life form. By working "methodically unmethodically" and presenting "speculation on specific, culturally pre-formed objects,"[12] Herzog intensifies rather than resolves the "forgotten dreams" of humanity's prehistoric ancestors, and the film never reaches a "definitive resting place in terms of explanation of argument."[13] As Timothy Morton writes, "at every turn [Herzog] announces his failure, thematizes it, makes it into part of the content rather than trying to erase it."[14]

What is more, Herzog's interpretations of prehistoric art and humanness echo and rearticulate an intellectual tradition which, in its attempt to tease out the impossible archaeologies of humanity's "birth," turns to originary figuration as the privileged space of human constitution. Maurice Blanchot, for instance, writes of the Lascaux cave (discovered in France in 1940, some 50 years before the discovery of Chauvet) that the birth of art

---

[11] Corrigan, *Essay Film*, 4. See 121–130 for Corrigan's reading of Herzog's "excursive essays."

[12] Adorno, "Essay," 13, 3.

[13] Johnson, "Science," 930.

[14] Morton, "From Modernity," 41.

opens up "a unique abode"[15] for humanity within the world. Elsewhere, Georges Bataille—who I will return to below—understands Lascaux to be the "cradle of humanity" and "the measure of this world."[16] In this sense Herzog is only the most recent in a line of continental thinkers and practitioners to reflect on prehistoric aesthetics as direct ontological signifiers. By emphasizing dreams over facts, and by "grow[ing] hazy in the half-light of prehistory,"[17] Herzog's film offers a speculative vision of humanity's inscriptive and speculative faculties.

SPECULATIVE FUTURES, TECHNICAL INSCRIPTIONS: BATAILLE, DERRIDA, AND STIEGLER

Yet *Cave of Forgotten Dreams*'s speculations about humanness are not only extended backwards to a prehistoric past, but also forwards towards an increasingly apocalyptic posthuman future. In other words, Herzog's film charts a trajectory from humanity's birth to its death. This pessimistic posthumanism has a precedent in previous Herzog films such as *Lessons of Darkness* (1992), *The Wild Blue Yonder* (2005), and *Encounters at the End of the World* (2007), in which images of the present world are re-presented as future catastrophes. Herzog's turning-upside-down of the present is closely related to an understanding of the world as fundamentally uncanny [*Unheimlich*], a space in which both human and animal life forms are isolated, alienated, and pushed into increasing degrees of insanity.[18] In this chapter, I would like to arrive at an understanding of *Cave of Forgotten Dreams*'s particular form of pessimistic posthumanism through a reading of Georges Bataille, Jacques Derrida, and Bernard Stiegler. By paying attention to the pharmacology of technics—that is to say, the way in which humanity's technical faculty functions as both a poison *and* a cure—and the aftershocks of its inscriptive capacities, I will show how Herzog's postscript envisions a speculative apocalyptic future. This posthumanist logic is deployed most concretely in Herzog's postscript and its attendant construction of an animal biography.

In a 1955 lecture on the Lascaux cave—the most famous European site of prehistoric cave paintings before the discovery of Chauvet—Georges Bataille uses a single rhetorical gesture to signal humanity's origin and its end:

---

[15] Blanchot, "Birth of Art," 11.
[16] Bataille, *Cradle of Humanity*, 145.
[17] Adorno, "Theories," 331.
[18] Sheehan, "Against the Image," 118.

It has become commonplace today to talk about the eventual extinction of human life. The latest atomic experiments made tangible the notion of radiation invading the atmosphere and creating conditions in which life in general could no longer thrive. [...] I am simply struck by the fact that light is being shed on our birth at the very moment when the notion of our death appears to us.[19]

Contemporaneous to the unfolding Cold War debates about mutually assured destruction, Bataille's lecture dwells on the likelihood of the apocalypse, this "prospect of absolute death." "Struck" by the crashing together of temporalities, Bataille's optical metaphors compound our sense of time by finding a disquieting connection between the deep time of prehistory and the imminent danger of catastrophe in the present. Indeed, Bataille warns his audience in the lecture hall that they are "at an exceptional turning point in history."[20] For Bataille, inspired by both Abbé Breuil's archaeological thinking on the cradle of humanity and Alexandre Kojève's philosophical formulation of the end of history, the Lascaux paintings indicate both the advent *and* the disappearance of humanity. Bataille therefore pictures the cave as a cradle and a coffin.

Bataille returns to such a compelling coupling of the birth and death of the *anthropos* in a short piece appositively titled 'Unlivable Earth?' Here Bataille speaks of two interrelated dangers: first, the possibility of an immense ecological collapse, and second, nuclear warfare. Taking a panoramic view of these potential catastrophes, Bataille writes that there is "something frightful in human destiny, which undoubtedly was always at the limit of this unlimited nightmare that the most modern weaponry, the nuclear bomb, finally announces."[21] The bomb here is taken to be a performative harbinger of the apocalypse, a radioactive speech act that, through the "announcement" of its presence, becomes the nightmare of humanity's future. To borrow Jacques Derrida's typically suggestive phrasing from his own essay on the threat of nuclear apocalypse, Bataille's bomb is envisaged as being "fabulously textual"[22]: it is humanity's last word.

And yet, as Derrida also reminds us, there is a pertinent question to be asked of the nuclear epoch from which Bataille writes: is the bomb, in fact, a new phenomenon, "or is it rather the brutal acceleration of a movement

---

[19] Bataille, *Cradle of Humanity*, 87.
[20] Ibid., 104.
[21] Ibid., 176.
[22] Derrida, "No Apocalypse," 23.

that has always already been at work?"[23] What Derrida has in mind here is the long history of technics itself, that is, the primary commingling between the human and the technical. This idea is best illuminated by turning to the central thesis of Bernard Stiegler's *Technics and Time* series (1994–present), which begins with the hypothesis that the human becomes human at the very moment that it becomes technical.[24] In other words, human life does not begin and then subsequently take up technics (tool use, inscription, painting). Rather the human *co-originates* with technics: the *who* (humanity) and the *what* (technics) are therefore *co-constitutive*. What this means is that the human is only human because of its technical faculties, because of its making and creating, because of its inscriptions and speculations. This relation is necessarily an ambivalent one, for humanity's technical life allows for simultaneously positive and negative interventions: on the one hand, technics leads to the creation of tools and technologies which make life easier for Paleolithic and twenty-first-century humans alike, but on the other hand it also leads to the creation of nuclear weaponry. In this sense, technics is described as a *pharmakon*, an aporetic "gift" which Derrida and Stiegler, following Plato, articulate as being both the remedy and the poison of the *who*.[25] To understand technics as imbricated with human life is, therefore, to understand why Derrida cautions us that the bomb might not be as radically new as Bataille understands it. For Derrida and Stiegler, the bomb is concomitant not only with the specific technological innovations of weapons production in the twentieth century but also with the deep time of human species-history as such. The bomb's eventual creation is therefore set in motion and—to use Bataille's phrasing—"announced" by the human's fundamental relation to technics.

If not a new phenomenon, then, but one that has always already been at work, then the bomb becomes a metonym for technics as such: the bomb is technics, and the nuclear age, turning our heads towards the future, is to be understood as an absolute and fabulous text of technics. This is because the bomb performs a seemingly paradoxical double-movement of erasure and inscription: the bomb at once annihilates the human species altogether, erasing it from the earth, but it also simultaneously writes the species' former presence onto the landscape. The bomb transforms the earth, inscribing humanity's presence into the earth as an

---

[23] Ibid., 21.
[24] Stiegler, *Technics 1*, 141.
[25] Derrida, *Dissemination*, 115.

archive of ruins and leftovers. This idea proposes a strange temporality in which humanity's remains would only be readable by a future archaeologist. As we will see below, one of the functions of Herzog's postscript is to imagine what would happen if radioactive crocodiles were to become future archaeologists that investigated the leftovers of the human species.

Owing to this future-oriented temporality, it is crucial to also keep in mind Stiegler's claim, made at the outset of *Technics and Time*, that "technics evolves more quickly than culture," causing time to consequently "leap outside itself."[26] Simply put, although technics co-originates with the human, Stiegler posits that technics is permanently and necessarily ahead of the human species; humans are always playing catch-up with technics. This is why Stiegler states elsewhere that his project revolves around the intertwined problematics of humanity and temporality. "Even when man is finished," Stiegler writes, "when he belongs to the past, this form of [technical] life may well continue on, becoming ever more complex—and perhaps man is *already* finished."[27] Stiegler's work therefore prioritizes the problematic of how technics continually inscribes itself onto the world even after the demise of the human species. Put differently, Stiegler argues that a posthuman world is never post-technics, and that *a posthuman world is therefore never post-script*. Humans remain through their remains, through the technical forces they have put in motion. This idea will become central when I analyse Herzog's postscript.

Before I do begin unpicking this postscript, though, it is crucial to point out that Stiegler, like Bataille, also looks to the Lascaux cave—and hence to prehistoric cave paintings, the explicit concern of *Cave of Forgotten Dreams*—in order to elucidate his thesis on technics. Stiegler's recourse to Lascaux comes in the third volume of *Technics and Time*, in which he quotes Bataille's meditations on the cave before then theorizing what he calls the fragile existence of an "immense We."[28] This "We," a species-community formed across deep time, is archived and made readable by technical artefacts such as the Paleolithic art found in the Chauvet cave. But this "marvelous" community is also a fragile one. This is because cave paintings also disclose a "disturbing vastness"[29] that threatens to overwhelm the humans of today. What Stiegler means by this is that, by

---

[26] Stiegler, *Technics 1*, 15.
[27] Stiegler and Hallward, "Technics of Decision," 158 (original emphasis).
[28] Stiegler, *Technics 3*, 110.
[29] Ibid.

looking at or reading these paintings, we are simultaneously thrown backwards and forwards. Backwards into the temporal gulf that tentatively unifies prehistory and the present, and forwards into a measureless vastness that necessarily succeeds us into the future. In other words, cave paintings reveal the smallness of the present moment as it is surrounded by deep times which precede and follow it. Such a claim, I think, works to decentre the *anthropos* and concomitantly anticipate a future without us, without the "immense We." But, as we have seen above, this future may indeed be posthuman but it cannot be post-technics, that is, post-script. Technics lives on after humanity's extinction. The questions I want to ask of such a future, then, are as follows: "who" might replace "man" as the *who* that continues co-originating with technics? And, in this posthuman world, what remnants of the human are left? As Bataille asks in his Lascaux lectures, "what would a humanity reduced to its material works be?"[30] Such a future is, I think, dramatized by Herzog's postscript.

READING HERZOG'S POSTSCRIPT

Cave of Forgotten Dreams has come to a close. The screen is engulfed in darkness. The word "postscript" appears in thin white typography. Herzog opens with a cloudy scene in which two nuclear cooling towers are pictured across the water. As waste heat is exhaled into the atmosphere, the camera pans from left to right, revealing a third cooling tower. Herzog's extra-diegetic narration begins:

> On the Rhône river is one of the largest nuclear power plants in France. The Chauvet Cave is located only 20 miles as the crow flies beyond these hills in the background. A surplus of warm water, which has been used to cool these reactors, is diverted half a mile away to create a tropical biosphere.[31]

Herzog then cuts to the inside of the "tropical biosphere" and continues:

> Warm steam fills enormous greenhouses, and the site is expanding. Crocodiles have been introduced into this brooding jungle, and warmed by water to cool the reactor, man, do they thrive. There are already hundreds of them.[32]

---

[30] Bataille, *Cradle of Humanity*, 102.
[31] *Cave of Forgotten Dreams*.
[32] Ibid.

Menacing music reverberates as Herzog directs us through this brooding jungle. There are shadowy trees, the leaves of which brush up against the camera's lens, while steam further veils our vision. Herzog approaches the crocodilians from an elevated walkway and spots a group of reptiles through the grates. Cutting a third and final time, Herzog focuses his camera on a small white crocodilian that rushes up and out of the water, snapping its jaws. Herzog's narrative then reaches its conclusion:

> Not surprisingly, mutant albinos swim and breed in these waters. A thought is born of this surreal environment. Not long ago, just a few ten thousands of years back, there were glaciers here 9,000 feet thick. And now a new climate is steaming and spreading. Fairly soon, these albinos might reach Chauvet cave. Looking at the paintings, what will they make of them?
> Nothing is real. Nothing is certain. It is hard to decide whether or not these creatures here are dividing into their own *Doppelgängers*. And do they really meet, or is it just their own imaginary mirror reflection? Are we today possibly the crocodiles who look back into an abyss of time when we see the paintings of Chauvet cave?[33]

As the music swells and grows more melodic, so too does Herzog's narration: it complicates temporalities by looking to the past ("Not long ago"), the present ("And now"), and the future ("Fairly soon"); it deploys anaphora ("Nothing is real. Nothing is certain.") and erotema ("what will they make of them?"; "is it just their own imaginary mirror reflection?"; and "Are we today [...]?"); and, furthermore, its vocabulary and phrasing is vibrant, even if occasionally clunky ("Are we today possibly"). At just over two hundred words, this short monologue is equivocal and satiric, mysterious and profound, even sonorous. It is, simply put, an enigmatic ending to the film (Figs. 10.1 and 10.2).

One way to approach this conclusion is to turn to what Herzog terms his stylistic technique of "fabrication and imagination and stylization," as outlined in his manifesto against *cinéma vérité*, "The Minnesota Declaration."[34] The postscript deploys what Herzog would call "ecstatic truth" rather than "mere facts," resulting in a sequence that explicitly plays with factuality, and that finds its aesthetic force in deliberate fictionality. We can illustrate this point by comparing Herzog's descriptions with the "truth" of those geographies and buildings he describes: the tropical biosphere, for example, is in

---

[33] Ibid.
[34] Herzog, "Minnesota Declaration," ix–x.

Fig. 10.1 Albino alligator. *Cave of Forgotten Dreams*, dir. Werner Herzog (2010). © Picturehouse Entertainment / Trafalgar Releasing. Reproduced under fair dealing

Fig. 10.2 Albino alligator close-up. *Cave of Forgotten Dreams*, dir. Werner Herzog (2010). © Picturehouse Entertainment / Trafalgar Releasing. Reproduced under fair dealing

fact not "half a mile" from the power plant, as Herzog tells us, but is rather 20 miles away; moreover the biosphere itself, depicted here as a "brooding jungle," is in truth a family-orientated tourist attraction.[35] And perhaps most important of all in this fabulation is Herzog's representation of the mutant albinos themselves: these reptilians are not crocodiles, but alligators. And, as I will discuss below, their "mutation" is not a mutation at all—or, at least not in the way Herzog presents it.

The question, then, is what does Herzog's willful fabrication achieve? Why fabulate inside the documentary form quite so explicitly? One reason is because Herzog has a longstanding reticence towards *cinéma vérité*, and has—in contradistinction to the logics of documentary realism and representation—developed a distinctive stylistic project which proposes imaginative affinities that speak to a different sort of truth. As Herzog comments in a recently published collection of interviews: "The line between fiction and documentary doesn't exist for me. My documentaries are often fictions in disguise."[36] It is from this position that Herzog conceives of *Cave of Forgotten Dreams*'s postscript as a speculative fiction. Herzog's falsification and misrepresentation are intrinsic to his aesthetic and ethical strategies, and I want to locate the albino alligator as the central figure in this formulation. Indeed I want to argue here that Herzog's postscript utilizes the alligator as both a material and an abstract marker, as what Akira Mizuta Lippit theorizes as an "animetaphor," namely, a "metaphor made flesh."[37] Envisioned, therefore, as both transcendental and embodied, the alligator's biography becomes the embodiment of humanity's continual inscription on the world. This is why Herzog's postscript suggests causality between nuclear waste and albinism. Moreover, Herzog even proposes that the radioactive material will one day transform the alligator's genetic code so substantially that this creature might understand the artefacts that adorn the Chauvet cave's walls. One way to read the postscript, then, is to say that it imagines a posthuman world in which technics (which includes both the nuclear waste *and* the Chauvet cave's artefacts) is absorbed and understood by the irradiated alligator. It creates a biography of a mutated crocodile in the future.

For all of this fascination with the future there is also a question of the relation between the past and the present: "Are we today possibly the

---

[35] For further information see the attraction's website: "La Ferme aux Crocodiles."

[36] Herzog and Cronin, *Werner Herzog*, 289.

[37] Lippit, *Electrical Animal*, 165.

crocodiles who look back into an abyss of time when we see the paintings of Chauvet cave?" Here Herzog's attention moves away from the mutated alligator and returns to thinking about the human itself. This critical perspective on the human sits in a conceptual relationship with a similar perspective articulated by Cary Wolfe, whose book *What is Posthumanism?* (2010) envisions posthumanism as a temporal aporia, both before and after the human. As Wolfe explains:

> before in the sense that [the posthuman] names the embodiment and embeddedness of the human being in not just its biological but also its technical world [… A]fter in the sense that posthumanism names a historical moment in which the decentering of the human by its imbrication in technical, medical, informatic, and economic networks is increasingly impossible to ignore.[38]

Rather than seeing posthumanism as transcending the human, Wolfe argues that it "requires us to attend to that thing called 'the human' with *greater* specificity, *greater* attention to its embodiment."[39] This is not to say that Herzog's postscript offers its own "embodiment" of Wolfe's posthumanism. Rather, it is to point out how Herzog's final question interrogates the human and its imbrication with technical matter. Herzog returns to the human life form with the "greater specificity" and "greater attention to its embodiment" that Wolfe calls for. Herzog imagines the humans of today, in this current nuclear epoch, as understanding as little about prehistoric art as reptiles: the abyss of time is also an abyss of ontological separation. Bringing contemporary humanity into contact with the alligator in an equalizing rhetorical configuration, Herzog's postscript even momentarily disrupts the vast unification of Stiegler's "immense We." Rather than seeing the paintings as communicating a techno-ontological connection between the prehistoric and contemporary *who*, Herzog's postscript instead suggests that "we" are in fact closer to these radioactive "crocodiles" than we are to our prehistoric ancestors.

Beyond Herzog's fanciful irradiation narrative, though, there is in fact another reading that I want to address. This will see me create my own brief animal biography of the filmed alligator. By moving outside of the postscript's speculative universe we find that this alligator is indeed a more "mutated" nonhuman animal than Herzog's biographical narration imme-

---

[38] Wolfe, *Posthumanism*, xv.
[39] Ibid., 120.

diately suggests. This is to say that, due to the inscription of technics onto the natural world, nonhuman animals are always irrevocably marked. As Gilles Deleuze and Félix Guattari write, "animals form, develop, and are *transformed* by contagion," that is, by the contagious forces of humanity's technical life.[40] Herzog's albino alligator is thus always already hybridized and mutated by the contagious speed of technical matter: first, the alligator has been removed from its natural habitat, presumably the swamps of Louisiana, and transferred to the south of France, where it is exhibited[41]; second, albinism occurs more frequently in captive populations than in the wild, hence meaning that the very conditions of the alligator's displacement and rehousing increase the probability of a transformed genetic code. Moreover, the rarity of albino alligators in the wild is predominantly due to their singularity and, therefore, vulnerability: as luminous white bodies they have no natural means of camouflage; they are easier to be preyed upon when young, and, for those that do reach adulthood, they do not have the same chances of completing successful kills because of their high visibility.[42] Captivity and simulation, then, two distinctly human and technical endeavours, are therefore the unnatural irradiating phenomena that transform and mutate these crocodilians' bodies. Humanity's technical life results in alligators being always already "post-crocodiles."[43] What I am suggesting, then, is that Herzog's tantalizing postscript opens our eyes to what is underneath it. In other words, underneath Herzog's fabulated scenario is a truth that is just as strange as Herzog's fiction. Namely, that the alligator's biography is already incredibly complex and "mutated," and that the postscript therefore has an intricacy that goes beyond our comprehension. It is incomprehensible to us just how radically the human world has written itself onto—that is, changed, mutated, transformed—the alligator's body.

SURVIVING TECHNICS: CONCLUDING WITH THE "CROCODILE"

Before concluding this chapter, I want to pause over the relationship between crocodiles and humans by way of Dan Wylie's *Crocodile* (2013). Published as part of Reaktion's *Animal* series, *Crocodile* takes a global

---

[40] Deleuze and Guatarri, *Thousand Plateaus*, 242 (emphasis added).
[41] Wickman, "Herzog's 'Ecstatic Truth'."
[42] Ibid.
[43] Lord, "Only Connect," 12.

approach to the biological and cultural history of crocodilians. From the Nile to the Amazon, Wylie surveys human-crocodile interactions through the ages, writing that crocodiles have been perennially "worshipped, appealed to, represented and treasured, albeit almost always with a tinge of fearfulness."[44] The final clause here points us towards what is a recurring motif in Wylie's short book, namely that crocodiles trigger in humans an uncanny fear. "Even in our secular, technologized era," Wylie continues, "crocodiles remain an unsettling reminder of humans' natural vulnerability."[45] This affective reminder is perhaps motivated by two intersecting notions: first, as Wylie succinctly puts it, crocodilians are "one of the Earth's most extraordinary survivors."[46] Current scientific research indicates that crocodilians have existed since the Eocene, some 55 million years ago; our intellectualizing of these reptiles is therefore intimately bound up in the speculative and imaginative space of prehistory.[47] Secondly, and as a consequence of their permanence, our thinking about crocodiles often orients us back towards our own bodies, our own vulnerable flesh. It is not merely that crocodiles survive, then, but that they are equally capable of ripping us apart.

Wylie's conclusion redeploys this sense of a "tinge of fearfulness." This time, though, it is on a much larger scale. He concludes: "One does not have to accept apocalyptic scenarios of humanity's demise to find it credible that, ultimately, the crocodiles might well outlive us."[48] For Wylie, this particularly human fear is therefore threefold: crocodilians have not only survived for the *past* 55 million years; and not only do they have the potential in the *present* to harm our bodies; but also, and more importantly, crocodilians might well continue to exist long after our departure, well into the earth's posthuman *future*. It should be evident, then, why Herzog's mutated albino alligator resonates the way it does: the postscript performs Wylie's complex threefold "tinge of fearfulness," with the alligator pictured as a "prehistoric monster" that threatens the order of the film *and* humanity; as Barnaby Dicker and Nick Lee put it, Herzog's postcrocodile even "aggrandizes and belittles the bold achievements made in Chauvet cave."[49] The postscript thus opens up an imagined posthuman

[44] Wylie, *Crocodile*, 8.
[45] Ibid., 9.
[46] Ibid., 7.
[47] Buchanan, "Kambara taraina," 473.
[48] Wylie, 198.
[49] Dicker and Lee, "Image Wants Danger," 49.

time-space that bears witness to technics necessarily leaping ahead of itself. Through the biography of this albino alligator, Herzog's *Cave of Forgotten Dreams* ends by visualizing the extent to which humanity has, through technics, irrevocably changed the natural world.

Cave of Forgotten Dreams's postscript invites viewers to see a projection of a posthuman planet, of "what the world looks like when we're not there."[50] This is a world in which the nuclear might have destroyed the *anthropos*; a world in which alligators might no longer be in captivity; a world in which reptilians not only exchange gazes with one another, but are also able to develop an aesthetic faculty that allows them to look at and understand the Chauvet cave's paintings. Herzog's postscript thus takes Bataille's lectures on Lascaux to their logical conclusion, forecasting a world that is indeed reduced to humanity's material remains. Herzog's radioactive alligator therefore imaginatively bears witness to technics as a catastrophic *pharmakon* that has leapt ahead of itself and eliminated the *who*. Although Herzog's creature survives long into the future, though, its irradiated body—even the posthuman habitat in which it exists—is inscribed with humanity's trace. The inscription of technics necessarily extends beyond the human, now and forever: it remains, and its remains remain. This idea finds an uncanny articulation in the postscript's fabulated biography: here we are, in the Chauvet cave, alongside an albino alligator that, somehow, can look at the cave paintings and contemplate the entire human species through these inscriptions. Herzog's postscript testifies to the radical exteriorization of technics, depicting a posthuman future that is decidedly not *post-script*. The human might be long gone but its presence—its archive, its trace, its touch—remains, painted onto the cave and written into the alligator's genetic code. The alligator's biography, should we be able to recover it at all, should we be able to read it, tells us as much about the human as it does about the nonhuman.

WORKS CITED

Adorno, Theodor W. "The Essay as Form." In *Notes to Literature*, edited by Rolf Tiedemann, translated by Shierry Weber Nicholsen, 3–23. New York: Columbia University Press, 1991.

---

[50] Wolfe, *Posthumanism*, 177.

———. "Theories on the Origin of Art: Excursus." In *Aesthetic Theory*, edited by Gretel Adorno and Rolf Tiedemann, translated by Robert Hullot-Kentor, 325–331. London and New York: Continuum, 2002.

Ames, Eric. *Ferocious Reality: Documentary According to Werner Herzog*. Minneapolis: University of Minnesota Press, 2012.

Bataille, Georges. *The Cradle of Humanity: Prehistoric Art and Culture*. Edited and translated by Stuart Kendall and Michelle Kendall. New York: Zone, 2009.

Blanchot, Maurice. "The Birth of Art." In *Friendship*, translated by Elizabeth Rottenberg, 1–11. Stanford: Stanford University Press, 1997.

Buchanan, Lucas A. "Kambara taraina sp. nov. (Crocodylia, Crocodyloidea), a New Eocene mekosuchine from Queensland, Australia, and a Revision of the Genus." *Journal of Vertebrate Paleontology* 29 (2009): 473–486.

Bullock, Marcus P. "Germany's Lost Son, Germany's Dark Dream: Werner Herzog, Ecstasy, and *Einfühlung*." *Discourse* 36 (2014): 232–260.

Cave of Forgotten Dreams. Directed by Werner Herzog. UK: IFC Films, 2010. DVD.

Clottes, Jean. *Return to Chauvet Cave: Excavating the Birthplace of Art*. London: Thames and Hudson, 2003.

Corrigan, Timothy. *The Essay Film: From Montaigne to Marker*. Oxford and New York: Oxford University Press, 2011.

Deleuze, Gilles. *Cinema 1: The Movement-Image*. Translated by Hugh Tomlinson and Barbara Habberjam. Minneapolis: University of Minnesota Press, 1986.

Deleuze, Gilles and Félix Guattari. *A Thousand Plateaus: Capitalism and Schizophrenia*. Translated by Brian Massumi. Minneapolis: University of Minnesota Press, 1987.

Derrida, Jacques. *Dissemination*. Translated by Barbara Johnson. Chicago: University of Chicago Press, 1981.

———. "No Apocalypse, Not Now (Full Speed Ahead, Seven Missiles, Seven Missives)." Translated by Catherine Porter and Philip Lewis. *Diacritics* 14 (1984): 20–31.

Dicker, Barnaby and Nick Lee. "'But the Image Wants Danger': Georges Bataille, Werner Herzog, and Poetical Response to Paleoart." *Time and Mind* 5 (2012): 33–51.

La Ferme aux Crocodiles. "La Ferme aux Crocodiles." http://eng.lafermeaux-crocodiles.com. Accessed August 18, 2015.

Herzog, Werner. "The Minnesota Declaration." In *Ferocious Reality: Documentary According to Werner Herzog*, by Eric Ames, ix–x. Minneapolis: University of Minnesota Press, 2012.

———. "Why Being rather than Nothing?" *Framework* 3 (1975): 24–27.

Herzog, Werner and Paul Cronin. *Werner Herzog: A Guide for the Perplexed*. London: Faber and Faber, 2014.

Johnson, Christopher. "Science in Three Dimensions: Werner Herzog's *Cave of Forgotten Dreams*." *Modern Language Review* 109 (2014): 915–930.

Koepnick, Lutz. "Herzog's Cave: On Cinema's Unclaimed Pasts and Forgotten Futures." *The Germanic Review* 88 (2013): 271–285.

Lippit, Akira Mizuta. *Electric Animal: Toward a Rhetoric of Wildlife*. Minneapolis: University of Minnesota Press, 2000.

Lord, Catherine. "Only Connect: Ecology Between 'Late' Latour and Werner Herzog's *Cave of Forgotten Dreams*." *Global Discourse* 6 (2016): 119–132.

Morton, Timothy. "From Modernity to the Anthropocene: Ecology and Art in the Age of 28 Asymmetry." *International Social Science Journal* 63 (2012): 39–51.

Pettitt, Paul and Paul Bahn. "An Alternative Chronology for the Art of Chauvet Cave." *Antiquity* 89 (2015): 542–553.

Rayns, Tony. "*Cave of Forgotten Dreams*: Director: Werner Herzog." *Sight and Sound* April (2011): 52.

Sheehan, Paul. "Against the Image: Herzog and the Troubling Politics of the Screen Animal." *SubStance* 117 (2008): 117–136.

Stiegler, Bernard. *Technics and Time, 1: The Fault of Epimetheus*. Translated by Richard Beardsworth and George Collins. Stanford: Stanford University Press, 1998.

———. *Technics and Time, 3: Cinematic Time and the Question of Malaise*. Translated by Stephen Barker. Stanford: Stanford University Press, 2011.

Stiegler, Bernard and Peter Hallward. "Technics of Decision: An Interview." Translated by Sean Gaston. *Angelaki* 8 (2003): 151–168.

Wickman, Forrest. "Fact-checking Herzog's 'Ecstatic Truth': Are Those Alligators Really Radioactive Mutants?" *Slate Magazine*, May 13, 2011. http://www.slate.com/blogs/browbeat/2011/05/13/fact_checking_herzog_s_ecstatic_truth_are_those_alligators_really_radioactive_mutants.html. Accessed May 3, 2017.

Wolfe, Cary. *What is Posthumanism?* Minneapolis: University of Minnesota Press, 2010.

Wylie, Dan. *Crocodile*. London: Reaktion, 2013.

PART IV

Experiments

CHAPTER 11

The Elephant's I: Looking for Abu'l Abbas

Radhika Subramaniam

1

You might say the elephant has not been shy. No more than a few lines bring him onto the historical stage but much more ink has been spilled in commentary. It is in 801 AD that he appears first in the Royal Frankish Annals when notice of his impending arrival comes to the newly crowned emperor Charlemagne. While in Pavia in Italy's Lombardy, following his Christmas Day coronation in Rome by the Pope, Charlemagne receives word that two envoys have arrived, one from Baghdad and the other from the North African territory of Ifriqiya. They bring news of the embassy he sent to Abbasid caliphate two years earlier. Two of his ambassadors, Lantfrid and Sigimund, have died but the third, Isaac, is returning bringing with him gifts from Harun al-Rashid, the caliph of Baghdad, among which is an elephant. Isaac has made a long slow journey from

This text is adapted from an ongoing longer work of narrative non-fiction, also called *The Elephant's I*, which explores the challenge of telling stories across space, time, and species. As such, it is written without heavy recourse to citations in the body of the text; all historical and biological information is drawn from the sources listed in the bibliography. Al-Hindi is a plausible fiction.

R. Subramaniam (✉)
Parsons School of Design, The New School, New York, NY, USA

© The Author(s) 2018
A. Krebber, M. Roscher (eds.), *Animal Biography*,
Palgrave Studies in Animals and Literature,
https://doi.org/10.1007/978-3-319-98288-5_11

Baghdad to Ifriqiya where he awaits instruction. Charles swiftly dispatches his notary, Ercanbald, to make arrangements to bring over the animal and anything else that has been sent. The notary is evidently an efficient and resourceful man because it is not long after, in October of the same year, that the elephant and Isaac set sail from today's Tunisia, arriving at Porto Venere in Liguria.

Winter is approaching making the Alps impassable, so they remain in northern Italy at Vercelli, crossing the mountains the following year to arrive in Aachen on July 20, 802. With this entry, we learn the elephant's name: Abu'l Abbas (or Abul Abaz). The next mention of him is a brief line in the year 810. While in Aachen, Charlemagne receives word of an incursion by Godofrid, king of Denmark. Hastening immediately northward, he stops at Lippeham, probably near today's Wesel where the Lippe meets the Rhine. The elephant evidently accompanied him too, whether as a matter of course or not we do not know but the sentence about him is as abrupt as his demise: here the annalist interjects tersely, the elephant suddenly dies.

Rare is the history of the period that does not make mention of "Charlemagne's elephant." In most accounts, he is summoned as a symbol—of Charlemagne's growing stature and legend, the expansiveness of his reach, of cordial diplomatic ties with the eastern caliphate (although Arab sources are silent on the subject), for insight into the political alliances of the time, and as an exotic gift exchange. He is a charismatic token in an intertwined story of the Franks and the Abbasids, indeed often between Islam and Christendom, mediated by the figure of Isaac the Jew. This symbolic valence together with his status as an exotic in Europe is taken to be sufficient explanation for his presence. And what more might we really derive from the gnomic account of the annals?

Although Abu'l Abbas is well caught in the net of history, his own story remains strangely threadbare. I am not the first to wonder about the life behind the filament of a name woven into a grander tale. Nor am I the first to be snagged enough to want to follow it elsewhere. When you lift your eyes, forgotten lives, overlooked histories, and sidelined figures call from the shadows. It is tempting to reach across the smudged divide and draw them into the brightness of the weave—to pick, as I do now, at the strand of the elephant.

*   *   *

20 August, Germany

Dear J,

I am still on the wild-goose chase of the elephant. Is that a mixed metaphor? I couldn't get to the museum in Berlin in time to look at the oliphants—quite frankly, it seemed so forensic an approach unless it is to remind me that our relationship to animals always includes death and incorporation. How strange it is anyway to speak of ivory and elephants separately as if it is not all one being.

It turned out that there is actually a bit of ivory in the Treasury in Aachen which "could be" made from AA's tusks. So said the acoustiguide, although there is no evidence for this at all. When I ask the local museum folks about such an embellishment, I get a shrug. It's as if the town realizes it is participant in a myth and by that, I mean the entire Charlemagne complex, and isn't about to shatter it. But if it is true, this is as much the elephant's reliquary as the emperor's. AA is actually quite alive here appearing in comics and cartoons as "Karl's elefant" who is let loose for the summer like many other pets!

Can't wait to see you. With love, R

*   *   *

2

Who was the elephant before he stepped onto the pages of the Royal Frankish Annals? What do we know of the experience of Abu'l Abbas himself? What can we say of the animal behind both the symbol and the name? An epistolary historical fiction written by Lebanese writer Jamil Nakhla al-Mudawwar, published in Cairo in 1888, proffers a story. Called *Hadarat al-Islam fi dar ul Salam* (Muslim culture in Baghdad), it depicts life in Baghdad in the heyday of the Abbasid caliphate as described by the son of a nobleman from Khorasan in a series of letters home. This Persian is appointed in 802 AD by caliph Harun al-Rashid to head an embassy being sent to the Franks to seek an alliance against the Spanish Umayyads. He takes a number of presents including a large white elephant, formerly owned by Khalifa al-Mahdi, Harun's father, to whom it had been gifted by an Indian "malik" or king. Well received in its time, the book was clearly written as fiction; however, it is described as a relatively serious account, complete with references to several Arabic sources, leading scholars to speculate that Abu'l Abbas's journey might have originated in India.

By this time, elephants had largely disappeared from North Africa and Mesopotamia. Long past was the era of the Roman *venationes* in which elephants, lions, and other animals were brought to the Colosseum to be pitted against each other. The war elephants of Hannibal's well-remembered cohort, who made a similar crossing from Africa, were more likely to have been members of the smaller species of African forest elephant. In any case, the elephant of the Greek and Roman worlds was far enough in the distance that Abu'l Abbas would have been a sensation in Europe. While it is possible that African elephants were brought to the Arab world in the Abbasid period, it is even more likely that the elephants of the Arab empires were sourced through a mixture of tribute and gifts from farther east in India where elephant domestication had a much longer history. Elephants were a particular mark of prestige and wealth; they bestowed power and status on those who received them, whether through warfare or diplomacy.

On trade, travel, diplomatic relationships with, and general curiosity about India, there is considerable Arab testimony. Records show that around 800 AD, during Harun's reign, a delegation was sent to get medicinal herbs and return with more information about Indian religions and political conditions. Baghdad's *Bayt al-Hikma* or House of Wisdom, founded by the caliph, was a prominent hub for both humanities and the sciences, responsible for facilitating connections to Greek, Persian and Indian scholarship. Trade and exchange between the Arabs and India and China was active and ongoing.

From the east came sweet cardamom for coffee, black pepper for a kick, aromatic spices like camphor and cinnamon, light muslin for harsh sunlight, deep indigo and other dyes, glowing jade, bright gems, silver and metals, sturdy teak for ship's planks, and ivory and elephants. Boats left the Indian peninsula, sailing before the monsoon winds across the sea. Or they might stay within shallower waters, stopping at port after port all along the coastline from the Persian Gulf, until they dropped anchor along the coast of western India. On these ships came juicy dates, finished goods, fragrant frankincense, gleaming gold and Arab thoroughbred horses, light, fleet, whinnying and much desired by Indian kings for their armies.

These animals were at the core of traditional Indian military structure, the *chaturanga*, which was organized around four arms: elephants, horses, infantry, and chariots. Historian Thomas Trautmann argues that the war elephant was actually an Indian invention. By this, he means that in India, an entire complex of technology and culture had been constructed around the human-elephant relationship that included techniques of capturing wild adult male tuskers and training them for warfare. War elephants were inextricably linked to kingship by the requirements in resources and forms of warfare; in fact, royal investment probably played a considerable role in the conservation of elephant habitats. The classic Indian treatise on kingship, the *Arthashastra*, describes eight elephant forests across the country and the caliber of animals found in each. The possession of an elephant forest was an attribute of a typical kingdom and it was recommended that its superintendent maintain a census of the wild population and impose a death penalty on anyone who killed an elephant. Elephants contributed to royal prestige: kings could maintain large stables—keeping an elephant has never been cheap—and elephants were part of the life of a kingdom—used in war, paid in tribute or, as in the case of Abu'l Abbas, presented as gifts.

Sympathy for our elephant together with the slim contours of the account in the Frankish annals has, more recently, resulted in an actual biography for Abu'l Abbas. In 2011, German historian Achim Thomas Hack published just such a slender volume in which he said that the animal should be pitied for never having played a role in this story despite being flaunted in the titles of articles and covers of books. Hack is sensitive to the silence that surrounds the elephant's own experiences—his long journeys, the separation from his fellows especially during the last ten years of his life as well as the damp cold weather of his new Frankish home. Yet, in this somewhat wry biographical provocation to historiography, he also points out that about as little actual source material is available about human beings in the Middle Ages so that in this respect, the elephant is actually not that ill-served. It is no more possible to definitively attribute traits to Charlemagne than it is to discern the temperament of Abu'l Abbas.

* * *

Still Aug, Germany

Hello J, Got a cab from the station and predictably, the driver was South Asian. It took us scarcely a minute to establish our antecedents. Here again is another taxicab tale of migration. He gave me a little potted history of the town, strangely proud of its panzer production during the war. He has two daughters who are growing up German, another matter of pride. Not since his parents died five years ago has he been back home to Sheikhupura. Yet another of many casual interchanges between supposedly hostile neighbors, only possible at a geographical remove from the subcontinent. It makes me wonder what separates and unites us—the cabbie and I as much as the elephant and I—and how distance and familiarity get configured to knit connections or create rifts.

I've bought an illustrated volume of Grimm's Fairy Tales from the museum as a gift and am trying to keep it from getting too thumbed with my own reading. Where do the animals that so abundantly populate the waking and dreaming worlds of childhood recede? And how can they return? It is through a dream that elephants spoke to bioacoustician Katy Payne when she was researching their communication at an Oregon zoo. She had just put two and two together about the vibrations she sensed near the Asian elephant enclosure. The elephants were communicating infrasonically. No sooner had she realized this than they appeared around her at night to say, "We did not reveal this to you so you would tell other people." Payne describes telling her parents about both the discovery and the dream at the end of a Thanksgiving meal. The account is folded into a larger tale of loss— of the family farm, of a marital relationship, of once being part of a "we" rather than an individual, and of a childhood in which she was introduced to trees by the taste of their sap, and surrounded by creatures in stories read and told to her—from Ratty, Mole and Toad of Wind in the Willows to a beloved familial character, Johnny Possum, a somewhat curmudgeonly, sleepy being created by her father. I too invented nighttime stories for my sister of a family of hedgehogs (an animal we'd never seen) who were friendly with an itinerant teapot. What else do we forfeit as age defamiliarizes an enchanted world of talking animals and travelling objects—when we lose our easy mobility between these worlds and with it, our comprehension of them? But perhaps, as the spells of enchantment recede in our minds, these objects and creatures are set free.

And indeed, I am looking at those escape artists, the Town Musicians of Bremen in their wonderful geometry, one atop the other, and trying to be—forgive the pun—less grim(m). Love to all, R

* * *

3

This is a tale of legends.

Charlemagne, born Charles, nicknamed David, once described as "the lion who reigns over all living creatures and wild beasts," kept a type of animal reserve in Aachen where they were maintained both for hunting and as "ornament." Unlike courtly menageries, this *brogilus*, as it was termed in medieval Latin, was more than a site of captive display; it included both game animals like stags, deer, and boar as well as exotic species such as peacocks, panthers and may well have housed our elephant. The bust reliquary in the treasury at Aachen shows Charles with long curling hair, trimmed beard and mustache, and erect head and shoulders. Glowing reddish gold, the bust is studded with the eagle heraldry that would come to symbolize his reign. His sarcophagus now lies near the beautiful octagonal cathedral in Aachen where he was once disinterred, two hundred years after his death, by Otto III, who, so the story goes, found his body seated upright with a scepter, in perfect condition, ready to be the stuff of legend. Otto refreshed the body with oils and before it was reburied, he wrapped it in a purple cloth decorated with elephants.

Harun al-Rashid, khalifa or caliph of Baghdad, *amir al-mumineen* or the Commander of the Faithful, acquired some of his legendary status through a series of tales in which he was often featured as the central protagonist. These tales of the *Thousand and One Nights*, sometimes known as the *Arabian Nights*, were cliffhangers recounted every night by master storyteller, Scheherezade to king Shahryar in a bid to save her life. The unbearable suspense hanging over the bedchamber as dawn rose would prompt the monarch to grant another night's reprieve in anticipation of the next chapter in the tale. Prominent characters in these stories were Harun, his Grand Vizier, Yahya al-Barmaki, and Yahya's son, Ja'far, also a dear friend to the caliph. A master of disguise, Harun was known to wander at night through the streets of Baghdad in Ja'far's company so he could eavesdrop on the daily lives of his subjects. The Barmakids were a family of great prominence who wielded tremendous influence in the affairs of the kingdom only to fall so far out of favor as to be executed in one of the caliph's bloody purges.

In Harun's time, the caliphate formed the center of an Islamic world that had expanded farther east since the Arab invasion of Sind in 712 AD. Baghdad, the relatively new Abbasid capital on the banks of the Tigris, was a well-designed cosmopolitan city with a vibrant intellectual life fostered by the patronage of the caliphs. Little is on record in Arabic sources of matters to the west so we cannot confirm the assertion of Einhard, Charlemagne's faithful courtier, who contends that the elephant was expressly requested by the emperor and that the caliph, as a mark of high esteem, sent him the only one he had. Was it more likely that Harun was preoccupied with the domestic intrigues of his court, or the establishment of another library or with a minor skirmish in his eastern periphery when the Frankish embassy arrived and the question was raised of the elephant? And perhaps irritated by the interruption on a matter from such a trifling quarter, did he wave a dismissive hand sanctioning this "re-gift" so that history could not catch this thread among the hundreds being spun every night in the royal bedchamber and weave them into the weft at number one thousand and two?

The Malik who was the source of the elephant gifted to caliph al-Mahdi, makes his appearance in al-Mudawwar's nineteenth century account of the renown of the Abbasids. If this was Ballahara, whom Arab sources of the ninth and tenth centuries describe as the greatest of all kings of al-Hind (India), *malik al-hikma*, lord of wisdom, his was a magnificent court, his cities of teak and bamboo, and his armies with innumerable horses and elephants. In fact, a Deccan inscription named him "the fierce lord of the elephant force" and in Arabic he was *malik al-fil* or "lord of elephants." Ballahara is believed to be Vallabharaja, an epithet meaning "beloved king" used by the Rashtrakuta kings of western and southern India. Arab writers were as eloquent about Indian kings and their wealth as they were silent about their European counterparts. The Rashtrakuta kings allied themselves with the Arabs against their mutual foes, the Gurjara Pratiharas, who stood to the north in opposition to Arab expansion beyond the Indus.

According to André Wink, until the tenth century, the largest settlements of Arab and Persian Muslim traders were in the welcoming territories of the Rashtrakutas along India's Gujarat and Konkan coasts; trade moved farther south to the ports of the Malabar only in later centuries when exchange shifted from the Persian Gulf to the Red Sea and Fatimid Egypt. When the matter of a gift to his Arab allies arose in his court, did Ballahara, in his infinite wisdom, issue a command to select an elephant from a royal *pilkhana* that had too many to count? Let us imagine that this was Abu'l Abbas who might have begun his life in one of the royal elephant forests, source of the stately *kumeriah* elephant.

The legend of Isaac is even fainter. Some historians have tried to follow his gentle trace in the archive if only to remind us that this was more than just an interchange between the Christian empire and the Islamic caliphate. The fact remains that for all his ambassadorial work, all we surely know of Isaac, so soon bereft of his Frankish companions, was that he was Jewish. His story is apparently preserved in Jewish tradition, with unknown sources, connected to the dispatch of Rabbi Makhir of Babylonia. According to legend, the rabbi was related by marriage to the Carolingians and a leader or "nasi" of the Jewish community in Narbonne. A slender and singular essay by F.W. Buckler on the relationship between Charles and Harun draws on Russian scholarship to outline some of the questions that have been raised about Isaac's role. Why did the envoys from Baghdad and Ifriqiya go on ahead and entrust the elephant and the gifts to Isaac? Under what circumstances could Isaac make his journey to Baghdad and back? The route the returning embassy took, over North Africa through the territory of Abbasid ally, emir Ibrahim ibn Aghlab, suggests that Isaac and his entourage planned their travel through regions that were friendly to the caliphate. Medieval Jewish merchants called Radhanites were active in trade networks across vast swathes of Europe and Asia. Perhaps Isaac was selected for the embassy because of a connection to these networks; yet, he may only have left a mark in the annals because his travel companions died—the two ambassadors who, despite their early demise, are mentioned by name. However, neither Isaac nor the dead envoys could be assumed to know anything about the care of animals, least of all one as imposing and foreign as an elephant.

No captive travels alone. Who, then, is the man who leaves no trace except one we can presume by the presence of Abu'l Abbas? Who rolled fodder and molasses into a ball to feed the elephant? Calmed him when frightened, coaxed him forward when recalcitrant or tempered his moods when raging with musth? Who stood ready to persuade him onto the boat in Ifriqiya at the end of a dusty trek, prepared to embark on what was certainly their last maritime journey together? Who might have ridden him forward to strike terror in the hearts of Charlemagne's foes?

From the time of Ptolemy II, mahouts or elephant handlers accompanied their Indian charges and were often recruited to train other elephants. For a long while, it was believed that elephants could understand only the language of these men, described by Scullard on the basis of Aelian's early commentary as "elephant talk," and would not respond to other commands. In Hellenistic usage, handlers or riders were generically called "Indian," no matter what their origin. Indian mahouts may well have eventually passed on their knowledge and training to local apprentices; nevertheless, "Indos" remained an appellation, signifying a relationship to elephants rather than any ethnic affiliation, and often used in a military context. A news report from a British colonial officer in 1927, speaking about an effort underway in the Belgian Congo to train African elephants, states that seven Indian mahouts were brought in as instructors. Neither the Belgians nor the Indians nor presumably the Azande training recruits spoke one another's languages. However, even after the Indian trainers left, what remained were not only the system of training they had imparted but also words of command in "distorted Tamil."

In the sixteenth century, a mahout from Kerala came along with the young Asian elephant, Hanno, acquired by Pope Leo X. As late as the 1970s, when Baghdad Zoo imported an Indian elephant, a mahout from Assam was in tow. While the *Arthasastra* lists many jobs in the royal stables from veterinarian to rider, forager to foot-chainer, decorator to foot cleaner, it is likely that each elephant had a single handler closely associated with him or her. Even in today's camps and temples in South Asia, there is usually a two- or three-member team associated with each elephant—mainly a mahout and a grass cutter. This mahout often trained an elephant from the outset, working through a series of semi-ritual, semi-constrained, repetitive activities, aided by other men and elephants. The time, care, and attention demanded by an elephant, from the vast quantities of forage to regimens of grooming, exercise, and training, have meant that the mahout's relationship to his elephant could even supersede that with his family. Did such a man, already torn between these relationships, make the journey with Abu'l Abbas to Baghdad? And was this man—let me call him *al-Hindi*, Arabic for The Indian—recruited for his necessary expertise by Isaac to take yet another journey with an animal that only he really knew? While the death of his fellow Franks could be responsible for thrusting the Jewish Isaac into the annals, the mahout is forever obscured behind the elephant. For now, think of them waiting together on the shores of the Mediterranean: Isaac, his heart and eyes turning toward home, standing as guide to two migrants: Abu'l Abbas and al-Hindi.

*   *   *

October, Italy

Dear J,

You're right—it gets harder every day to think of this Mediterranean crossing. The news is terrible. Every face I see demands that I try to imagine the arduous and desperate journeys that lie behind it. I think once more of the encounter in Athens in 2011. Do you remember my telling you?

At the height of the Greek recession, the city was volatile with frequent protests and demonstrations, often with strong anti-immigrant sentiment. We'd sit with a drink in one of the roadside tavernas after our sessions, often accosted by immigrant hawkers and peddlers selling cheap children's toys and small trinkets. Most were obviously Bangladeshi. One evening, one of them proffered something. I smiled, ready to initiate a little conversation.

Bangla? Bengali? Though our eyes met more than once, it was as if without recognition. He turned away. I remember characterizing it as a "wild encounter," one beyond comprehension, beyond relationship. What lay behind those eyes—the rigors of his journey, daily fear and vulnerability, a life lived on the edge of precariousness? I felt shamefully unable to find a bridge as I did so casually the other time with the cabbie from Sheikhupura.

What flashes into my mind is the description of the eyes of the chimpanzee from whom Kafka's Red Peter—the ape who learns to be human and makes a report to the academy about his transformation—derives comfort some nights. The eyes that the ape says still held the insane look of bewilderment of the "half-trained." Struggling to respond to the enigma presented by those eyes is sometimes what I feel I'm up against—wild eyes, beyond sight, beyond shared experience, beyond recognition.

When an elephant is brought into the control of humans, say the Sanskrit verses of the *Matanga-lila* (Elephant Sport) describing the process of making a village elephant, it is an experience of grief, fear and bewilderment. There is that word again, bewilderment: where sense and the senses go astray. Notice how the word 'wild' hides within it. The longing for its former freedom and the memory of its forest life on mountain ridges and lotus pools and among other elephants never leaves the animal; thus, he or she may be tamed but is never quite domesticated. So, perhaps it's right that AA should elude my grasp. You seem out of reach too. It's my turn to be perplexed. R

*   *   *

4

Why conjure up al-Hindi, you might ask? Why not propel our imaginations toward a sympathetic conception of the elephant itself? There is often a headlong rush to "give voice" that follows a glimpse of the erasures and silences of history. Such giving voice to the assumed voiceless, especially alongside a longstanding characterization of animals as "dumb creatures," in all senses of the term, permits all too easy forms of ventriloquism. Placing the mahout between us is like being asked for a password into another world. His knowledge and familiarity proffers an invitation, a possibility, but it is simultaneously a barrier against easy access. We may reach across the channel he opens but the centuries of interspecies contact embodied in him reminds us that entry isn't quickly gained. There is no rosetta stone for "elephant talk." And indeed, rather than thrusting forward in our effort to give voice or even to communicate, what if we instead held back and tried to listen? What story might be told *to* us not *by* us? Listen. What passes in the space between Abu'l Abbas and al-Hindi? What makes or has made worlds that are both elephant and human?

For all that we think about the trumpeting of elephants, it actually isn't always easy to hear them. Beyond and below the rumbles, squeals, trumpets that are part of the elephant language repertoire, they also communicate infrasonically. Anywhere from 14 to 24 Hz, these mostly fall below the human auditory threshold of 20 Hz. When Katy Payne first identified this in the mid-1980s, she described it as a "throbbing in the air." She and her fellow researchers recorded the environment around the elephants at the zoo. These recordings included what was audible to their ears and what seemed to be vibrations, which they were later able to identify as infrasonic communication between the elephants themselves. Spectrographs visually register sounds at the low end of the frequency spectrum and if the sound recording itself is sped up several times, it can be made audible to the ear.

Low frequencies carry across vast distances, their overtones less attenuated across space. Researchers in Southern Africa found that large herds went into hiding in advance of an organized elephant cull, either indicating that they could, at a great distance, pick up the low frequency sound of the helicopter from which the elephants were being shot or that an infrasonic alarm was sent out across the expanse of the park from herd to herd. In the oceans, fin whales communicate in infrasonic frequencies across the entire Atlantic. On land, elephants are one of the very few to do the same.

In Oregon, Payne and her fellow researchers had been watching the elephants closely as they recorded. When they sensed the vibrations, it seemed that there was also a slight fluttering in the skin of the elephant's forehead. This was something keepers at the zoo had already observed—a reminder of how informal knowledge and expertise are often made to wait in the wings for public recognition—and it was also a sign that the elephants might be behind the throbbing in the air. It is when the team returned to the lab and identified the strange shudder as infrasonic waves that the elephants came to her in a dream to warn against revelation. The next day, she writes, the dream continued to drum on her heart.

Deep listening drums in the body. Elephants know this. They produce low vocalizations at such high amplitudes that they run along the earth's surface separate from their airborne counterparts. This collaboration of sound waves with the earth is picked up by elephants' bodies in a literal manifestation of what Caitlin O'Connell-Rodwell calls "keeping an 'ear' to the ground." Seismic information is sensed through the feet, up the bones to the ear. A cushion of acoustic fat keeps the elephant's foot quite literally on its toes and ever alert to sound waves. The elephant turns its body toward the sound, sometimes lifting a foot, which has cells within sensitive to vibration. There are few other percussionists on this channel except for thunder so it offers a quiet and discreet line of communication, one that is often perceived by us as a premonitory or telepathic "secret sense."

Mahouts have probably long known about various forms of elephant communication. Elephant training itself is a discipline of both sound and body. Most mahout traditions use a mixture of speech, song, touch, and pressure to develop their relationship with an elephant. In his work among Khamti mahouts in Arunachal Pradesh in India, Nicolas Lainé recounts the different songs that are sung at the first stage of training, when the elephant, tied to a stake, is rubbed and caressed in order to make it accustomed to human contact. Other songs and rhymes follow as the elephant is taught to respond to words of command. Chants, songs, and music are key to the metamorphosis of a forest elephant. Piers Locke's research in Nepal and other accounts from Southern India also describe folk and other songs that accompany the various stages of training. But together with words and chants is touch. While the *ankus*, the curved elephant goad or bullhook, is one of the earliest icons of human mastery over elephants, an experienced mahout might only display it in a symbolic manner. As he sits on the back of an elephant, the mahout presses his bare feet behind the elephant's ears, communicating with the animal through a language of pressure.

It may have taken more than pressure behind the ears to impel Abu'l Abbas forward at various stages of his journey. Before his journey across the Mediterranean, the elephant was probably well into the fourth or fifth decade of his life. Poised to step into the annals as a gift that signified the magnificence of both giver and recipient, he is not much younger than his new patron, the almost 60-year old emperor. Soon he will be Abu'l Abbas. The name itself has been a source of some speculation. Scholars have suggested that Abul Abaz, as the annals first have it, or Abu'l Abbas, the more likely Arabic term, simply signified his origins as an Abbasid gift. The name, meaning "father of Abbas" might refer to the progenitor of the Abbasids, the first caliph Abu'l Abbas al-Saffah. Or perhaps it referred to the elephant who appears in the *surah al-fil* of the Qur'an whose patronymic is Abu'l Abbas. Might Abu'l Abbas therefore have been some kind of generic Arab usage for elephant? Another theory uses a linguistic route to suggest that the name could mean "father of frowns" or "father of wrinkles" based on the folds and furrows of an elephant's skin. Whatever the source, the fact remains that an Indian elephant usually acquires a name in the transition from forest to village. So he would have had one from the moment of his earliest training. This is probably the one by which al-Hindi, if not history, continued to address him. Al-Hindi's own name may have disappeared in this transition. In some mahout traditions, naming conventions involve the mahout incorporating the elephant's name into his own. Describing the mahouts or "*ane-mottans*" of Mudumalai in southern India, Zvelebil says that the mahout of an elephant named Bommi, for instance, is likely to be called Bommimottan rather than by his own personal name. A name is one step in a series of transformations that happen together between mahout and elephant.

Surely the elephant's feet grew sore and abraded by the long journeys outside the soft floor of his native forests and required care. How did his digestion deal with the continual changes in forage and browse? An elephant's enormous requirement for fodder would have meant that sating his appetite was a full-time job—as it would have been in the elephant stables of India where the task of a grass or forage cutter is one of the key roles in an elephant management team. Bathing was essential and finding the source for a daily plunge or watering was probably one of the most trying imperatives. It is possible that they were occasionally obligated to travel at night in order to keep the animal away from the blazing sunlight along the journey.

Did Abu'l Abbas, like any full-grown male elephant in his prime, go into *musth*—a period of sexual potency with elevated testosterone levels that, several times a year, makes male elephants eager to mate and fight off competitors? The sides of his face would be streaming with fluid from his temporal glands, his demeanor wild and fierce. Musth was often regarded as an ideal attribute of a war elephant. An array of towering animals, fearless and aggressive, their faces streaming, was a sight that cowed many an opposing army. War elephants were also roused to battle by plying them with alcohol. Off the field of battle, it requires an experienced handler to control a male elephant during a period of musth, one who might not only chain the animal but also curb his food intake or use special herbs to stem the ferocity. While the journey surely took its toll on everyone in the party, the responsibility of keeping Abu'l Abbas in fine fettle for his presentation to the emperor could have made it especially burdensome.

Is it possible that the Baghdadi envoy who accompanied this unconventional entourage was sorely tried by the many demands placed on it by his fellow traveler? The needs of an elephant are neither simple nor easily fulfilled—and an irritated swipe from a trunk could knock a man to the ground. Spying the chance for a reprieve, perhaps he leaped at the chance to accompany his Aghlabid counterpart, foregoing the spectacle of arriving with an elephant for a quiet appearance before Charlemagne in advance of Isaac. Was the still inconsequential Isaac left behind to deal with difficulties of the elephant and his man? In Hannibal's time, centuries earlier, Carthaginians had managed to ship elephants to Sicily and Spain but this knowledge had receded with time. So, the envoys and Charlemagne's notary probably relied on the ingenuity and know-how of Genoese and Ifriqiyan seafarers to build an elephant transport.

We cannot be sure if this was only the second sea voyage that elephant and mahout took together but it is possible. Their journey from India could have begun, as Barry Flood has suggested, through a series of ritualized gift exchanges from the eastern edge of the empire in Sind from governor to sultan to petty king all the way to the Khalifa. However, if the elephant began his career in the Rashtrakuta stables before he was gifted to the caliph, it is just as likely that he and the mahout avoided the hostile territories of the Pratihara empire to their north and traveled by a different route to Baghdad. Let us say they came by ship, cradling the coastline, crossing the waters up the river to the capital. With their maritime experience, elephant and man may have crossed the Mediterranean with greater fortitude if not less trepidation. Did al-Hindi now sing those songs of first encounter and transformation, reminding himself more than Abu'l Abbas that there were new experiences ahead? Did it now occur to him how he and the elephant were once thus made one together?

*   *   *

Leaving soon.

J, I am trying to listen to you. Our own communication needs more elephant-like tricks that can travel across distances. I've been looking at the recordings from the Elephant Listening Project at Cornell—and look is what I mean since here you can see spectrographs that show us elephant calls made at frequencies below the hearing threshold of humans. Such sounds travel farther as their overtones are less diminished across space.

I find myself dreaming of al-Hindi, already so obscure and passing into oblivion. When did the realization hit that his own language was just rattling like rotting teeth in his mouth? All he had left from home was "elephant talk," a language only the animal would understand. Did he repeat instructions just to savor the sounds, or whisper again and again the chants and words that only he and Abu'l Abbas shared together? Did he trace their journeys on the pressure points of the animal's body waiting for Abu'l Abbas's trunk to reach out with a reassurance of their shared tongue? What did he do after the death of his fellow migrant? Did he reach out in his dreams for Abu'l Abbas?

It's always been surprising to me that most references to Katy Payne's complex account of elephants and humans reduce it to "infrasonic communication" because there is so much more in her book, *Silent Thunder*, about her own attempts to come to terms with science, conservation, indigenous people in the wildlife game and the elephants themselves. When the elephants appear with their injunction in her dream, Payne says, that is the elephant as subject. Many dreams appear in the book for they are the ways in which the Shona and Ndebele scouts and trackers with whom she worked often communicate across long distances, in parallel to, although this remains unsaid, the elephants' own communication. In her scientific articles, elephants are the objects of discovery. In her dreams, she receives them because she listens. Listening implies being attentive but is that enough any more?

Think of the speaking buffalo of Pietro Marcello's film Lost and Beautiful (*Bella e Perduta*). Have you seen it? It's a semi-documentary fantasy in which a foolish servant, Pulcinella, is sent from deep within Mt. Vesuvius to Campania to rescue a young buffalo calf named Sarchiapone. The calf can speak and he eloquently describes his condition as they travel through the countryside. As long as the fool Pulcinella remains the masked figure of commedia dell'arte, he is able to hear and understand the animal. But at some point during the journey, he falls in love, gets distracted and removes his theatrical mask. Suddenly, his comprehension ceases. The buffalo becomes nothing special, just an animal that is eventually led to slaughter— as the calf goes, he says, when men do not believe you have a soul, being a buffalo is an art. It is as if theatre and art—the worlds of make believe and belief—are essential to access the revelations of animals.

I imagine al-Hindi lying awake some nights, sensing underneath a low vibration that he cannot hear. I close my own eyes to listen. For it is only in that open channel of wild yearning and deep hallucination that is the mind's eye that I think I might find the elephant's I.

Yours, R

*   *   *

5

When a figure obscured in the historical record catches our attention, the search for textual and material traces often begins—in archives and documents, architecture and museums—in a hunt for the small pieces through which to build a picture. For Abu'l Abbas, I could go looking for ivory oliphants, carved chessmen, sculptural elements on buildings, for drawings, paintings, and mosaics that depict elephants. But surely this strategy and anything unearthed by it says more about our forensic imagination than anything about the elephant himself. If our approach to animal biography is to track animals, even with all the attunement of a hunter, do we not also risk creating only the carcass of a life? How do we respond to the demand placed not only upon forms of expression but also on modes of research by lives that overlap with but exceed our experience? What can we learn from Sarchiapone the buffalo's assertion in the film that where there is no recognition of one's being, the act of being itself must become an art?

Is there an art to hearing Abu'l Abbas? What call travels outward from him, skirting under the human ear to reach across space, its harmonics multiplying from that first fundamental note? What does it say? Did it once start and keep oscillating steadily outward until, through time, it reached through to pull in the willing earwitness against whose ossicles it now vibrates just enough to become perceptible? Finnish composer, Kaija Saariaho, insists that all composers work with full awareness of the ways in which a listener's ear is manipulated. Composition is about movement and time. In my attempt to stop time, she says in an interview, I have the irrational feeling that, if I succeed, time will become space and I'll be able to enter a secret realm where I've never been before. ... the physical parameters are muddled; it's like a secret invitation to find the celestial pattern that would contain the solution.

Can sounds really travel across time, you ask? Musician and writer David Rothenberg in his book *Why Birds Sing* describes scientific claims that mockingbirds might be imitating the calls and songs of birds now extinct. If 85% of the mockingbird's song is not composed of easily identifiable imitations, he continues, then they might be the sounds of birds no longer with us, making the song of the mockingbird not a fanfare but an elegy. Might we conjecture that the actions regarded as premonitory, telepathic and part of what has been called "the hidden life of elephants," respond, in part, to information gleaned by them from ancestral communication transmitted from one to another over millennia?

Is it fanciful to wonder whether the throbbing in the air that Payne described, that al-Hindi would have felt near Abu'l Abbas, was the elephant calling out a message to his own, reaching, searching for those far-flung and left behind, telling them of new dangers, new experiences, new futures to come? A throbbing in the air that rolls as a wave across the planet. Listen. Sense it in the ground beneath your feet. Feel it in the skin behind your ear.

Here's your invitation. Listen to the earth as you walk forward. Stand still with your feet on the ground. Sense your sole and feel the long limbs of your legs as tuning forks above the earth. Listen. Perhaps you can feel a fluttering on your own forehead, between your eyes, a low throbbing that sends a thrill through your body. That is the drumming of your heart, the call of your mind's eye, the secret channel of communication that only you dare enter. Heed it. Is it the elephant? It's your call.

Acknowledgments I am grateful to André Krebber and Mieke Roscher for the generative context they created at the Animal Biographies conference in Kassel; to Carla Freccero for comments on an earlier version of the essay; to Philip Schauss who translated several sources from the German for me; to Frank Pohle for the introduction to the cartoon world of "Karl's elefant"; and to John Bruce who introduced me to the film *Bella e Perduta*.

References

Aelian. *On the Characteristics of Animals.* Translated by A.F. Scholfield. Cambridge: Harvard University Press, 1959.

Ahmad, S. Maqbul. *Indo-Arab Relations: An Account of India's Relations with the Arab World from Ancient Up to Modern Times.* New Delhi: Indian Council of Cultural Relations, 1969.

Altekar, A.S. *The Rashtrakutas and their Times.* Poona: Oriental Book Agency, 1934.

Alter, Stephen. *Elephas Maximus: A Portrait of the Indian Elephant.* New York: Harcourt, 2004.

Bedini, Silvio. *The Pope's Elephant.* Manchester: Carcanet Press, 1997.

Buckler, F.W. *Harunu'l Rashid and Charles the Great.* Cambridge, MA: The Medieval Academy of America, 1931.

Clot, André. *Harun al-Rashid and the World of 1001 Nights.* London: Saqi Books, 2005.

Edgerton, Franklin W., trans. *The Elephant-Lore of the Hindu: The Elephant-sport (Matanga-lila) of Nilakantha.* New Haven: Yale University Press, 1931.

Einhard and Notker the Stammerer. *Two Lives of Charlemagne*. Translated and with an introduction by Lewis Thorpe. London: Penguin Books, 1969.

Dutton, Paul Edward. *Charlemagne's Mustache and Other Cultural Clusters of a Dark Age*. New York and Hampshire: Palgrave Macmillan, 2004.

Flood, Finbarr Barry. *Objects of Translation: Material Culture and Medieval "Hindu-Muslim" Encounter*. Princeton: Princeton University Press, 2009.

Hack, Achim Thomas. *Abul Abaz: Zur Biographie eines Elefanten*. Badenweiler: Wissenschaftlicher Verlag Bachmann, 2011

Hall, Tarquin. *To the Elephant Graveyard*. New Delhi: Penguin Books India, 2009.

Haraway, Donna J. *When Species Meet*. Minneapolis: University of Minnesota Press, 2008.

Hart, Lynette and Sundar. "Family Traditions for Mahouts of Asian Elephants." *Anthrozoos* 13.1 (2000): 34–42.

Hart, Lynette and Piers Locke. "Indian and Nepali Mahouts and their Unique Relationship with Elephants." In *Encyclopedia of Human-Animal Relationships Vol. 2*, edited by Marc Bekoff, 510–515. Westport CT: Greenwood Press, 2007.

Heuschkel, Gunnar. "Zum Aachener Tiergehege zur Zeit Karls des Grossen." In *Ex Oriente: Isaak und der weisse Elefant: Bagdad-Jerusalem-Aachen*, 144–155. Mainz am Rhein: P. von Zabern, 2003.

Hodges, Richard. "Charlemagne's Elephant." *History Today* 50.12 (2000): 21–27.

Hourani, George F. *Arab Seafaring in the Indian Ocean in Ancient and Early Medieval Times*. Princeton: Princeton University Press, 1951.

Kistler, John M. *War Elephants*. Lincoln and London: University of Nebraska Press, 2007.

Lahiri Choudhury, D.K. "The Indian Elephant in a Changing World." In *Contemporary Indian Tradition: Voices on Culture, Nature and the Challenge of Change*, edited by Carla M. Borden, 301–321. Washington and London: Smithsonian Institution Press, 1989.

Lainé, Nicolas. "Pratiques Vocales et Dressage Animal: Les Melodies Huchées des Khamti a leurs Éléphants (Nord-est Indien)." In *Chant pensé, chant vécu, temps chanté: Formes, usages et representations des pratiques vocales*, edited by Charlotte Poulet and Nicolas Bénard, 187–203. Sampzon: Éditions Delatour France, 2016.

Locke, Piers. "History, Practice, Identity: An Institutional Ethnography of Elephant Handlers in Chitwan, Nepal." Phd diss., University of Kent, 2006.

Mao-Takacs, Clément. "A Conversation with Kaija Saariaho." *Music and Literature*, No. 5, September 25, 2014.

Moss, Cynthia. *Elephant Memories: Thirteen Years in the Life of an Elephant Family*. Chicago: University of Chicago Press, 2000.

Payne, Katy. *Silent Thunder*. New York: Simon and Schuster, 1998.

Rothenberg, David. *Why Birds Sing.* New York: Basic Books, 2005.

Scholz, Bernhard Walter and Barbara Rogers, trans. *Carolingian Chronicles. Royal Frankish Annals and Nithard's Histories.* Ann Arbor: University of Michigan Press, 1970.

Saramago, José. *The Elephant's Journey.* Translated by Margaret Jull Costa. Boston: Mariner Books and Houghton Mifflin Harcourt, 2010.

Scigliano, Eric. *Love, War and Circuses.* New York: Houghton Mifflin, 2002

Scullard, H.H. *The Elephant in the Greek and Roman World.* Cambridge, UK: Thames and Hudson, 1974.

Shalem, Avinoam. *The Oliphant: Islamic Objects in Historical Context.* Leiden: Brill, 2004.

Sukumar, Raman. *Elephant Days and Nights: Ten Years with the Indian Elephant.* Delhi: Oxford University Press, 1994.

Sypeck, Jeff. *Becoming Charlemagne.* New York: Harper Collins, 2006.

"Taming African Elephants." (From our Kenya Correspondent) *The Times of London,* April 9, 1927.

Trautmann, Thomas R. *Elephants and Kings: An Environmental History.* Kindle edition. Chicago: University of Chicago Press, 2015.

Wink, André. *Al-Hind: The Making of the Indo-Islamic World.* Leiden: Brill, 1990.

Zeier, Kristin. "Baghdad, Jerusalem, Aachen: On the Trail of the White Elephant." *Deutsche Welle,* July 21, 2003. http://dw.com/p/3sG9. Accessed September 17, 2017.

Zvelebil, K.V. "'Elephant Language' of the Mahouts of Mudumalai Wildlife Sanctuary." *Journal of the American Oriental Society* 9.4 (1979): 675–676.

CHAPTER 12

Topsy: The Elephant We Must Never Forget

Kim Stallwood

INTRODUCTION

They say an elephant never forgets. If only we were equally capable of remembering every elephant whose life was ended by hunting, poaching, habitat loss and destruction, and human greed for their ivory, we may not be witnessing their impending extinction. There are fewer than 50,000 elephants in Asia and half a million in Africa.[1] About 100 years ago, there were 100,000 elephants in Asia and 5 million in Africa.

There is one Asian elephant whose biography recounts a tragic life and a gruesome death we should never forget. Topsy's biography reveals archaic animal cruelty unimaginable today; nonetheless, harm to individual elephants and threats to entire populations are as significant now as they were in her time. Moreover, this elephant, who was born around 1875 and came to an untimely death in 1903, unwittingly played a prominent role in the development of the USA as an industrial empire and producer of films and entertainment. In writing Topsy's biography, I draw from contemporaneous newspaper reports and other sources, including

[1] Mathiesen, "Elephants."

K. Stallwood (✉)
Independent Scholar, Hastings, UK

© The Author(s) 2018
A. Krebber, M. Roscher (eds.), *Animal Biography*,
Palgrave Studies in Animals and Literature,
https://doi.org/10.1007/978-3-319-98288-5_12

elephant traders and trainers, regarding key moments in her life; information about other elephants who also lived in zoos and circuses during that period; and current research regarding the sentience of elephants living in the wild and in captivity that also yield insight into their thoughts and emotions. Topsy's life mattered to her, and her biography deserves to be known. The function of a biography is to make the subject visible by recovering and reconstructing the life of an individual, regardless of species. Empowered with this enlightened perspective, the false claims of anthropomorphism and anthropocentrism in writing the biography of nonhuman animals are rejected. Empathy and compassion for nonhuman animals empower a connection and imagination about Topsy's life as an individual sentient being. Accordingly, humans are referred to as human animals and animals as nonhuman animals, and as subjects, not objects.[2]

The once prevailing view of René Descartes (1596–1650) that nonhuman animals are machine-like, devoid of self-intentions or self-drive is no longer generally held to be true.[3] Charles Darwin (1809–1882) recognised that the difference between "man and the higher animals, great as it is, certainly is one of degree and not of kind."[4] In 2012, a prominent group of scientists released the Cambridge Declaration on Consciousness, which formally acknowledges that nonhuman animals possess "the neurological substrates that generate consciousness."[5] This emerging awareness of nonhuman animal sentience is welcomed as it encourages more enlightened relationships between human animals and nonhuman animals. But this sensibility to nonhuman animal sentience challenges our relationship with them. Historian Keith Thomas saw the relationship between human animals and nonhuman animals as a "mixture of compromise and concealment."[6] The sleights of hands and tricks of minds that hide and sustain the institutional use and commercial exploitation of nonhuman animals to manufacture products and services for our consumption are increasingly revealed as speciesism.[7] Psychologist Richard D. Ryder first used the word speciesism to "Describe the widespread discrimination that is practised by man against the other species, and to draw a parallel between it and racism."[8]

---

[2] Dunayer, *Animal Equality*, 182.
[3] Regan and Singer, *Animal Rights*, 60–66.
[4] Ibid., 72–81.
[5] Frederick Crick Memorial Conference.
[6] Thomas, *Man*, 303.
[7] Hawthorne, *Hearts*.
[8] Ryder, *Victims*, 16.

In short, we use nonhuman animals because we can. We have power and control over them. But the growing recognition of nonhuman animal sentience forces us to learn a new understanding about nonhuman animals and reorder our relationship with them.[9] Their lives are as important to them as ours are to us. They, like us, live lives rich in emotional, psychological, and behavioural experiences. To deny them the right to have their lives written as enlightened biographies is to refuse to recognise their existence as individual sentient beings. To write Topsy's biography is to narrate her life as a *subject of a life*. In *The Case for Animal Rights*, Tom Regan defines a subject of a life as a human or nonhuman animal or human animal who has

> beliefs and desires; perception, memory, and a sense of the future, including their own future; an emotional life together with feelings of pleasure and pain; preference- and welfare-interests; the ability to initiate action in pursuit of their desires and goals; a psychological identity over time; and an individual welfare in the sense that their experiential life fares well or ill for them, logically independently of their utility for others and logically independently of their being the object of anyone else's interests.[10]

From what we know about her life and death, and what we know from contemporary research into the complex emotional, psychological, and behavioural lives of elephants, Topsy was undeniably a subject of a life—and, consequently, could be murdered.

LIFE

The elephant known as Topsy was born in Southeast Asia—India, Sri Lanka, Indochina, or Indonesia—in about 1875. She was probably captured with her mother in a keddah. Frank Buck, who captured nonhuman animals living in the wild and sold them to circuses and zoos in the 1930s, described a keddah as "an area of several acres that comprised the main keddah. Connecting with this, by means of a gate, was a smaller corral."[11] Elephants were forced to enter the keddah by a "demoniac hullabaloo" made by "hundreds of natives" who in a "final assault on the ears of the all-but-trapped pachyderms, tin-pans, guns, lungs and what not were

---

[9] Balcombe, *Second Nature*. Bekoff, *Emotional Lives*.
[10] Regan, *Case*, 243.
[11] Buck and Anthony, *Back Alive*, 202.

called upon for a last epic outburst designed to stampede the frantic beasts through the opening of the great prison."[12]

Today we know elephants to be intelligent, social animals with complex emotional, psychological, and behavioural needs.[13] Adult elephants both nurture their young ones and care for their sick and elderly. Baby elephants suckle up to 3 years of age and reach sexual maturity at 9–15 years of age. They can live up to 60 years or more and grow up to 10 feet high at the shoulder weighing 2.25 to 5.5 tons. They eat as much as 300 pounds of food a day, which requires walking about 10 miles a day. Elephants in a herd will defend themselves against predators, including human animals and nonhuman animals. Elephants acknowledge death and pay respects to the dead. They communicate over great distances and recognise themselves in mirrors. Each has his or her own individual personality. Their matriarchal society prospers under the tutelage and leadership of elder elephants.

But this was a life denied to this baby elephant.

Most likely Topsy witnessed the murder of her mother when she was captured and taken from her family. It was—and still is—customary for hunters and poachers to kill mothers to capture their babies. She was abducted and held hostage as she was shipped thousands of miles from Southeast Asia across land and sea to the USA via Germany, a journey that took four to six months. She travelled as cargo, chained in place, in the dark holds of merchant ships and goods wagons pulled by steam trains.

Young Topsy was sold by Carl Hagenbeck, the international wildlife dealer based in Hamburg, Germany. His clients included America's leading circus impresarios and arch rivals: P. T. Barnum and Adam Forepaugh. Both had bought elephants and other nonhuman animals caught from the wild from Hagenbeck for their circuses.[14] Her arrival in America coincided with the country celebrating its centenary in 1876. Barnum opened his show with a 13-cannon salute—one each for the original colonies. Forepaugh called his circus the Great Centennial Show.[15] Moreover, Forepaugh knew that for the young country, which at that time was welcoming thousands of immigrants from Europe, having the first American-born elephant would resonate with the celebration of independence,

---

[12] Ibid., 205.
[13] Moss, *Memoires*. Payne, *Thunder*. Sukumar, *Elephants*.
[14] Hagenbeck, *Beasts*. Rothfels, *Savages*.
[15] Daly, *Topsy*, 12.

national pride, and pioneering spirit. To be among the first American-born is to be part of America's exceptionalism—even if you are an elephant and a nonnative species.

But Forepaugh did not have the first American-born elephant, although he had already imported wild-caught young elephants since launching his circus in 1867. He did have a baby Asian elephant who arrived in New York during the winter of 1876. Unlike previous elephants and other wild-caught animals whose arrivals in the USA were greeted with much public celebration and press attention, this baby elephant was discreetly unloaded in New York and secretly brought to Forepaugh's winter quarters in Philadelphia. This furtive behaviour, Forepaugh assumed, would help him to pull off a major publicity stunt. In February 1877, he announced to have the first elephant born in the USA, a male who stood 18 inches high.[16] But Barnum suspected Forepaugh was lying and had bought the baby Asian elephant from Hagenbeck. So Barnum issued a public challenge. "It is an established zoological fact that elephants do not breed in captivity," he claimed. Maybe Forepaugh suspected Barnum had found out the truth about the baby Asian elephant. Or maybe Barnum was simply calling Forepaugh's bluff. Regardless, Forepaugh quietly withdrew his first American-born claim.[17]

When she was born, she weighed about 200 pounds and stood about 3 feet tall. She consumed as much as three gallons of milk a day and increased her weight by as much as 30 pounds a week.[18] Upon her death in 1903, she was 10 feet high and almost 20 feet long from trunk to tail. Her quick growth most likely inspired her name. In Harriet Beecher Stowe's 1852 novel, *Uncle Tom's Cabin*, Miss Ophelia asks the young slave Topsy, "Do you know who made you?" "Nobody, as I knows on," she replies. "I spect I grow'd. Don't think nobody never made me." It is not unreasonable to speculate that the book's popularity and her "I spect I grow'd" comeback inspired the figure of speech to "grow like Topsy."

Life for elephants in American circuses in the late 1800s was not that much different from how they live today. Topsy was held captive and lived a peripatetic life, travelling on foot and by train across the USA. She was shackled and restrained in rail cars as she was shipped around the country. Prolonged periods of chained boredom were alleviated only by short peri-

---

[16] Ibid., 14.
[17] Ibid., 16.
[18] Ibid., 5.

ods of intense activity when she was moved, trained, or performed. She was provoked by men whose machismo behaviour was emboldened by alcohol. She was beaten to behave in ways that had no meaning to her, but this ensured the paying audience was entertained by the silly tricks. Elephants do not, of course, perform in the wild. They have to be trained. This can be done with positive reinforcement, including praise and reward, or with blows and jabs from a bullhook,[19] a metal pole with a hook and sharp point at one end. Topsy had a series of trainers throughout her life. The first were Forepaugh's son, Addie Forepaugh, who abused her, and Moses "Eph" Thompson, a young African-American man who treated her more kindly.

In 1900 when she was touring with the Forepaugh & Sells Brothers Circus in Texas, Topsy allegedly killed one keeper in Waco and another in Paris.[20] Then, in 1902, she was involved with two fateful incidents. First, James Fielding Blount, a drunkard, attached himself to the Forepaugh and Sells Brothers Circus. One day, he teased the resting and sleeping elephants, with a glass of whiskey in one hand and a cigar in another. When he reached Topsy, his glass was empty but he still teased her with it. Elephants learned to associate the smell of alcohol and the sight of the bullhook with threatening behaviour from men. Blount threw sand in her face because she did not pay him any attention. Then he stabbed his lit cigar into her extremely sensitive trunk. This was too much for Topsy; she wrapped her trunk around his waist, held him up high in the air and threw him to the ground, crushing him to death with her body.

The second incident occurred some days later. Elephants were being unloaded from a train and were waiting to walk to the next location. Topsy was approached by Louis Dodero, a local young man, who used a stick against her. She seized him around the waist, hoisted him into the air and threw him to the ground. She raised her right foot to crush him but was stopped by a circus worker; Dodero survived. But the sequence of events that led to Topsy's murder had been set in motion. The Forepaugh and Sells Brothers Circus knew that they could no longer keep Topsy. Later

[19] The bullhook is banned in California and Rhode Island, see Pacelle, "Ringling Announcement."

[20] Nance, *Elephants*, 184. Daly challenges Topsy killed two keepers in Texas. He refers to one keeper in Paris being attacked by Topsy and the one in Waco as a "fabrication" (Daly, *Topsy*, 282.) He could not find any mention of the incident in town records or local newspapers.

that day, they announced she had been sold and become the property of Frederick Thompson and Elmer "Skip" Dundy.

At the 1901 Pan-American Exposition in Buffalo, New York, Thompson and Dundy operated a virtual ride called a "Trip to the Moon," which featured an airship called Luna. In late 1902, they were establishing Luna Park on Coney Island. Thompson and Dundy bought Topsy and assigned a handyman, Frederick "Whitey" Ault to be her trainer. Ault, a drunkard, abused Topsy as she was forced to drag the popular "Trip to the Moon" ride along the boardwalk to its new location and help build Luna Park. Ault was arrested twice for beating Topsy but there is no evidence of any significant penalty.

Thompson and Dundy realised that, with Luna Park's opening only months away, they had to maintain positive relationships with residents, police, and the press. This meant they had to resolve the related problems of Ault and Topsy, who would follow only Ault's instructions. Thompson and Dundy knew they could fire Ault. But what about Topsy?

Death

Although far from being an everyday occurrence from the mid-1800s to mid-1900s, elephants were killed by circuses and zoos when they were deemed to be uncontrollable and dangerous. Elephants were poisoned, shot, strangled, and hanged. As every elephant trainer knew, you could take a wild animal out of the wild and *believe* you can tame them. But you cannot take the wild out of a wild animal and *make* them tame. In his memoir *I Loved Rogues*, George "Slim" Lewis, the circus and zoo elephant trainer, wrote: "Dozens of elephants, most of them males, have been executed in the past twenty years because of a killing or simply because they were periodically unmanageable. Black Diamond, Major, Romano, Joe, Sammy and Teddy are only a few given death sentences for running away or attacking somebody."[21] Historian Susan Nance describes several incidents involving the deaths of elephants who performed in circuses in America.[22] Nance chronicles elephant mortality involving accidents (e.g., drowning, electrocution, train accidents, and collisions) and the murder of elephants who went *rogue*—the term used to describe "bad" elephants. "Bad" behaviour was caused by inadequate healthcare (e.g., inappropriate diets, insufficient care

---

[21] Lewis and Fish, *Rogues*, 6.
[22] Nance, *Elephants*, 108–113.

for their feet and teeth, lack of socialisation with other elephants), cruel training techniques, aggressive provocation by elephant trainers and the public, accidents, and musth (a hormone-fuelled period in male elephants that can cause a dramatic increase in aggression). For example, Mary, a five-ton Asian elephant, who performed with the Sparks World Famous Shows circus, was hanged in Erwin, Tennessee, in 1916 after killing a trainer and becoming known as "Murderous Mary." Black Diamond, a nine-ton Asian elephant who performed with the Al G. Barnes Circus, injured his long-time former trainer and killed his current employer in Texas in 1929. A firing squad killed him with 50–100 shots. In 1994, an African elephant named Tyke who performed with Circus International killed her trainer and trampled her groomer during a performance in Honolulu, Hawaii. After she charged out of the ring into the nearby streets, local police officers fired 87 shots to kill her.

Perhaps the most celebrated elephant ever, Jumbo, who was bought by P. T. Barnum from the London Zoo and brought to the USA in 1882, was killed in 1885 after being hit by a freight train in St. Thomas, Ontario. Unlike Mary, Black Diamond, and Tyke, Jumbo's death was an accident and not from going "rogue." Nonetheless, the impression is made that circus proprietors and elephant trainers treated elephants, who were valuable income-generating assets, with neglect and callous indifference to their welfare and safety needs. Lewis noted in *I Loved Rogues* that

> When the victim is a spectator or a zoo keeper, the elephant usually pays with his own life these days, and in recent years, even the circuses have become touchy about elephants killing people. It used to be cheaper to hire another handler than it was to buy an expensive elephant, and if it was only a circus roustabout who got it, the incident was hushed up.[23]

As for Topsy, we know more about how her life ended than how it began. She first was considered a liability after she reportedly killed two people in separate incidents Texas. But such allegations were often forgotten by circus proprietors, who were known to give elephants with bad reputations new names to hide their dangerous past.

Topsy's liability returned when she killed Blount and attacked Dodero in 1902. She was also a problem because she would only follow instructions from Ault, whom Thompson and Dundy found difficult to super-

[23] Lewis and Fish, *Rogues*, 4.

vise. In its story about Topsy's electrocution, *The New York Times* reported that Ault had a "habit of taking more stimulant than was good for him, and on these frequent occasions it was hard telling what he would do with Topsy."[24] Topsy was then in her mid-twenties and an adult elephant with strength and intelligence, and capable of single-minded determination to get whatever she wanted. Having been denied a natural existence in the wild, she was forced to cope in an alien society, deprived of any nurturing from her own kind to help her learn how to behave. She was not a dangerous animal when left alone, but became one when she was provoked. She defended herself in the only way she knew.

The New York Times explained why Thompson and Dundy finally made the fateful decision for Topsy:

> The beginning of the end was on Oct. 30, [1902] when "Whitey" proceeded to conduct Topsy on a tour of Coney Island, and wound up in the police station, with Topsy trying to get her fat head in through the door with doubtful success. From that time until Friday of last week "Whitey" was kept in control, and consequently Topsy behaved herself, very dutifully pushing around big beams which were being used in construction at Luna Park, and hauling loads too heavy for ordinary beasts of burden. But last Friday "Whitey" decided that such work was too degrading, and Topsy agreed with him. So he led her out of her stable on the grounds, and after the elephant language told her to "Sick 'em", the "'em" being a force of Italian workmen, who promptly took to the tall timber being used in the construction of electric towers and other such things. It was so little time before "Whitey" was persuaded, partially by threats and partially by force, to call his elephant, and from that time Topsy's life was doomed.[25]

Thompson and Dundy fired Ault and decided to kill Topsy, which they wanted to use as an opportunity to attract maximum attention to Luna Park's opening. But how to kill Topsy? Shooting her was not an option; it was impossible to find an elephant gun in the USA. The American Society for the Prevention of Cruelty to Animals stopped them from hanging her, partly because they were concerned with it becoming a public spectacle. But the ASPCA could not prevent her from being killed by other means. It was also agreed that only invited people could attend Topsy's execution.

[24] Anon., "Coney Elephant."
[25] Ibid.

An audience of at least 800 onlookers and 100 photographers witnessed Topsy's murder.

On the day of her execution on January 4, 1903, Topsy was fed carrots laced with 460 grams of potassium cyanide, which appeared to have no effect. Then she was electrocuted with 6600 volts of electricity for 10 seconds, which killed her. *The New York Times* reported:

> At 2:45 the signal was given, and Sharkey [of the Edison Company] turned on the current. There was a bit of smoke for an instant. Topsy raised her trunk as if to protest, then shook, bent to her knees, fell, and rolled over on her right side motionless. All this took a matter of ten seconds. There had been no sound and hardly a conscious movement of the body, outside the raising of the trunk when the current was first felt. In two minutes from the time of turning on the current [veterinarian] Dr. Brotheridge pronounced Topsy dead.[26]

Topsy was electrocuted because she was typecast as a villain in a much larger drama playing itself out on the human-animal stage. Yes, she killed people, but she also became collateral damage in the so-called War of Currents, a battle fought for about 10 years in the late 1880s between Thomas Edison and George Westinghouse.[27] They each wanted the electricity that their companies generated to fuel America's growing industrial empire. Edison wanted direct current (DC) and Westinghouse lobbied for alternating current (AC). In 1887, in an attempt to discredit Westinghouse and his preference for alternating current, Edison electrocuted 44 dogs, two calves and one horse to prove AC was more dangerous than DC. The press were invited to watch these experiments. Even though he opposed capital punishment, Edison also secretly paid for the first electric chair to be built for the State of New York to demonstrate that AC was deadlier than DC. He believed if he could show the danger of AC, only then he would be able to win the War of Currents and empower Americans with DC.

Thompson and Dundy were entrepreneurs in America's emerging industrial empire and producer of films and entertainment. They wanted to capitalise on Topsy's death to attract publicity to Luna Park and its forthcoming opening as a public attraction. They recalled their time at the Pan-American Exposition in Buffalo in 1901, the first event of its kind to

---

[26] Ibid.
[27] Essig, *Edison*. Stross, *Wizard*.

make full use of electricity, including electric lighting. The expo even advertised the electrocution of an elephant named Jumbo II, but that killing never took place. The Buffalo expo occurred in 1901 after the War of Currents had ended, but they both cast long shadows over Topsy's electrocution. Ironically, by 1901, both Edison and Westinghouse had lost control of their business empires, and alternating current had become the way in which electricity was delivered throughout the USA. The War of Currents is sometimes cited as the reason why electrocution was chosen as the method for Topsy's killing. Edison reportedly wanted to show that AC was so dangerous that it could even kill an elephant. As a result, Topsy's death was filmed by The Edison Moving Picture Company and called "Electrocuting an Elephant." Edison was neither present at Topsy's electrocution nor did he own the film company, but the association of his name fed the belief that the gruesome event was associated with him and the War of Currents.

"Electrocuting an Elephant" subsequently became important footage in the history of film-making. It was recorded for posterity and came to symbolise America's global presence as an industrial empire and producer of films and entertainment. Further, the film captured the power and control human animals had over nonhuman animals and the natural world. Anat Pick wrote that "Electrocuting an Elephant could be declared the 'ground zero' of animal cinema. It combines the prowess of the cinematic apparatus, the ambivalence of electricity as an animating and lethal agent, and the spectacle of the vulnerable animal body that arouses both compassion and cruelty."[28]

Forty years later another "dramatic" film featuring an elephant performing in a circus became popular and the most financially successful Disney film of the 1940s. While Topsy's biography ended in her death, the life of fictional Dumbo, beginning with his fanciful entrance as a baby elephant with unusually large ears and delivered by a stork, is a success story in which he is celebrated for being a star in the circus ring. Nothing, of course, could be further from the truth about the life of elephants in circuses. Nonetheless, Walt Disney's "Dumbo" has its moments of animal rights insight. For example, Dumbo's mother, Mrs. Jumbo, loses her temper when she sees boys torment her son. She is incarcerated for being "mad" when she was only protecting him, caregiving behaviour that we credit elephants for today based on field studies of the wild populations

[28] Pick, "Sparks," 106.

from which individuals like Topsy were once taken. Even in Disney films, where the deaths of maternal characters are common, it is some comfort that Mrs. Jumbo's fate for acting "rogue" was not as dire as Topsy's.

CONCLUSION

Thompson and Dundy made the decision to kill Topsy because she was a "big, man-killing elephant."[29] They no longer had power and control over her and her trainer; they saw no choice but to kill her and fire him. The latter was easy, but the former was slightly more difficult. But to read her biography simply as Topsy the elephant who was electrocuted to death because she went "rogue" is to tell an unfinished story.

Topsy's alleged crime was to be a "killer," for which she was sentenced to death. Even though she attacked and killed, I believe she was innocent of being a "big, man-killing elephant." Topsy's true crime—if indeed it was an offence—was simply to be an elephant. To be more precise, it was to be guilty of being a wild-caught elephant held captive in an unsuitable environment. Why should we be shocked when elephants like Topsy kill people? They are traumatised by the murder of their own kind, including quite possibly either or both of their parents, when they are captured. They are deprived of the close companionship of their own relations and extended family who live in close-knit matriarchies. They are hijacked and held hostage against their will. They are confined and transported across land and sea to new continents whose native fauna is unlike anything they or their ancestors are familiar with. They are beaten until they behave in ways meaningless to them. They survive in an existence that prevents them from fulfilling their emotional, psychological, and behavioural needs. Indeed, we should be surprised that they do not attack and kill more often.

To be found guilty and sentenced to death is not that unusual for non-human animals, of course. E. P. Evans's *The Criminal Prosecution and Capital Punishment of Animals* describes more than 500 years of nonhuman animals being tried and found guilty and sentenced to death.[30] In addition, millions of nonhuman animals are routinely killed to manufacture products and services for the consumption of human animals. Whether it is for products or productions, we use nonhuman animals because we can. "The day *may come*," noted Jeremy Bentham (1748–1832), "when the

---

[29] Anon., "Coney Elephant."
[30] Evans, *Criminal Prosecution.*

rest of the animal creation may acquire those rights which never could have been withholden from them but by the hand of tyranny."[31] Again, we should be surprised that nonhuman animals do not rebel against their oppressors more often. Perhaps they are, and we are only beginning to notice the "animal resistance" that Jason Hribal describes in *Fear of the Animal Planet*: "Captive animals escaped their cages. They attacked their keepers. They demanded more food. They refused to perform. They refused to reproduce. The resistance itself could be organised. Indeed, not only did the animals have a history, they were making history. For their resistance led directly to historical change."[32] To acknowledge "animal resistance" is to recognise the subjectivity of the lives of nonhuman animals. When Forepaugh named the baby elephant Topsy, he authorised people to view her as an individual nonhuman animal ("subject of a life"), but it was also with the understanding that in doing so it licensed human power and control over her. Topsy had no power and control over her own life except when she acted in her own defence. Ironically, her self-defence became the reason why those who had power and control over her were empowered to end her life as a "rogue" elephant.

Writing this biography of Topsy as the subject of her own life is intended to make some amends to her and return some power and control back to her—for her own life to be recognised as the subject of a life. This begs the question: Who speaks for Topsy? Certainly, not anyone who had power and control over her life or any economic or political gains to be made from her exploitation. In restitution of her tragic life and gruesome death, this biography seeks to make amends for past injustices and prevent their reoccurrence. Whomever is recognised as speaking for Topsy has power over her. But the power in this biography is not for any material gain on the author's part; it is the commitment to restorative justice and a sense of duty for her life should not have been so wasted.

Topsy, of course, never asked to be captured. Or to be forcefully relocated to another continent. Or to be kept by people who did not understand her needs. She never asked to be beaten or abused in the mistaken belief that doing so would give her keepers power and control over her. And yet, this was her fate. Topsy killed out of fear and retaliation. And she paid for it dramatically with her life. In 1903, awareness about elephants and their psychological and behavioural needs was not as evolved as it is

---

[31] Regan and Singer, *Animal Rights*, 130.
[32] Hribal, *Fear*, 29–30.

today. There were no elephant sanctuaries that could have sheltered Topsy for the remainder of her life. She was doomed to die, as were many other elephants in circuses and the entertainment industry. It would be reassuring to believe that the poisoning and electrocution of elephants no longer happens, but this is the not the case. Ivory poachers commonly use poisoning to kill elephants, such as when more than 80 elephants died after poachers used cyanide to poison a water hole in Zimbabwe's Hwange National Park in September 2013.[33] The London-based NGO, Elephant Family, reports scores of endangered Asian elephants are accidentally electrocuted and killed by low-hanging power lines each year in India.[34]

There is today reason to hope that the era of using elephants in circuses is waning. The decision by Ringling Bros. and Barnum & Bailey Circus, the biggest circus in the USA, to discontinue its use of performing elephants reflects a major shift in how these animals are viewed philosophically and used commercially.[35] Elephant sanctuaries around the world continue to promote the well-being of animals previously held captive in zoos and circuses, and work to relieve their exploitation. For Topsy, all of that came more than a century too late. Expediency and spectacle conspired with power and profit to make her life, and her death, a tragedy. But perhaps her biography will serve not just as documentation of archaic animal cruelty, but more importantly a recognition that what she suffered will no longer be tolerated by civilised society.

Acknowledgements The author wishes to express his appreciation for advice and professional assistance from Jill Howard Church in the writing of this paper.

WORKS CITED

Anonymous. "Coney Elephant Killed: Topsy Overcome with Cyanide of Potassium and Electricity." *The New York Times*, January 5, 1903.
———. "Zimbabwe's Elephants Poisoned by Cyanide." *BBC News*, September 25, 2013. http://www.bbc.co.uk/news/world-africa-24234927. Accessed September 30, 2017.
Balcombe, Jonathan. *Second Nature: The Inner Lives of Animals*. New York: Palgrave Macmillan, 2010.

[33] Anon., "Zimbabwe's Elephants."
[34] Elephanfamiliy.org, "Elephant Electrocution."
[35] Maslin and Schweber, "Ringling Brothers."

Bekoff, Marc. *The Emotional Lives of Animals: A Leading Scientist Explores Animal Joy, Sorrow, and Empathy – and Why They Matter*. Novato, CA: New World Library, 2007.

Buck, Frank and Edward Anthony. *Bring 'Em Back Alive*. New York: Garden City Publishing Company, 1930.

Daly, Michael. *Topsy*. New York: Atlantic Monthly Press, 2013.

Dunayer, Joan. *Animal Equality: Language and Liberation*. Derwood, MD: Ryce Publishing, 2001.

Elephantfamily.org. "Elephant Electrocution." http://www.elephantfamily.org/what-we-do/campaigns/elephant-electrocution/. Accessed September 30, 2013.

Essig, M. *Edison and the Electric Chair*. Stroud, UK: Sutton Publishing, 2003.

Evans, E. P. *The Criminal Prosecution and Capital Punishment of Animals*. London: Faber and Faber, 1987.

Frederick Crick Memorial Conference. Cambridge, UK, July 7, 2012. http://fcmconference.org. Accessed September 23, 2017.

Hagenbeck, Carl. *Beasts and Men: Being Carl Hagenbeck's Experiences for Half a Century Among Wild Animals*. London: Longmans, Green, and Co., 1909.

Hawthorne, Mark. *Bleating Hearts: The Hidden World of Animal Suffering*. Winchester, UK: Changemakers Books, 2013.

Hribal, Jason. *Fear of the Animal Planet: The Hidden History of Animal Resistance*. Oakland, CA: AK Press, 2010.

Lewis, George "Slim" and Byron Fish. *I Loved Rogues: The Life of an Elephant Tramp*. Seattle, WA: Superior Publishing Company, 1978.

Maslin, Sarah and Nate Schweber. "After 146 Years, Ringling Brothers Circus Takes Its Final Bow." *The New York Times*, May 21, 2017. https://www.nytimes.com/2017/05/21/nyregion/ringling-brothers-circus-takes-final-bow.html. Accessed September 30, 2017.

Mathiesen, Karl. "Elephants on the Path to Extinction – The Facts." *The Guardian*, August 12, 2016. https://www.theguardian.com/environment/2016/aug/12/elephants-on-the-path-to-extinction-the-facts. Accessed September 23, 2017.

Moss, Cynthia. *Elephant Memories: Thirteen Years in the Life of an Elephant Family*. Chicago: University of Chicago Press, 2000.

Nance, Susan. *Entertaining Elephants*. Baltimore: Johns Hopkins University Press, 2013.

Pacelle, Wayne. "Ringling Announcement an Indicator of Broader Shift Toward Animal Protection." http://blog.humanesociety.org/wayne/2017/01/ringling-bros-shuts-circus-animal-acts.html?credit=blog_post_020817_id8772. Last modified January 16, 2017. Accessed September 23, 2017.

Payne, Katy. *Silent Thunder: The Hidden Voice of Elephants*. London: Phoenix, 1998.

Pick, Anat. "Sparks Would Fly: Electricity and the Spectacle of Animality." In *Animalities: Literary and Cultural Studies Beyond the Human*, edited by Michael Lundblad, 106. Edinburgh, UK: Edinburgh University Press, 2017.

Regan, Tom. *The Case for Animal Rights*. Berkeley, CA: University of California Press, 1983.

Regan, Tom and Peter Singer, ed. *Animal Rights and Human Obligations*. Englewood Cliffs, NJ: Prentice-Hall, 1976.

Rothfels, Nigel. *Savages and Beasts: The Birth of the Modern Zoo*. Baltimore: The Johns Hopkins University Press, 2008.

Ryder, Richard D. *Victims of Science*. London: Davis-Poynter, 1975.

Stowe, H. *Uncle Tom's Cabin*. Originally published in 1852. London: Wordsworth Classics, 2002.

Stross, R. *The Wizard of Menlo Park*. New York: Crown Publishers, 2007.

Sukumar, Roman. *The Living Elephants: Evolutionary Ecology, Behaviour and Conservation*. Oxford: Oxford University Press, 2003.

Thomas, Keith. *Man and the Natural World*. London: Allen Lane, 1983.

CHAPTER 13

Online Animal (Auto-)Biographies: What Does It Mean When We "Give Animals a Voice?"

Margo DeMello

Introduction

Since the early 2000s when what are called the "second generation" social media platforms appeared, sites like MySpace and Friendster (then) and Facebook, Instagram, and Twitter (now) have allowed people to reach across borders and connect with other people, widely expanding the range of their social contacts, while at the same time allowing companies, organizations, public figures, and political movements to expand their reach. They also play an important role in creating community and individual identity.[1]

These platforms also allow people to create profiles for nonhuman animals. Some sites, like Catster, Dogster, Hamsterer, and Bunspace, were created specifically for this purpose, while the more mainstream sites, like

---

[1] See DiPerna, "Web connector"; Ellison, "Social Network."

M. DeMello (✉)
Canisius College, Buffalo, NY, USA

Animals & Society Institute, Ann Arbor, MI, USA

© The Author(s) 2018
A. Krebber, M. Roscher (eds.), *Animal Biography*,
Palgrave Studies in Animals and Literature,
https://doi.org/10.1007/978-3-319-98288-5_13

Facebook and Twitter, are created for people. Dogster and Catster, as examples of the former, host millions of profiles, share dog- and cat-related news, and feature advertising from hundreds of pet-related companies. Catster members create profiles for their cats, write diaries from the point of view of their cats, message other cats, buy their cat friends gifts and treats, use the online forums, and the site features a cat of the day, a veterinary blog, and more. Bunspace is a much smaller site, with over 16,000 profiles, community forums, shared interest groups (a popular one is for special needs or disabled rabbits), adoption postings from rabbit rescue groups, a newsletter, contests, and limited advertising from a handful of rabbit supply companies. Forums cover issues like health, adoption/rescue, behavior, diet, bonding, rabbit-related books, the Rainbow Bridge (where rabbits, like other animals on other Internet sites, go after they die), and Bunday (which is one day a week, generally Monday, where Bunspace members eat vegetarian).

On all of these sites, people create profiles in the names of their animals, and then interact with each other through the created personalities of their animals; for the most part, the human's names and identifying characteristics are completely absent on the sites. On some sites, users speak in a constructed language which attempts to simulate how those animals would speak, if they could speak English—the most well-known of these languages is "catois." Through these sites, users transfer the characteristics of their animals to the people behind the profiles, creating a sort of joint human-feline/canine/lapine identity.[2] But cats, rabbits, dogs, and hamsters do not really speak. Do they? Can an animal tell his or her life story?

A better question might be, how can a nonhuman animal tell his or her life story, when they cannot speak, much less write? This chapter addresses this question and attempts to answer it by looking at animals on social media. We know that animals are not just popular, but are ubiquitous, on social media. A handful of animal celebrities are among the most followed and "liked" individuals on the major social media platforms today, and beyond that, "ordinary" animals now routinely have profiles made for them. The question for me is: how do social media sites allow animals to tell their own stories, as well as wider stories about animal suffering and need? Further, what are the potentials and limitations of creating and sharing animal biographies online, and in particular, on social media? How can these online practices act as a form of activism? What happens when we allow animals, via social media, to "speak for themselves?"

[2] Golbeck, "On the Internet"; DeMello, "Identity"; Schally and Couch, "Creating Feline."

THE VOICELESS

As we know, it has long been thought that nonhuman animals do not possess the capacity for symbolic language (i.e., a form of communication which allows for the conveyance of thoughts, feelings, and information not confined to the here-and-now). And while research in the communication systems of many nonhuman animals is challenging this belief,[3] one cannot deny that animals can, at the very least, communicate important information to those of their own species—and those of other species—through their native call systems. So why is it so hard for us to understand—or even hear—them? The idea that animals, thanks to their supposed lack of language, are "voiceless" has a long history.

Those who possess language possess something that is a critical prerequisite for being human, while those who lack it are rendered "dumb." In Old English, dumb—a term which dates to the eleventh century—simply means "unable to speak." But its second meaning—to lack intelligence—may be almost as old, as the old High German *thumb* carries both meanings. (The contemporary German word *dumm* refers to the latter only.) Since the origin of the term, dumb has been used to refer to animals, whether with reference to their lack of speech, their lack of intelligence, or, since at least the nineteenth century, their vulnerability and need for human assistance.[4] Even today, dumb continues to be used to refer to animals in all three senses of the word: Florida's animal cruelty statutes define "animal" as "any living dumb creature," an animal welfare group in Denver calls itself the Denver Dumb Friends League, and Buzzfeed recently published an article called "23 Dumb Animals that I Can't Believe Are Really Real."

But being dumb also means, to many, that animals are easily ignored, or can be killed without concern. Rabbits, for example, do not vocalize at all. It is not coincidental that these animals are among the most exploited of all animals. Small, silent, and feminized rabbits cannot easily protest mistreatment, and are essentially silenced as a result. That is one reason why laboratory dogs often have their vocal chords cut—so they cannot

---

[3] Gardner and Gardner, "Sign Language"; Patterson, "Language Acquisition"; Herman and Austad, "Knowledge Acquisition"; Savage-Rumbaugh et al., "Ape Consciousness"; Pepperberg, *Alex Studies*; Slobodchikoff and Perla, *Prairie Dogs*.

[4] See Harriet Beecher Stowe's 1869 essay, "Rights of dumb animals," or *Dumb Animals*, the monthly newsletter published in 1868 by George Angell, the founder of the Massachusetts Society for the Prevention of Cruelty to Animals.

bark or scream. Being dumb is, essentially, a justification for these animals' deaths. (The expression, "too stupid to live," used for both people and animals, concisely makes this point.) Early animal advocates, like many activists today, thought that because animals could not speak, that they needed our assistance. This supposed lack of language has also been the rationale for humans to "speak for" nonhuman animals who are rendered silent by this construction. Being "voiceless" thus means to lack the physical ability to speak, but also the ability to convey one's beliefs, attitudes, or opinions. Those who, due to their socio-economic position, ethnicity, race, religion, or gender—or species—have no voice consequently have no power.

Animals, whether they can bark, squeak, or oink, or make no sounds at all, have no voice in this sense, and are, by this construction, effectively silenced. This is why, from the rise of the western animal protection movement in the nineteenth century, animal advocates have claimed to be the "voice of the voiceless," as groups like Animal Rights Action, Friends of Animals, Serbian Animal Voice, and Voice for the Voiceless claim. But who has, and uses, the voice has the power, not only to speak for others, but to translate their needs into human language. As we know, in communication exchanges, the more powerful of the actors exercises control over what is said, when interruptions occur, and when the exchange is over.[5] This dynamic is also apparent in situations wherein the more powerful actor exercises the right to say what the less powerful actor "really means" or would "like" to say, as we know today from the popularity of the term "mansplaining." Even with this obvious problem of translation, many activists and animal protection groups continue to attempt to give voice to animals, rather than simply speak for them, with a variety of important implications.

CONSTRUCTING IDENTITIES

Since their inception in the 1990s, social media sites provided an important tool for the construction of identities. As Schally and Couch[6] note, it is the fact that we can now join multiple virtual communities that have allowed us to develop not just a singular identity but multiple identities. The very act of creating a public profile on sites such as Six Degrees (pos-

---

[5] Tannen, *Gender and Discourse.*
[6] Schally and Couch, "Creating Feline."

sibly the first true social media site) in the early 2000s or Instagram today allows the user to consciously think about what type of identity to construct, as well as what type of community to join.

Animal social media sites like Catster and Bunspace differ from the mainstream sites in that they are aimed at companion animals—not people. These sites allow the user to create profiles for individual animals, which means that the user must interpret their animals' personalities in order to create online identities for those animals, and, in turn, themselves. For example, users upload photos of specific companion animals onto these sites, which then represent not only the cat, dog, or rabbit pictured in the photo, but also, by extension, the person who uploaded the photo, controls the account, and "speaks for" the animal to other animals (or more accurately, to other humans speaking for their own animal).

Sociologists Clinton Sanders and Arnold Arluke, in an article about speaking for dogs,[7] argue that dog owners must "translate" their dogs' feelings and desires, for example, to the veterinarian, thanks to the dog's inability to speak (in human language) for himself. This process serves both a practical purpose—that is, letting someone else know something important about the dog—but it goes further than that, and also allows the person to essentially construct the dog's identity through speaking for him. When a human creates a social media presence for an animal, the process is very similar. Schally and Couch,[8] in their study of Catster, found that 75% of their respondents said that while they use what they know of their cats' personalities in constructing their feline identities, their own personalities also came through when, for example, communicating with other "cats." The online identity becomes, then, a dual human/feline persona. The animal part of the identity is just as important, if not more so, than the human part, because it allows the users to express different thoughts or emotions, as well as make different connections, than they otherwise might, if they were just speaking as themselves. Here, the feline aspect of the Catster identity then becomes an important feature of the human identity.

Bunspace members also create a joint human/rabbit identity on the site, and, like Catster members, feel that they can discuss different ideas, in a different way, on Bunspace than they can in either "real life" or on a different social media platform. In that sense, both sites function in a similar

---

[7] Sanders and Arluke, "Speaking for Dogs."
[8] Ibid.

way, in that the use of the animal actually provides the human with a new "voice." In addition, like Catster users, Bunspace members actively interpret their rabbits' personalities when constructing identities for them; but because rabbits are somewhat more inscrutable than cats, Bunspace members must arguably work harder in trying to interpret their silent companions' personalities. Bunspace also differs from Catster in that, because of the rabbit's minority status as a pet, and their shorter life expectancies, Bunspace fills a greater need for community among its users than other animal networking sites. Many members live in areas with very few people like themselves—house rabbit lovers—and Bunspace allows them to communicate with other people who share their love of rabbits, and who understand the unique issues, including sudden death, that house rabbit guardians face.

Animals with profiles on other sites also have carefully constructed personas which reflect both their own personalities (as interpreted and translated through their human caregiver), as well as the interests of their humans. Marnie, a rescued elderly Shih Tzu, comes across on her Instagram page as funny, quirky, and silly (her long tongue that lolls out of her mouth helps with this perception). Wally the angora's public persona reflects the interests of his social worker caretaker, who takes the time to ensure that his message is somewhat therapeutic. Doug the Pug, on the other hand, calls himself the "King of Pop Culture" and is rarely seen without one of his elaborately fashionable outfits. The biggest celebrities of all, like Grumpy Cat and Lil Bub, have public personas which are as carefully cultivated (by their human handlers/PR specialists) as those of Tom Cruise or Beyonce. And yet the millions of followers of these celebrities are happy to ignore the fact that there is a human (or sometimes a marketing team) behind the persona. We are only interested in the animal.

While the very nature of online animal autobiographies may be anthropomorphic, in that it is, after all, humans who are interpreting and constructing these online identities, they also, I argue, can create space for a new understanding of animal subjectivity which can lead to real changes for animals—if those humans who are creating the accounts, and "speaking" for the animals, do so with sensitivity. For example, most Bunspace users that I spoke to told me that they found their rabbits' voices by thinking about their personalities. Fluffy's mom, for instance, told me about how she knows how to express his voice: "I write his blog as how I hear him 'speak' to me, with little quirks and inflections and I try very hard to write it in a way that helps others to get to know his personality. And I think they do."[9] The work that people spend in creating their animals' profiles goes a long way toward making these animals more than just feline or lapine avatars—they make them real.

One of the most well-known Internet animal celebrities is Grumpy Cat, whose claim to fame is the unusual appearance of his face, which makes the cat seem angry. His (or her: Grumpy Cat is the public name of Tardar Cat, a female cat who is, unlike her online persona, said to be very sweet) online presence is primarily used as an entertaining image, but also, increasingly, to sell merchandise. Other online celebrities, such as Maru, the Scottish-fold Youtube celebrity whose major talent involves jumping into boxes, are also primarily used to entertain viewers. But even those animals who appear to exist only to entertain us may do more than that. They help make the animals *real*; they humanize them. By showing that animals have personalities, that they have wants and desires, that they have emotions like love, joy, being sorry, and frustration, makes them appear more like us, and thus, more worry of our consideration.

Anyone who lives with a companion cat or dog knows that these animals do have personalities. But a surprising number of people do not believe that other animals—like cows, sheep, chickens, rabbits, or wild animals like deer or lions—share these same capacities. Seeing videos of cross-species animal friendships (like Roscoe the dog and Suryia the orangutan, Owen the hippo and Mzee the tortoise, and the (multiple) rabbit and deer friends known only as Bambi and Thumper), or strange or moving behaviors like an octopus carrying a coconut, former captive lions feeling the grass for the first time after their rescue, a rat dragging a piece of pizza into the subway, or a dog bringing food to other homeless animals, shows us some of the capabilities and emotions that other animals share with us. Through watching these videos, we recognize that in some ways, these animals are just like us. They make friends with others, they like pizza, they experience joy, and they make tools. Likewise, following animals on Facebook, Twitter, or Instagram gives us a window into the interesting lives that some of them lead.

For instance, Suryia is an orangutan who lives at the Institute of Greatly Endangered and Rare Species in South Carolina, who was befriended by Roscoe, a stray hound who wandered onto the sanctuary grounds. Their friendship, seen by millions in Youtube videos uploaded by sanctuary staff

[9] Personal communication.

as well as in a picture book, has inspired countless people with their cross-species friendship. Owen and Mzee's story, too, has been featured in a book, as well as a documentary. A story about a street dog named Lillica, who lives at a trash dump in Brazil and was filmed walking miles each night to deliver food to her friends (who include chickens, a dog, and a cat) at the dump, likewise was seen by millions of people who were moved by her selfless act of friendship. Stories like this show viewers that animals are not just like us—in many ways, they seem *better* than us.

"Giving" Animals Voice: Suffering

The attempt to let animals speak for themselves, via human media, did not begin with contemporary social networking sites. It dates back to the nineteenth century, when the first wave of the animal protection movement was emerging. British and American (mostly female) writers published a number of animal autobiographies which focused on the mistreatment of the animals involved. Anna Sewell's 1877 novel *Black Beauty*,[10] for example, is an autobiography told by a horse named Black Beauty. His narrative includes the stories of a number of horses that he meets, many of whom, like Black Beauty, suffered from the cruelty of their human owners. Sewell's intent in writing the novel was to change the treatment of horses in American society. Both women and animals, at that time, were considered to be (and effectively were) voiceless, through books like Black Beauty, were given a voice (and an audience to hear that voice). Russian writer Leo Tolstoy wrote movingly of the death and suffering of animals, often through the animal's point of view, as in the 1886 story "Strider: The Story of a Horse."[11] While "Strider" has been interpreted by critics as using the perspective of the horse as a way to expose human vanity and selfishness, as Josephine Donovan[12] points out, there can be no doubt when reading the agonizing description of Strider's death that Tolstoy did not simply use the horse as a metaphor. In works like this, animals do not act (only) as stand-ins for something else, but demonstrate, baldly, their own suffering, generally at the hands of humans.

The nineteenth century saw the passage of some of the first pieces of animal welfare legislation in Britain and the United States, and the first

[10] Sewell, *Black Beauty*.
[11] See "Strider" in Tolstoy, *Shorter Fiction*.
[12] Donovan, "Tolstoy's Animals."

animal protection organizations (the RSPCA in Great Britain and the ASPCA in the United States) emerged at the same time to enforce those laws. These developments were assisted by the publication of books like *Black Beauty* and other works of fiction that attempted to give animals a (human) voice. But this movement can trace its roots back even further, to publications that date back to the eighteenth century and even earlier. For example, in 1749, the *Gentleman's Magazine*, a London periodical, printed the speech of a dying hen, appealing for an end to the practice known as cock throwing. The hen said:

> Hold thy hand a moment, hard–hearted wretch! if it be but out of curiosity, to hear one of my feather'd species utter articulate sounds—What art thou, or any of thy comerades, better than I, tho' bigger, and stronger, and at liberty while I am ty'd by the leg? What art thou, I say, that I may not presume to reason with thee, tho' thou never reasonest with thyself? I appeal to thyself, who has known me for many months, What have I done to deserve the treatment I have suffer'd this day, from thee and thy barbarous companions? What have I ever said or done amiss? Whom have I ever injur'd?[13]

A few years later, in "The Mouse's Petition" by Anna Laetitia Barbauld,[14] a mouse, caught in a trap, opens by saying:

> O hear a pensive prisoner's prayer,
> For liberty that sighs;
> And never let thine heart be shut
> Against the wretch's cries!
> For here forlorn and sad I sit,
> Within the wiry grate;
> And tremble at the' approaching morn,
> Which brings impending fate.

The poem ends with the following plea:

> So when destruction lurks unseen,
> Which men, like mice, may share,
> May some kind angel clear thy path,
> And break the hidden snare.

---

[13] Anonymous, "Strange and Wonderful," 147.
[14] See "The Mouse's Petition" in Barbauld, *Poems*, 36–37.

According to Barbauld's autobiographer, the petition was actually success-ful in that it was delivered to Joseph Priestly, a friend of Barbauld's and an animal scientist, and resulted in the freeing of a mouse from his lab.[15] Even if that were not her intention, it is difficult to imagine either a modern reader or a contemporary of Barbauld's failing to perceive, even in a small way, some of the mouse's suffering.

Using an animal's voice to represent that animal's suffering remains one of the most enduring themes in animal protection rhetoric today. Animal rights activists have long used pictures, film, and animal voices to plead for better treatment of animals. A common image in vegetarian advertising today is a picture of a cow, pig, or chicken with the words "don't eat me," "love me, don't eat me," or a similar phrase. Activists understand that without triggering an empathetic response among the public—giving peo-ple the opportunity to relate to and share the feelings of an animal—the public will not respond to their message. By giving animals human voices to express their suffering, people are thought to be much more likely to listen to the message, and to relate. For example, Soi Cats and Dogs (SCAD) is a Bangkok-based non-profit organization dedicated to improv-ing the lives of Bangkok's street dogs and cats, known as "soi cats" and "soi dogs." One way that the organization does this is through the online autobiographies that they create for their animals, whether or not they are up for adoption. For example, one dog named Som writes:

> I don't really remember much of the first few years of my life. I know I was living on the Sois (streets) and in the temples of Bangkok, and I remember always being hungry and thirsty. I also remember that sometimes people weren't very nice to me [...] I was emaciated, had no fur, my skin was cracked and bleeding, and my toe nails were severely overgrown. It hurt. Also, because I was so malnourished, my teeth turned black and grew hori-zontally instead of vertically.[16]

Later, she writes: "I am now so happy that I can't wipe the smile from my face. My mum and dad say that I am 'the happiest, skippiest, most loved and most loving dog anyone could hope for.' All I wish for now is for all the other dogs and cats who are living rough on the Sois can have as happy an ending as I do."[17]

[15] Milne, "Speaking Animal's."
[16] Savvides, "Speaking for Dogs," 233.
[17] Ibid.

As Nikki Savvides writes in an analysis of the organization's practices,

> The biographies of Mr Daeng and Bashful differ from the majority of stories told about soi dogs which mainly view them as 'a blight on the city' [...], or representing 'a health risk' [...] Instead, SCAD's biographies discuss the problem from the dogs' perspectives, building up a picture of them as beings with distinct, unique personalities. By couching dog personalities in terms we humans understand, SCAD engenders identification between human and animal [...] The notion of 'speaking for' soi dogs could be criticized as a form of anthropomorphism, yet it can be utilised in a more positive way by allowing humans to attempt to understand animals not only as having 'feelings' but as having consciousness and subjectivity, just as humans do.[18]

The profiles on Bunspace, a website which allows users to create profiles for their pet rabbits, also serve the interests of alleviating rabbit suffering. Rabbit rescuers are a prominent part of the Bunspace community. Rescue organizations reach out to Bunspace users by posting about their financial needs, advertising rabbits for adoption, and seeking help with big rescues, or with transportation. Rescue groups can create profiles for their adoptable rabbits, can blog, and can post on forums and groups. Because of their interest in rabbit rescue, Bunspace's founders also create fundraisers every year, which raise funds for rabbit rescue groups. Bunspace is unique among animal networking sites because of the activism of its members, and the vegetarianism of many of its users. Many Bunspace users are vegetarian, and they created a forum on Bunspace called Bunday to encourage the eating of a vegetarian diet (i.e., a rabbit's diet) on one day of the week, usually Monday.

In *Stories Rabbits Tell*, my co-writer Susan Davis and I wrote:

> The fact that a species is unknown—as the rabbit is—means that we as humans can project all sorts of characteristics on the animals that would deem them unworthy of protection. We can even project a trait of blankness on them; that is, because we don't understand the rabbit, we assume there is nothing to understand, that the rabbit is a creature with neither sentience nor subjectivity. And once we assume that, creating what in other species we would recognize as 'suffering' becomes acceptable.[19]

---

[18] Ibid., 241.
[19] Davis and DeMello, *Rabbits Tell*.

Social media accounts featuring rabbits (or other silenced animals, like pigs or chickens) help make these animals visible by giving them a voice—and by giving them a voice, they make them visible. In fact, social media has given animal advocates a major new platform from which to advocate for animals, and creating profiles for individual animals is the simplest way to do that.

Lil Bub, for example, a cat who suffers from a bone disorder which both compromises her health and makes her cuter, and her phenomenal online presence is geared, in part, to publicizing the plight of other rescued animals and promoting animal rescue. She has 1.4 million followers on Instagram, 2.9 million likes on Facebook, and almost 1 million Twitter followers, and has raised hundreds of thousands of dollars for animals in need. Wally and Molly, a pair of English angora rabbits, have a busy Instagram account (319,000 followers) which show off not only their adorable personalities and loving relationship with each other, but, according to their caretaker, a social worker, their personas are also geared toward helping both people and animals, via Wally's advice column and the way in which the rabbits' comments are crafted. Wally, like Lil Bub, Romeo the Cat, and countless other internet personalities today, encourages animal adoption.

One of the downsides to the rise of these literal animal activists is that these animals, and the stories they tell, often emphasize the individuality of that animal, and the particularities of his or her rescue and salvation, rather than emphasizing the structural problems that allow animal suffering to continue. When the public enjoys stories about the exploits of a rescued animal like Boo, known as "the world's cutest dog," with 17.5 million Facebook likes, they empathize with him and learn that abandoning dogs is "bad." But do they actively work to help other homeless dogs? One might argue that by focusing on the heartwarming stories of individual animals, all of whom have had a "happy ending," viewers and readers might not need to go further and care about other animals who are not as charismatic, do not have social media profiles, and suffer in silence and obscurity. Perhaps the focus on the extraordinary individual animals even obfuscates our understanding of animal suffering on a wide scale. Another problem, which has been pointed out by Elaine Laforteza,[20] is the way in which the fame of many of these animals (Lil Bub is a good example, as is Turbo Roo the disabled dog, Hofesh the sea turtle with prosthetic fins,

[20] Laforteza, "Cute-ifying Disability."

and Tuna the chihuahua with a severe overbite) relies on the animal's disability to captivate the audience. Laforteza writes that these animals' celebrity serves to both cuteify and turn disability into a spectacle.

Ecofeminist Carol Adams[21] has written that in intimate human-animal relationships we come to recognize an animal's individuality, or perhaps even personhood. I would argue that when we follow internet celebrities, we also come to see those animals as individuals, or even as persons, and, we mourn them when they die. When Biddy the hedgehog died in 2015, over 200,000 people publicly mourned him in comments on his Instagram page. Interestingly, Biddy's online popularity has only increased since his death, as has been the case for a number of other animals made popular through social media. The fact that Biddy was so mourned (as was Loki the corgi and Colonel Meow the cat) after his death is a testament to the power and importance of his online presence and the connection that people feel that they have made to the animal in question. These are animals who were only personally known by a few dozen people, but hundreds of thousands of people were affected by their deaths. On the other hand, it may also be the case that for some animals, their posthumous popularity indicates something perhaps more troubling: the potential irrelevance of the animal him- or herself.

An example of this may be Oolong. Oolong was a brown and white Dutch rabbit who lived from 1994 to 2003 with photographer Hironori Akutagawa in Japan. Akutagawa made Oolong famous in the 1990s through photos he took of Oolong with objects on his head (mostly Japanese pastries); he called it "head performance art." During Oolong's lifetime, his photos were beloved by animal lovers around the world, and in particular, by the house rabbit community, which was emerging at that same time, who recognized the love shared by Oolong and Akutagawa. After Oolong's death, however, in the late 2000s, his photos went viral, taking the form of a popular image macro, which used a photo of Oolong with the caption, "I have no idea what you're talking about ... so here's a bunny with a pancake on its head."

The Oolong meme, in which Oolong lost his name, his identity, his relationship with Akutagawa, and even his subjectivity ("its"), demonstrates a downside to viral popularity. Here, Oolong has become an absent referent, to borrow Carol Adams' term.[22] The real animal, through his

---

[21] Adams, *Neither Man.*
[22] Adams, *Sexual Politics.*

re-construction into a meme, has been erased, leaving us with a photo that derives its humor from the fact that, without context, it no longer makes sense.

CONCLUSION

The philosopher Ludwig Wittgenstein once wrote: "If a lion could talk, we could not understand him,"[23] demonstrating the impenetrability of animal minds. In addition, one could take Wittgenstein's statement another way, and say, following Erica Fudge,[24] that if a lion (especially if that lion were living in a zoo) could talk, we may not *want* to understand him, as understanding him might make us feel bad, because of what it reveals about his life and those of other animals. When we do hear what they have to say, it opens up a whole Pandora's box for us—don't we need to then respond? I think that some of us do.

Esther the Wonder Pig changed the lives of the two men who rescued her, but also, perhaps, the lives of countless others. Derek Walter and Steve Jenkins were living outside of Toronto in 2012 when they were asked to give a home to what they were told would be a mini-pig. They brought Esther home as a baby, and soon found that she was no mini-pig: she grew to over 600 pounds. Esther was actually a commercially raised "meat pig." After falling in love with Esther, Walter and Jenkins stopped eating meat and began promoting Esther online, through her own website, as well as through Facebook, Twitter, Youtube, and Instagram. They also bought a large piece of land and now run an animal sanctuary, which is focused on rescuing other animals like Esther. She has an online store which sells a variety of merchandise, and her website includes a section called "The Dark Side," which offers videos about the lives of factory-farmed animals from animal rights organizations. Her posts on her various platforms are both humorous—giving followers insight into her pushy, funny personality, her likes and dislikes, and what she does with her days— but also does not shy away from sharing information about animal agriculture, veganism, and more. With about 1.5 million total followers, as well as a best-selling book and countless media appearances, Esther is perhaps the most influential pig to have ever lived, in terms of her ability to impact the beliefs and practices of people around the world. Her social media

[23] Wittgenstein, *Philosophical Investigations*, 190.
[24] Fudge, *Animal*.

presence—even if she herself is unaware of it—has given her a measure of agency that other pigs could only hope for.

According to the cute cat theory of digital activism,[25] social activists have used Twitter, Facebook, Flickr, Blogger, and other social media sites—sites which were created for online community formation, identity creation, and, of course, the sharing of cute animal videos—because those sites are safer—and more public—for activists than would be sites specifically created for activism. If activists are targeted by governments, corporations, or others interested in silencing them, they would have a very difficult time shutting down or even censoring sites like Facebook. Because of this concern, we have social movements, which largely take place, or at least find structure, on social media, like Egypt's "Facebook Revolution" or Iran's "Twitter Uprising." So the presence of cute cats, ultimately, has helped propel some of our modern social movements. But those cute cats may be helping cats too. Just as some of the eighteenth and nineteenth century animal autobiographies may very well have played a role in the passage, in England and the United States, in some of the world's first anti-cruelty laws, the modern, online version of these biographies may eventually reap similar results. By creating, liking and following animals on Facebook, Twitter, and Instagram we may indeed be giving these animals as much significance as those of their human counterparts, which may result in concrete changes for the animals behind the profiles—and perhaps, for other animals as well.

WORKS CITED

Adams, Carol J. *The Sexual Politics of Meat: A Feminist-Vegetarian Critical Theory.* New York: Bloomsbury Publishing, 2015.

———. *Neither Man nor Beast: Feminism and the Defense of Animals.* London: A&C Black, 1995.

Anonymous. "A Strange and Wonderful Relation of a Hen that Spake at a Certain Ancient Borough in Staffordshire on the 17th of February being Shrove Tuesday; Together with her Dying Speech." *The Gentleman's Magazine* 19 (1749).

Arluke, Arnold and Clinton Sanders. *Regarding Animals.* London: Pearson Education, 2010.

Barbauld, Anna Letitia. *Poems.* London: Joseph Johnson, 1773.

---

[25] Zuckerman, "Cat Theory."

Davis, Susan E. and Margo DeMello. *Stories Rabbits Tell: A Natural and Cultural History of a Misunderstood Creature*. Hemden, VA: Lantern Books, 2003.

DeMello, Margo. "Identity, Community and Grief: The Role of Bunspace in Human and Rabbit Lives." In *Speaking for Animals: Animal Autobiographical Writing*, edited by Margo DeMello, 115–129. London: Routledge, 2013.

DiPerna, Paul. "The Web Connector Model: New Implications for Social Change." *Journal of Information Technology Impact* 7.1 (2007): 15–20.

Donovan, Josephine. "Tolstoy's Animals." *Society & Animals* 17.1 (2009): 38–52.

Ellison, Nicole B. "Social Network Sites: Definition, History, and Scholarship." *Journal of Computer-Mediated Communication* 13.1 (2007): 210–230.

Free, Amy. "Can 'Dumb' be Undone? What the Human Proclivity for Speech Means for Non-Human Animals." Phd. diss., Canisius College Anthrozoology program, 2015.

Fudge, Erica. *Animal*. London: Reaktion Books, 2004.

Gardner, R. Allen and Beatrice T. Gardner. "Teaching Sign Language to a Chimpanzee." *Science* 165.3894 (1969): 664–672.

Golbeck, Jennifer. "On the Internet, Everybody Knows you're a Dog: The Human-Pet Relationship in Online Social Networks." Paper presented at the Conference on Human Factors in Computing Systems, Florence, Italy, April 5–10, 2008.

Herman, Louis M. and Steven N. Austad. "Knowledge Acquisition and Asymmetry Between Language Comprehension and Production: Dolphins and Apes as General Models for Animals." In *Readings in Animal Cognition*, edited by Marc Bekoff and Dale Jamieson, 289–306. Cambridge, MA: MIT Press, 1996.

Laforteza, Elaine M. "Cute-ifying Disability: Lil Bub, the Celebrity Cat." *Media/ Culture Journal* 17.2 (2014). http://journal.media-culture.org.au/index. php/mcjournal/article/view/784. Accessed September 19, 2017.

Milne, Anne. "The Power of Testimony: The Speaking Animal's Plea for Understanding in a Selection of Eighteenth-Century British Poetry." In *Speaking for Animals: Animal Autobiographical Writing*, edited by Margo DeMello, 163–177. London: Routledge, 2013.

Patterson, Francine G. "The Gestures of a Gorilla: Language Acquisition in Another Pongid." *Brain and Language* 5.1 (1978): 72–97.

Pepperberg, Irene M. *The Alex Studies: Cognitive and Communicative Abilities of Grey Parrots*. Cambridge, MA: Harvard University Press, 2009.

Sanders, Clinton R. and Arnold Arluke. "Speaking for Dogs." In *The Animals Reader: The Essential Classic and Contemporary Writings*, edited by Linda Kalof and Amy Fitzgerald, 63–71. London: Bloomsbury, 2007.

Savage-Rumbaugh, Sue, William Mintz Fields, and Jared Taglialatela. "Ape Consciousness – Human Consciousness: A Perspective Informed by Language and Culture." *American Zoologist* 40.6 (2000): 910–921.

Savvides, Nikki. "Speaking for Dogs." In *Speaking for Animals: Animal Autobiographical Writing*, edited by Margo DeMello, 231–243. London: Routledge, 2013.

Schally, Jennifer and Stanley Couch. "Catster.com: Creating Feline Identities Online." In *Speaking for Animals: Animal Autobiographical Writing*, edited by Margo DeMello 103–113. London: Routledge, 2013.

Sewell, Anna. *Black Beauty.* New York: Scholastic Paperbacks, 1877.

Slobodchikoff, Constantine Nicholas, Bianca S. Perla, and Jennifer L. Verdolin. *Prairie Dogs: Communication and Community in an Animal Society.* Cambridge, MA: Harvard University Press, 2009.

Stowe, Harriet Beecher. "Rights of Dumb Animals." *Hearth and Home* 1.2 (1869): 24.

Tannen, Deborah. *Gender and Discourse.* Oxford: Oxford University Press, 1994.

Tiffin, Helen. "Speech of Dumb Beasts." In *Considering Animals: Contemporary Studies in Human-Animal Relations*, edited by Carol Freeman, Elizabeth Leane, and Yvette Watt, 137–152. Burlington, VT: Ashgate Publishing, 2011.

Tolstoy, Leo. *Collected Shorter Fiction: Volume 1.* Translated by Louise Maude and Aylmer Maude. London: Everyman's Library, 2001.

Wittgenstein, Ludwig. *Philosophical Investigations.* Hoboken, NJ: Wiley-Blackwell, 2010.

Zuckerman, Ethan. "The Cute Cat Theory of Digital Activism." Paper presented at the E-Tech Conference, San Diego, California, March 3–6, 2008.

Index[1]

---

[1] Note: Page numbers followed by 'n' refer to notes.

© The Author(s) 2018
A. Krebber, M. Roscher (eds.), *Animal Biography*,
Palgrave Studies in Animals and Literature,
https://doi.org/10.1007/978-3-319-98288-5

Lightning Source UK Ltd.
Milton Keynes UK
UKHW01n0603241018
331102UK00009B/318/P